What's
Theology
Got to Do
with It?

What's Theology Got to Do with It?

Convictions, Vitality, and the Church

Anthony B. Robinson

THE
ALBAN
INSTITUTE

Herndon, Virginia
www.alban.org

The Alban Institute
2121 Cooperative Way, Suite 100
Herndon, VA 20171

Scripture quotations, unless otherwise noted, are from the New Revised Standard Version of the Bible, copyright © 1989, Division of Christian Education of the National Council of Churches of Christ in the United States of America, and are used by permission.

Cover design by OffPiste Design, Inc.

Library of Congress Cataloging-in-Publication Data

Robinson, Anthony B.
  What's theology got to do with it? : convictions, vitality, and the church / Anthony B. Robinson.
     p. cm.
  Includes bibliographical references.
  ISBN-13: 978-1-56699-320-3
  ISBN-10: 1-56699-320-2
  1. Theology, Practical—United States. 2. Protestant churches—United States. I. Title.

  BV3.R64 2005
  230'.044—dc22

                                    2005032260

  09   08   07   UG   2   3   4   5

Dedicated to Rev. Dr. Teruo Kawata—
mentor, friend, pastor, and
teacher of the church

Contents

Foreword

Members of the worship committee are arguing. Madeline, a member since 1965 says, "Look, it makes no sense to do away with the confession of sin." Howie, who owns the bookstore in town, says, "All I know is that they don't confess their sins at my niece's church. Their worship center is packed." Madeline responds, "So, if we don't confess our sins does that mean we don't sin anymore?" She leans toward the group. "When I used to say to my Dad, 'I hate to hurt people,' he'd say, 'Madeline, think straight, you sin against people every day.'" The debate continues. They make no decision at the meeting. However, the committee members decide to think more about sin before they do away with confessing it.

Where could this group turn to plan a conversation about sin? They could turn to this wise book. These lay theologians could read chapter 6, "Why Nice Is Not Enough," and talk about the meaning of sin and redemption. They could acknowledge, as Anthony Robinson suggests, that they participate in personal and corporate sin. The group could name ways in which their sins are sometimes a result of willfulness and sometimes a sign of what Robinson calls will-lessness. Then, after they have practiced the suggestions in this book regarding conversation about sin, the worship committee members could talk about the other theological convictions that Robinson addresses: Revelation, Scripture, the Trinity, Christology, the Holy Spirit, and Ecclesiology.

How a congregation thinks matters. Thinking creates feelings. Feelings motivate actions. The way parishioners think about their life together shapes their practice. How a faith community thinks determines the practices of that congregation. How worship committee members think about sin will effect whether or not there is a confession of sin in their congregation's liturgy.

What does it mean for a congregation to think theologically? It means that parishioners use theological language. It means that members of a congregation are more conscious of a worldview infused with God. They follow a logic predicated by faith in God. The logic of the marketplace or the logic of therapy may be helpful. Yet such ways of thinking are secondary to thinking rooted in the ways of faith, through which people are able to see patterns to their lives. "Oh," Madeline from the worship committee might observe, "I pray for forgiveness. I sense mercy. Then I sin and, well, it starts all over again." As the patterns of faith become more apparent, parishioners can learn to trust God's remarkable logic. Congregations achieve a more abundant expression of faith through theological reflection.

As Anthony Robinson reminds us, when we are intentional about theological reflection we enter a conversation started long before us, one that will continue long after we are gone. In this relevant book, Robinson uses the language, grammar, and practices of theology to support conversations about congregational vitality.

Some might suggest that participants in congregational life are not able to use the thought patterns of theology. Some suggest that as we move away from Christendom, the language of theology lacks relevance. I disagree. On every page of this book, Anthony Robinson shows us ways to reclaim the richness of theology for congregational life. Parishioners are capable of using the language of theology. In other areas of life, people of faith use sophisticated, nuanced ways of thinking. So why not apply the same sophistication to matters of faith? I believe people of faith can know as much about the way of faith, the grammar of faith, as they know about other interests in their lives.

What happens when congregations learn to think theologically? They become more accurate. Sin is not the same as "messing up." Grace is not the same as "good luck." Theological thinking is precise. It is rooted in narrative; God's story told in Scripture and God's story revealed through specific activities of faith communities. Theological reflection does not always bring agreement. It certainly does not make it easier to practice our faith. Yet clear theological thinking does allow us to see the object of our reflection more truthfully. Honesty is expressed when a pastor says, "Look, we didn't just make a mistake, we sinned." Something truthful occurs when the board of a faith community asks members to wonder, as Robinson recommends, "What part of the Trinity does our ministry most reflect?" Such questions lead to conversations that have depth. Depth supports accuracy. Moreover, accuracy generates health.

Theology has plenty to do with congregational health. Theological reflection is a way to align what we believe with who we are. Careful thinking about theology helps a congregation preach what it practices and practice what it preaches. If a congregation neglects core categories of faith, it is possible for the congregation to become, in practice, something other than a *faith* community.

So, let us be accurate about the reality of congregations. All life is theological. We neglect the responsible use of theology at our own peril. Congregations are God infused. It takes God-logic to understand congregational life. This book reminds us of something that we dare not lose. Theology is the best tool for congregations to speak the truth about the relationship between the human and the divine. There are many voices telling people of faith how to shape stronger congregations. The way most congruent with congregational life is the way of theological reflection. What has theology got to do with it? It has to do with what is true and healthy. It has to do with congregations responding to their unique vocations. Ultimately, it has to do with loving God fully, with our hearts and our minds.

Tim Shapiro
President, Indianapolis Center for Congregations

Preface

I wrote this book because I believe two things: First, I believe that congregations matter. They make a difference in the lives of individuals, families, and communities. Second, I believe that congregations are vital when they are clear about the core convictions of Christian faith. I offer this book in support of congregations and their leaders across North America. If it proves of use in other settings, such as college or seminary classrooms, or in the consultations of denominations and their leaders, then it shall be an added blessing. To facilitate the book's use, questions for reflection and discussion are included at the end of each chapter.

I want to offer some words of thanks and acknowledgement. First, I recognize the Louisville Institute and its director, Jim Lewis, for their support of this project. Part of what the Louisville Institute made possible was the convening of a working group of theologians and pastors where the guiding questions of the project were explored. That working group included Cheryl Clementson, Don Mayer, Kristine Anderson Ostrem, Rick Steele, Mark Taylor, Robert Wall, and Angela Ying. I am grateful both for their contributions to the project and for who they are as colleagues: a splendid group!

That group also included my editor for the book, Beth Gaede. Beth not only knows writing, she knows theology. Her assistance has been invaluable. I also wish to acknowledge the excellent assistance of my copy editor, Andrea Lee, who saved readers from many unnecessary words.

Finally, I dedicate this book to one of my own best mentors and friends in ministry, Rev. Dr. Teruo Kawata. "Teri" is a pastor-theologian who cares deeply that congregations be theologically funded and alert. He has guided many congregations and pastors—including me—in, as the apostle Paul wrote to his protégé Timothy, stirring into flame "the gift of God that is within you" (2 Tim. 1:6).

I pray that this book may stir into flame the faith that is within you.

Introduction

F ive years ago a presbytery of the United Church of
Canada invited me to lead a three-part series over a year's
time for their pastors and lay leaders on the subject of
healthy congregations. Suggested subtopics were healthy leadership and healthy presbyteries. It seemed a good challenge, so I
happily accepted the invitation, and I then set to work to prepare
the series of presentations and workshops.

Because healthy congregations was not a specific topic upon
which I had taught or spoken in the past, I did several things to
prepare. First, I began looking at literature on the topic. Second,
I asked colleagues what the words "healthy congregations" suggested to them. (Often their first response was a joking rejoinder,
"Gosh, I'm not sure I've ever seen one!") Third, I mentally reviewed my own pastoral experience for ideas, taking notes on
different themes, questions, and ideas. And, fourth, I pondered
what Scripture has to say, both directly and indirectly, about healthy
congregations. The Acts of the apostles and the Pauline and Pastoral Letters seemed the best candidates, but of course the entire
corpus of Scripture is concerned with God's attempt to create a
faithful people.

1

My review of current literature on healthy congregations revealed a heavy reliance on that work on "systems theory," much of it inspired by the work of Murray Bowen and Edwin Friedman on family systems. Peter Steinke, informed and taught by Bowen and Friedman, has been a leader in the field, applying family systems approaches to congregations. Much of this work is insightful and extremely useful. I recommend it. A second category of current literature particularly relevant to the topic of vital congregations falls in the area of leadership studies. Some of the best work on leadership and its relationship to organizational health comes from various secular disciplines, including business, politics, and organizational theory. The work of Peter Senge on learning organizations, Ron Heifetz on adaptive change, and Jim Collins on "fifth level" leadership and the role of leaders in moving organizations from "good" to "great" are among the most notable contributions. Additional material within the larger leadership genre focuses on the specific tasks of pastoral leadership and its importance to congregational vitality.

A third major category of literature bearing on healthy congregations focuses on conflict in organizations and churches and how to use, survive, and resolve conflict. The Alban Institute and its staff and consultants are among the leaders here. Again, this body of work is rich in insight and helpful suggestions for congregations and their leaders. Beyond systems theory, leadership studies, and the congregational conflict genre, other approaches to healthy congregations include congregational typologies, personality-type analysis applied to congregations, and material from the field of group dynamics. Finally, a wealth of material focuses on specific aspects of church life from stewardship to music to outreach to youth ministry, all of which promise greater health and vitality to churches and their leaders. As in all fields, some contributions are excellent while others are, at best, so-so. Clearly, a lot of material either directly or indirectly addresses what a healthy congregation looks like and how you move toward such a reality. Indeed, for any one person to fully master all that is out there is probably impossible.

What I did not discover as I went hunting in the fields on healthy congregations was much that was explicitly theological or biblical in nature. To be sure, many of the studies I have mentioned would surface general theological or religious themes, and sometimes Scripture was deployed. But by and large, congregational health seemed, to judge by the literature, not to have much to do with either the core convictions of the Christian faith, theology, or the Bible.

Meanwhile, I was continuing to make notes to myself about my own experience as a pastor and teacher. When I pulled the various slips of paper together and tried to bring order out of chaos, I noted—with the force of a revelation—that my thoughts steered steadily toward theology. I was stunned to note the things that seemed most important to me and to my practice of ministry and leadership were consistently theological convictions and teaching. Time and again, it seemed theology was integral, at least in my own practice and experience, to healthy congregations.

For example, I made notes to myself about a church fight I had walked into fresh out of seminary and at my first church. There some notions of ecclesiology and Pauline teaching about the church as the body of Christ proved to be central in finding our way out of a morass. I also recalled my efforts to help another congregation that had lost its center and sense of purpose by turning them to the category of revelation and the nature of Scripture and its function in the church. In another setting, as issues swirled around the respective roles and responsibilities of ordained clergy and laity, the utility of a clear understanding of baptism and ministry crystallized for me. How were the roles and callings, that is, the ministries, of each to be understood theologically? In short, my ruminations headed not toward systems theory, leadership studies, or conflict resolution techniques, but toward theological teaching and conviction. I noted this with interest and fascination. Could it be that theology has something to do with healthy congregations? I seemed to believe so.

Do not misunderstand me here. Much can be learned from these auxiliary fields, and I have greatly benefited from them. In particular, I have paid significant attention to the leadership genre and built on the insights of Heifetz and others in my work and in my writing. Nevertheless, from my preparation for that series for the United Church of Canada, a conviction, which is the thesis of and inspiration for this book, began to take shape. My thesis is that an integral and absolutely vital relationship exists between our core convictions, our theology, and our health as congregations. Where we are reasonably clear about our core convictions and their relevance to our life and purpose as church, chances of vitality are great. Conversely, where we are fuzzy about our core convictions and unsure of their meaning or value, disarray is likely. Organizations, including congregations, that lack norms and convictions and the ability to interpret their ongoing significance for their life and mission, are organizations that are likely to be ingrown, conflicted, and driven (often off the road and into a ditch) by personalities of leaders and members.

One can see an analogy to this thesis in reasonably healthy people. Those that we think of as healthy seem fairly clear about who they are. They know themselves. They know what is important to them and why. They are capable of making decisions and choices and of giving an account of their actions. Moreover, such self-knowledge and integrity does not close a healthy person to others or to ongoing learning and exploration. In reality, such self-knowledge makes further growth and exploration possible. Knowing ourselves, we are free to explore. An apt analogy might be spelunkers, those who enjoy exploring underground caves and caverns. Before descending into the dark bowels of the earth, spelunkers tie to themselves a rope that is attached to a fixed point outside the cave. In a wonderful paradox, that fixed point allows the spelunker to explore!

Likewise, when individuals are reasonably clear about who they are and are at peace with themselves, other things become possible. They are free to welcome the stranger and to be open to continuing growth and learning. Those who lack such a point of reference or self-knowledge seem more likely never to set out on a journey or to condemn all that differs from them because other perspectives seem only threatening to their fragile sense of self. Social groups and congregations are much the same, in this respect, as people. Being clear about our identity and purpose, our core convictions, and where our rope is tethered enables vital life. Lacking such core convictions and points of reference, congregations are more likely to circle the wagons against the outside world, engage in unending internal struggle and scapegoating, and lose their way altogether.

To look in another direction, lack of theological content and reasonable clarity may also be at the core of the current malaise of many mainline Protestant congregations and denominations. "The weakest link is theology," argues Princeton Theological Seminary professor and youth ministry leader Kenda Creasy Dean in her recent and notable book, *Practicing Passion: Youth and the Quest for a Passionate Church*. "By the late twentieth century, youth ministry analysts had launched a cottage industry of lament, blaming youth ministry's failures on everything from insufficient leadership training and lack of denominational support to sociological cycles and the invasion of secular culture. The literature flourished, but on the whole youth ministry did not. Something remarkable was missing from all these explanations," writes Dean. "Nowhere did we suggest that *theology* may be partly responsible for the church's diminishing influence on young people. While youth ministry has routinely capitalized on the passions of adolescents, little (if any) attention has been given to connecting them to the Passion of Christ."[1]

For this leader in the field of youth ministry, the issues are not limited to youth or youth ministry. The struggles of youth ministry are unavoidably related to the larger malaise of the mainline Protestant world, and that malaise cannot be blamed on a need for better technique or new tricks to entice young people. The challenge is theological. It is regaining, or gaining for the first time, theological content, integrity, and passion. "What if mainline Protestantism's disappointing track record with young people (in and beyond the church) has not been primarily a failure of models, educational strategies, historical cycles, or institutional support, but a failure of theology?"[2] We tend, as Dean implies, to look everywhere for an explanation or help—except at what might be the most obvious place of all, namely what we believe and confess and the difference it makes.

What Dean sees in youth ministry, Douglas John Hall sees in the broader church. Hall claims that the real problem before us is a theological one. We have lost touch with our core convictions, he argues. "Insofar as we are committed to genuine renewal in the churches we represent, there are no shortcuts: *we must begin with basics.*" Like Dean, Hall is not enamored of the latest methodology for creating cultural relevance, church growth technique, leadership strategy, or model of ministry. These represent only shortcuts. There are no shortcuts. "We have two or three generations of people in and around the churches now who are, most of them, not only unfamiliar with the fundamental teachings of the Christian traditions but ignorant even of the Scriptures." Please note, neither Dean nor Hall are fundamentalists, nor even conservatives in any usual sense of the term. Both are in the forefront of historically liberal denominations and share their commitments to progressive public witness. But both believe theological focus and renewal is at the heart of the renewal and vitality of the church. Notes Hall:

> Some denominations have been more diligent than others in the area of Christian education, but I doubt that any North American Protestant denominations stemming from the central streams of the Reformation could measure up to the minimal standards of catechesis assumed by the sixteenth-century reformers. We have even to ask ourselves whether we have a well-educated professional ministry, or at least a ministry whose basic theological education is continuously renewed and supplemented, and then incorporated into preaching and congregational leadership.[3]

A third respected voice, saying much the same thing from the vantage point of the pulpit and preaching, is that of Fleming Rutledge. In her essay "A New Liberalism of the Word," in the recent collection *Loving God with Our Minds,* Rutledge argues that the core problem contributing to the inability of mainline Protestant churches and clergy to occupy a vital center that contributes to public discourse and public life is theological in nature. "Speaking as one who has traveled extensively through the mainline churches and listened to hundreds of sermons over a number of years, I believe that the essential problem can be precisely identified in the words of Jesus to the Sadducees: 'Is not this why you are wrong, that you know neither the scriptures nor the power of God?' Jesus' point against the Sadducees is that the power of God is able to create an entirely new reality that transcends all human categories."[4] As Rutledge points out, the Scriptures and the power of God are inextricably related. The Scriptures mediate the power of God, a power that has in it the potential to transform and make new.

Again, it is not my contention that we cannot or ought not learn from fields and teachers whose primary focus is other than theological. We can certainly benefit from such contributions. But, in the end, there is no substitute for the heart of the matter, that is, Christian theology and those core convictions of faith that have the power, to quote Rutledge, "to create an entirely new reality." We do well in this challenging time to remember the wisdom of Bernard of Clairvaux, who observed that we must drink from our own wells.

The wells of Scripture, theology, and historic Christian faith are deep and refreshing, and they are largely untapped in the ongoing life of contemporary congregations. We have been eager, it sometimes seems, to search in far places and have forgotten the admonition of Moses to the Hebrew people: "Surely, this commandment that I am commanding you today is not too hard for you, nor is it too far away. It is not in heaven, that you should say, 'Who will go up to heaven for us, and get it for us so that we may hear it and observe it?' Neither is it beyond the sea, that you should say, 'Who will cross to the other side of the sea for us, and get it for us so that we may hear it and observe it?' No, the word is very near to you; it is in your mouth and in your heart for you to observe" (Deut. 30:11-14).

What Happened to Theology?

How does it happen that, like the pop song "Looking for Love in All the Wrong Places," we in the church sometimes seem to look for life and health in the wrong places? Or if not in the "wrong places," at least seldom in the most promising and obvious of places, namely our faith and theology and the difference they may make. This question has a number of answers. Some have to do with the way we have come to understand the term *theology*. These will be taken up more fully in the next chapter, which continues to lay the groundwork and foundation for the body of this study. Here I want to focus on the recent past, that is, the past few centuries of church life and history, and the consequences of the modern era for the matter at hand. In many ways, modernity has rendered the church theologically underfunded. This is, of course, a considerable irony: a church without theology. This would be like schools that no longer educate or quite know what education is, businesses that provide no real product or service, governments that fail to govern, and leaders who do not lead. The fact that all of these phenomena occur so regularly suggests that "there is need of only one thing," as Jesus put it to Martha (Luke 10:42), is not peculiar to the church. It is a human proclivity and problem. We lose our way. We become preoccupied with personal and institutional survival. We cast about for the next new thing that will save us. We conduct focus groups and take polls, hoping that the market will tell us what to do. We come up with the latest reform movement or some new and improved product or technique. But, to adapt a line from the prophet Jeremiah, we heal the wounds of our people lightly, not in fact healing them at all (Jer. 8:11).

Besides the apparent human proclivity for majoring in the minors and minoring in the majors, other factors have contributed to the theological underfunding of churches. These reflect the churches' journey in the eras of Christendom and modernity. Both eras, each in its way, tended to turn the church away from theological conviction. But both Christendom and modernity are arguably now over, creating not only the opportunity but also the necessity for theological recovery. How did Christendom and modernity contribute to our theological amnesia?

Christendom combines two words that some would argue should never have been combined in the first place, *Christian* and *dominion*. Christendom represents the wedding of Christianity and the governing powers of nation or empire. It can be dated to the Constantinian settlement by which Christianity moved, over time, from a minority and suspect faith in the Roman Empire to the majority and dominant religion. While the roots of Christendom can be traced to the fourth century and Constantine, for our purposes here, we need not go so far back. We can limit ourselves to Christendom's particular expression in North America, or "American Christendom." Though an official separation of church and state is part of the founding inspiration and remains legally the case for the United States, Christianity has been the de facto, if unofficial, religion of the nation and continent for most of the country's history. North American Christendom has been different from the Christendom of Europe, where state churches reflected the actual legal establishment of the church. In North America, the establishment has, for the most part, been a cultural establishment rather than a legal one.

When I was an elementary school student, for example, the school day began with a pledge to the United States flag, a reading from the Bible, and a prayer. Moreover, there was no discussion about which God we were praying to! It would not have occurred to us to have such a discussion. Nor would it have occurred to us to question the amalgamation of national and religious symbols. At Christmas programs, the Christian carols were sung and the Christian nativity story rehearsed. Sunday, the church's day of worship, was a cultural sabbath with stores closed and few other activities offered. Ministers, mostly Protestant clergy, played the role of social leaders, experts, and cultural commentators. The Bible served a symbolic role in courts and at inaugurations. In these and a hundred other ways, Christianity enjoyed a certain dominion and de facto cultural place. Moreover, within the Christian faith in general, mainline Protestant denominations, those descended from the Protestant Reformation in Europe, were especially dominant and were in reality the religious establishment of North American culture. The story is familiar, as is the rapid erosion of Christendom that has taken place in the last half-century.

Yet if Christianity, and particularly Protestant and Reformed Christianity, had such dominance, how could this have adversely affected the theological identity and theological funding of the churches? Though this theological diminishment may be paradoxical, it is not a great mystery. Anytime a group is the dominant or established religious body of a culture and nation,

its distinctive qualities, peculiar language and practices, and particular ways tend to be eroded in favor of the more moderate,
generally accessible, and seemingly universal. As a part of this
general acculturation, Christianity came to be characterized not
so much by its theological content as by its moral content. To be
Christian did not so much mean to hold a set of beliefs or distinctive practices formed by and formative of those beliefs. It
meant being a nicer sort of American, one who watched out for
his neighbor, played a part in the community, and was law-abid-
ing as well as civic and family minded. In other words, the term
Christian was emptied of theological content. To say someone
was a "good Christian" did not mean that he or she had a deep
understanding of the historic Christian faith and an ability to
articulate it. It meant she was an especially nice, a particularly
considerate human being. To be sure, this is a generalization to
which there were many exceptions. Still, the overall effect of
Christendom was not so much a Christianizing of America as an
Americanization of Christianity! Such is the danger of being the
religious establishment. Given the additional predilection of
Americans for the pragmatic, and a certain, constant strain of
anti-intellectualism in America, theology could be easily dismissed
in favor of the more practical and relevant. Many have been the
laypeople (as well as clergy) who have said, in essence, "Don't
bother me with theology; let's focus on what matters!"

Not only did American Christendom tend to minimize theological content of the Christian faith and the church in favor of
moral understanding and behaviors, this reduction has had the
dubious benefit of tilting the churches in America toward chirpy
moralism of the Ben Franklin variety, as well as moralistic versions of Christian faith. The emphasis of this established faith was
less on God and what God has done and more on us and what
we should do, think, and feel. Of course, religion, including Christianity, does and should have moral content and application. That's
not the point. The point is that when that's all the faith is, such a
religion tends to become moralistic. It becomes, as I have written elsewhere, a religion of good works and achievement, focused on becoming a "good Christian" and not a religion of
grace.[5] Grace is, by definition, grace to sinners. But increasingly

in the world of American Christendom, Christianity became the endowment of the "better sorts," not a religion for sinners at all but a benediction upon the saints, who are the upright and the virtuous. In this shift, something crucial was lost, and theology was downplayed and even viewed with suspicion.

The other partner in our theological devolution has been modernity, which for my purposes here can be dated to the seventeenth century, the end of the Thirty Years War in Europe, the Enlightenment, and the founding of the colonies that became the United States. Modernity was marked by a series of values and qualities not limited to but certainly including great emphasis on reason and rationality, optimism, universality, objectivity, and enthusiasm for grand narratives or an all-encompassing story.

Modernity was characterized by a huge confidence in reason and the capacity of human beings to comprehend, explain, and master the world through the exercise of reason in its theoretical and applied forms, science and technology. The explosion of science and technology led to a spirit of optimism about humanity's capacity to solve its most vexing and persistent problems (poverty, disease, ignorance), as well as confidence in the human capacity to conquer the vicissitudes and threats of nature. Particular cultural, linguistic, and ethnic traditions, values, and stories were downgraded and forgotten in the melting pot of a new and universal human identity. Moderns believed that people could stand apart from history, conditioning, and context, attaining an objective viewpoint and perspective. Finally, modernity had confidence in grand narratives, and particularly the big story that through science, reason, and technology humanity would usher in a new age of plenty and peace, with leisure and luxury for all. (To heck with liberty and justice!) Clearly, the contributions and gifts of modernity have been great, but they have not come without a price, nor have they quite fulfilled their utopian promise. The cheap hydroelectric power of massive dams has destroyed native fish stocks and the cultures of indigenous peoples. Modern science and technology have enabled us to kill one another more efficiently. The proliferation of communication technologies has meant a proliferation of media filled with violence and pornography available to all. One could go on. The point is that now in the postmodern world we are aware that modernity was a blessing, but a mixed one.

One of other consequences of modernity—the one relevant for this book—is exemplified by a slender volume known as *The Jefferson Bible*. Thomas Jefferson was a man of modernity, fascinated by science, versed in the arts of modern agriculture, a gifted inventor, fluent in modern political philosophy. Religiously, Jefferson was a deist, which means he believed something like God had created a universe that was a wondrous machine and then retired, leaving us in charge. Not being entirely comfortable with the received Bible, Jefferson the deist decided to create his own. He started by omitting the "primitive" Old Testament. Turning to the New Testament, he snipped out everything that did not square with a modern, rational man's devotion to reason and natural law. This meant the miracles had to go. Healing stories too were out. In the end, his Bible was a slender volume, composed mostly of the teachings of Jesus, the moral teachings of the man of Nazareth. The consequence of modernity, illustrated by Jefferson and his Bible, was much like that of establishing Christianity in American Christendom itself. Christianity was reduced to morality, a faith without revelation or theology. It was a practical faith, a faith without God or at least without a God who was in any way present or active. To be sure, God or some divine intelligence had created the world, but we were in charge now. The point, for our purposes, was that the world was demystified and religion rendered a-theological. Modernity's effect on Christian faith was decidedly reductive, a shift well symbolized by Jefferson's slender, reduced Bible.

A wonderful example of the shift from modernity to postmodernity has been the tale of Mount St. Helen's, one of the mountains of the Cascade Range in the western United States, near where I live. Twenty-five years ago, in 1980, Mount St. Helen's astonished nearly everyone by erupting. I remember the reaction well. We were surprised and disturbed, perhaps even a little offended. We were, after all, modern people. We had tamed nature, or so we thought. Volcanoes didn't erupt here any more. That sort of thing happened in other places, in the world called "Third." Twenty-five years later, when Mount St. Helen's again began to build toward eruption, the reaction was different and very postmodern. Now people began to make pilgrimages by the hundreds to the sacred mountain. People spoke of the mountain in tones of hushed awe. We postmoderns are no longer so confident of our ability to figure everything out through reason and science. We have discovered other ways of knowing—the mystical, emotional, and intuitive. We are intrigued by miracle and we long for mystery. These shifts in popular culture and consciousness have not been accompanied, for the most part, by resurgent interest in theology per se. They have rather spawned new interest in spirituality, in religious experience, and in encounters with the sacred, the numinous, and the divine.

But that is precisely where theology comes in. As Anselm said long ago, "Theology is faith seeking understanding."[6] The vast new interest in spirituality calls for a renewed and articulate theology to give expression, definition, and meaning to raw religious and spiritual experience. Theology is, at least in part, the attempt to make sense of religious experience. If postmodernity's turn to spirituality has not given rise to similar interest in theology, it may be because much extant theology was hammered out for a different time and a different need.

The next chapter, a continuation of this introduction, turns to the nature and function of theology, suggesting that theology as we have known it in the modern era may not be the theology we need for a postmodern era. But to summarize this brief excursion in American Christendom and modernity, both movements gave rise to a reductive ethos. Christianity became morality without spirituality. It was activism and work to do but without transformation or new birth. It was the Ten Commandments without either the burning bush or the exodus. It was the Sermon on the Mount without miracle or healing, without crucifixion and resurrection. It was a reduced, minimal faith, with theology relegated to departments of religion, academic specialists, and people who wrote books mostly for themselves and members of their guild. This is not to say that some theologians did not try to serve the church. Many did and some succeeded. But, by and large, theology and church parted ways, just as had theology and Christianity.

Perhaps one additional, more chronologically recent development also deserves brief comment in this connection. By the middle of the twentieth century and with gathered force in the 1960s and the following decades, popular and religious culture turned therapeutic. Religion was increasingly seen as an aspect of life having the purpose of enhancing my personal life or that of my family. It was supposed to contribute to our well-being and happiness with ourselves. In times of change, people turned to religion for comfort but not as often for challenge. What proved challenging but not comforting seemed, under such a popular therapeutic impulse and mentality, less welcome. Thus, for example, the idea of a God who commanded, required obedience, and judged, and before whom human beings were accountable, seemed to fade to be replaced by a God who was eager to bring us abundant life on our terms and according to our definitions. Moreover, if aspects of the faith once-received proved disturbing or troubling, we increasingly gave ourselves permission to amend, abridge, and discard what did not suit us. In other words, if there were problems in our experience of Christianity and the church, we changed Christianity and the church. Don't ask us to change. I'm okay and you're okay, but Christianity and the church are due for an overhaul. Such a sensibility has spawned nearly countless efforts to remake and refashion Christian faith. Less often did it occur to us therapeutically influenced moderns that we ourselves might also be in need of overhaul, repentance, or change of heart and mind.

Of course, efforts to alter and update the faith have a place. New occasions do teach new duties, and time does make ancient good uncouth, as hymnist James Russell Lowell wrote. Too often, however, a therapeutic sensibility resulted not only in some updating but also in revision and perhaps loss at the core. Instead of clergy and churches calling themselves and their congregants to be transformed "by the mercies of God" and not conformed to this world (Rom. 12:1-2), we preferred adjusting the faith to suit us. Such impulses did not further the cause of taking theology seriously.

All three—American Christendom, modernity, and a popularized therapeutic sensibility—tended to erode the theological content and authority of Christian faith. When we looked up and around sometime in the latter half of the twentieth century, it seemed, at least in some mainline Protestant congregations and denominations, there was no longer any "there" there, to adapt Gertrude Stein's legendary remark about her childhood in Oakland.[7] Christian faith had been so shorn of theological substance that it became, in the worst-case scenarios, a cobbled together mish-mash of being really nice and pursuing the latest social causes and enthusiasms, with a dash of new age spirituality. As a new century dawned, those who turned to the churches of the once mainline traditions to encounter God and to be formed and transformed by the gospel and a way of life congruent with the gospel too often found little of substance. Many wondered, "Where's the beef?" to borrow a once popular advertising slogan. What they found instead, not always but certainly too often, were congregations that were increasingly bedeviled by dysfunction, decline, and discouragement. Congregations and clergy of the once mainline suffered a loss of theological confidence. Seekers found congregations and denominations that had lost touch with their core convictions and what difference they made.

The aim of this volume is to contribute to a theological refunding of mainline Protestant churches. This effort is undertaken in the conviction that theology has something, a great deal really, to do with healthy and vital congregations. But before we turn to the particular core theological convictions most salient in this project, dwelling briefly on the nature and definition of theology is important. This is the topic of the next chapter.

Chapter 1

Theology and Vital Congregations

Defining Terms

The focus of this chapter is two key terms in my title, *What's Theology Got to Do with It? Convictions, Vitality, and the Church*. One of those terms is *theology*, and the other is *vitality*, particularly as it applies to congregations. More than providing textbook or dictionary definitions of each term, my intent is to reflect on their various meanings and particularly how I understand and use them. Moreover, when I turn to *vitality*, or as I often think of it, *health*, I suggest some of the marks of unhealthy and healthy congregations as I see them frequently evidenced in contemporary congregations.

Theology

Early on in my work on this book, I had the opportunity to address a group of pastors and lay leaders about the topic, "Healthy Congregations: What's Theology Got to Do with It?" As I concluded one portion of my presentation and began a dialogue with audience members, one said, "I really found what you said helpful, but I wonder why you insist on using the word *theology*. I just don't think it helps." I suspect this pastor would not be alone in her objection. To many pastors and laity, *theology* suggests heavy tomes, multiple volumes, dense and abstract language. Theology may have been something a person had to study as a student preparing for ordination, but when that was done, that was it for theology. It just was not the kind of thing that was very useful in parish ministry or in the ongoing life of the church and its members. Oh, an occasional work of theology or a theologian here or there might ignite the imaginations of people in some congregations, but even then such theological study might seem like an interesting mental exercise, not something you could practice or use. You just don't open up a warm and friendly conversation around the backyard barbeque with a line like, "What do you think about eschatology?"

On the other hand, some such conversations have a lot to do with eschatology. For example, someone might speak of a crisis brought on by illness or loss of a job, and then say, "You know that experience really put in perspective the things that are important in life." That statement would qualify as a comment of great eschatological meaning having to do with the ends for and to which we live. But the technical vocabulary of academic theology is more often a conversation ender than a conversation starter. In this respect, the word *theology* is somewhat similar to a few other words that generally appear as subheadings or rubrics within theological works—*doctrine* and *dogma*. These are perfectly respectable and useful words. *Doctrine* means a teaching or set of teachings regarding a topic or theme. *Dogma* means a system of doctrines or principles arranged coherently. And yet, when either word is used in popular discourse, that use is often accompanied by a pejorative tone or rhetorical sneer. *Doctrine* seems to connote something stale or boring. *Dogma* inevitably seems to be thought of as oppressive. Like these words, *theology* may suffer from a bad reputation that is not entirely deserved or helpful.

My point is that for many, theology is thought of negatively. It is, it seems, primarily viewed as something practiced by academic specialists, mostly in seminaries or university departments of theology or religion, but not something of great interest or relevance to the ordinary Christian or even the ordinary pastor. To a significant extent, this sense of irrelevance and even bewilderment may only have been amplified by the turn in recent decades to what Luke Timothy Johnson, a New Testament scholar, described as "adjectival theology." By that Johnson meant that suddenly every theology, or so it seemed, was preceded by one adjective or another. There was process theology, liberation theology, womanist theology, neoorthodox theology, feminist theology, and black theology. If you wanted to push a little further you could find queer theology, geek theology, and chick theology. Citing the latter examples is not meant to trivialize, only to point out the bewildering array of choices—a peculiarly modernist development that emphasizes the parts but in the process may have neglected the whole, or any notion that a whole exists. While there is no doubt a rich ferment of creativity brewing in all the various adjectival theologies, the risk is that theology becomes ever more the province of elites, those who have the time and background necessary to negotiate the world of microtheologies. Moreover, such adjectival theologies may seem to suggest that all theology or theologies are in service of some predetermined agenda or cause. Various adjectival theologies have given new and needed voice to some groups and experiences, but the proliferation itself may have left many a pastor and layperson mumbling, muttering, and tongue-tied. The result is that theology is neglected, avoided, dismissed, discounted, or limited to certain affinity groups. Of course, the academic discipline of theology is not wholly to blame for this state of affairs. Sometimes, truth to tell, pastors and laity are simply lazy. They do not want to do the work of challenging reading and conversation or of interpretation and application. No doubt, many theologians are as frustrated by the marginalization of theology as anyone.

Nevertheless, an abstract or academic understanding is probably the dominant understanding of theology that my questioner had in mind when she suggested that I keep doing what I'm doing but "lose theology, at least in the title, or lose readership—it's up to you!" Although such is the dominant understanding of theology abroad in the land, another understanding exists, possibly formed in opposition to the more academic and scholastic models. Such an alternative finds expression in such course titles as "Creating Your Own Theology" and "Do-It-Yourself

Theology" or when people speak of "my personal theology," as if highly personal and individualized theologies were the only kind of theology there is. To be sure, nothing is intrinsically wrong with such courses or with the attempt to articulate one's beliefs or theology. Much is right with it. But these titles and phrases do hold within them a certain danger, namely, the implicit notion that theology is pretty much a matter of personal choice and opinion: "You've got your theology and I've got mine. End of conversation."

The danger of the first type of theology is a certain scholasticism and dominance of a professional guild, while the danger of the latter notion of theology is a kind of antinomianism. The logical end game of the "my personal theology" understanding is the example discussed by Robert Bellah and his coauthors in *Habits of the Heart*. A woman named Sheila described her personal faith and religion as "Sheila-ism." Bellah focused on Sheila and Sheila-ism not because she was so unique but just the opposite—because she so well exemplified a common trend, that is, the perception that religion or theology is personal, private, and individual, and nothing more.

I aim to chart a course between scholasticism on one hand and antinomianism on the other, and to do so by turning to older, premodern definitions and understandings of theology. Scholastic versions of theology seem very much of the modern era with their divisions, subdivisions, categories, specialties, and subspecialties. In a way, this specialization reproduces or mimics the way of modern medicine and the modern university with their fragmentation of people and knowledge. As suggested, the antinomian variety can be seen as a kind of "to hell with you" reaction against the same. "Church and theologians, if your theology doesn't make any sense to me, I'll create my own!"

Is there an alternative, a different way to understand theology? In his collection of essays on theological education, *The Fragility of Knowledge: Theological Education in the Church and the University,* Edward Farley, a theologian who taught for many years at Vanderbilt University, claims that the contemporary situation is not far removed from what it was prior to the Protestant Reformation, namely, virtually all theological education is directed at clergy. "The church continues on the assumption that ordered learning with respect to matters of religion, its texts, its history, beliefs and practices, is not a possibility for the believer." Beyond noting that too much theological education is focused on a professional class of clergy and not enough on ordinary believers, Farley suggests we are helped to do worthwhile theological education or teaching by adopting an earlier, premodern, understanding of theology. "In the older sense, theology was not just for the scholar or teacher but was the wisdom proper to the life of the believer."[1] Wisdom proper to the life of the believer! Not mastery of insider language, but the capacity to articulate the language of faith and devotion and relate it to one's life. Not possessing encyclopedic knowledge of various schools and theologians, but possessing wisdom, the wisdom proper to the Christian believer.

Professor of Christian Education at Princeton Theological Seminary Richard Osmer points in a similar direction when he suggests, "What persons desperately need in most mainline churches today is help in gaining the kind of knowledge and skill that is necessary to allow them to make moral and religious meaning out of their everyday lives."[2] The emphasis falls on the closing words: "meaning" and "everyday lives." Does theology do that? Could it? Could a postmodern understanding of theology reclaim the notion of theology as the province not of professionals or elites, but of the life of the ordinary believer who seeks to make moral and religious sense of his or her life and experience?

A somewhat similar notion of theology was also suggested by ethicist James Gustafson, who spoke of theology as a perspective and a way of construing life. The word *perspective* literally means "to see through." What is the perspective through which we see life? Is it a perspective formed and shaped by cross and resurrection or by some other story or theology or doctrine? There are plenty of perspectives, doctrines, and dogmas available in the contemporary marketplace of worldviews and ideas. We are shaped by the perspectives, doctrines, and dogmas of nationalism, consumerism, materialism, and modernity, among others. Postmodern theory and thinkers suggest that none of us sees life simply as it is. We all see life through some lens, through some perspective, some story. Is Christian theology a lens through which to see life and to see it truthfully? I believe that it is. Moreover, I believe that if pastors and congregations are not hard at the work of forming and transforming people in this way of seeing, others—often backed by huge advertising and marketing budgets—will have their way with our fellow citizens, neighbors, and children—and with us.

Thus, when I speak of theology in what follows, I do not have in mind an academic subspecialty for which advanced degrees are required, though I hope that those who do possess such degrees may be increasingly helpful in funding the theological thinking and living of ordinary believers. Nor do I have in mind an understanding of theology that is so highly personal as to be idiosyncratic and not available for discussion or evaluation. I have in mind theology as wisdom proper to the life of the believer, as a way of construing life and making sense of it, and as a foundation for experience. Such theology forms and transforms lives. It forms and informs the growth of human character and moral substance. Or, if it doesn't, we who do theology and lead congregations had better find something better to do with ourselves!

In this regard, one of the earliest stories in the Gospel of Mark is both noteworthy and provocative. In Mark 1:21-28 Jesus is repeatedly reported to be "teaching" and "teaching with authority." What's odd about this early story is that there is not a word about the content of his teaching. Instead, in the midst of this presentation of Jesus as teacher and as one who taught with authority, Jesus casts out a demon. How does this add up? What in the world is the point of a story about Jesus as teacher without any teaching, but instead an exorcism? Possibly this: Mark would have us know that when Jesus teaches, lives are changed and healed, evil is confronted and named, people are set free and empowered. In other words, Mark wants us to know that when Jesus teaches it is not just an interesting sideline. No, when Jesus teaches, something is at stake! Could this be true, or become true, of the teaching, the theology, of the church? Could it change, even save, lives?

Beyond this life-changing capacity of teaching, I would hope that Christian theology would suggest neither the academic world nor the individual as its primary context but rather the church. When I speak of theology, I have in mind both "wisdom proper to the life of the believer" and the faith of the ecumenical and orthodox church. I understand that the ecumenical and ortho- dox church is a wide river through which flow many channels. Moreover, the many channels have their origins in many differ- ent places and events. The church cannot be easily narrowed down or reduced, nor should it be. Nevertheless, there is some- thing identifiable as the faith of the church. That faith has found expression in the ecumenical creeds of the church, the Apostles and Nicene Creeds. In the early centuries of the Christian church, creeds served as a kind of rule of faith, with *rule* meaning some- thing like *canon*, that is, "norm" or "measuring rod." The rule of faith, spoken of by Irenaeus, even preceded the first of the creeds, the Apostles' Creed. It attempted to guide Christians, congrega- tions, and pastors in the basics of sound and healthy teaching. (In the Pauline epistles, *sound* and *healthy* are the same Greek word.) Only later during the era of Christendom did creeds take on their more negative associations and usages as tests of loyalty to the empire or emperor. In their early stages, these summations of the faith were not loyalty tests so much as guides and direction markers, summations of the essentials of the faith, often ham- mered out in the face of persecution and temptations.

Another way to state the point regarding creeds is to say that the ecumenical church and the Christian faith can be known by a set of core convictions about God, humanity, the Scriptures, Jesus Christ, and so on. What do we, as Christians and as the church catholic and ecumenical, believe and affirm? My conten- tion in this book is that a fluid and flexible yet discernible core of Christian conviction exists, and that this core has the capacity to serve as wisdom proper to the life of believers and as norm, source, and resource for forming and sustaining healthy congregations. In this sense, theology might not only be taught and offered by the church's pastors and elders; it might also be deployed as a corrective to call those same pastors and elders to account and keep them faithful. In other words, theology as core convictions and wisdom proper to the life of all (not just clergy) believers, like the Bible, can be itself not only our best friend but also our best critic. Good theology, owned and embodied by ordinary Christians, can serve not only to form and inform the church and its members, but also to keep the churches and their leaders honest.

One additional note before I move on to discussing vital and healthy congregations. Recent decades have seen a rich and growing interest in Christian and spiritual practices. The focus on practices can largely be traced to the seminal work of Alasdair MacIntyre in the early 1970s and its further development by Stanley Hauerwas, Craig Dykstra, Dorothy Bass, and Diana Butler Bass, among others. Sometimes these practices are contrasted with and set over against beliefs. Some proponents of practices have even remarked that Christianity is not, in fact, about beliefs at all but about practices. While I understand the hyperbole of such statements, they seem to me misleading. We ought to want beliefs or core convictions, on one hand, and practices or a way of life, on the other, to go together and not to be set in opposition. It seems to me that the challenges of our postmodern, post-Christendom time call for our best work and attention to both—to practices and to beliefs. While I would certainly agree that Christianity ought always to be more than beliefs and that right living must accompany right belief, I can't imagine that right living is helped by a lack of clarity or conviction about our core beliefs. Because, at present, a great deal of attention and effort are being focused at least in some quarters on Christian practices, I hope this essay on theology, beliefs, and convictions only complements such efforts and does not compete with them or appear indifferent to them.

Vital and Healthy Congregations

The driving force behind this book is not an indifferent or idle one. It is a deep concern for the vitality of congregations, which of course suggests an equally deep concern about congregations that are not vital. Too many congregations are stuck, dysfunctional, toxic, or simply boring—in a word, unhealthy. I care about congregations, their leaders, and their participants. I do understand that every congregation has dysfunctions, failures, and disappointments. Perfection is neither a worthwhile nor in this life an attainable goal. But a greater degree of health—of faithfulness and vitality—is attainable and to be sought. So what does a healthy congregation look like? And what does a lack of health, or congregational pathology, look like?

When I asked these kinds of questions of colleagues, both lay and clergy, their initial responses often included remarks like, "Health is not merely an absence of conflict. Sometimes we think that the absence of conflict, or the seeming absence of conflict, equals health. That's misleading. Conflict can be a sign of health. Moreover, seeming harmony is sometimes an inability to deal with the tough questions or to be honest with one another." Others said, "Health is not be equated with numerical membership growth, or lack of health with membership decline. It's more complex than that." What, then, does a vital and healthy congregation look like, and how does a lack of health or vitality manifest itself? While most pastors, lay leaders, denominational executives, and seminary teachers have their own list of characteristics of a healthy or unhealthy congregation, I note seven unhealthy patterns based on my experience as pastor, consultant, teacher, and person who works widely with congregations, clergy, lay leaders, and denominations. These seem to be some of the most common forms of disarray.

The Church as a Club

One of the ironies of church life is that the same congregation can be described by two different people in opposite ways, and both descriptions can be accurate. One person will describe a particular congregation as "the warmest, friendliest church anywhere." Another person will describe the very same congregation as "cold, difficult to join, and not very friendly." What's the difference? It is usually whether or not a person is part of the group or marginal to it. When the church has become a club, those on the inside typically describe it as "close, warm, caring, and friendly." Someone who is not on the inside describes the same church as "cold and unfriendly."

But something else marks the congregation that has become a club, or is tending in that direction, and is no longer fully the church: its primary purpose has been lost or forgotten. Instead of focusing on people growing in faith and discipleship and growing in the image of Christ, the club church's purpose has become satisfying the members. The job of the pastor, along with a few lay leaders, seems primarily to be keeping the members happy. This may make for a pretty good club, but it may not be the church. Purpose has been displaced. To put it positively, a healthy congregation has reasonable clarity about its purpose or reason for being, and its life and mission serve that purpose. When the purpose is growing people of faith, that is, helping people grow in the image of Christ, then the church is likely to be healthy. Moreover, when this purpose is in place, a congregation is more likely to be a strong fellowship marked by a sense of belonging *and* a community that is hospitable to the stranger, guest, and sojourner.

The Church Where Leadership Is Ineffective

Congregations, like all social groups and organizations, require effective leadership. Effective leaders who are people of integrity enable congregations to be faithful to their essential purpose and to deal with the toughest problems and challenges. An absence of leadership creates a vacuum, and congregations abhor a vacuum nearly as much as nature does. People will step or push forward to fill the vacuum. But these self-appointed leaders may lack both the gifts and the training for leadership. Moreover, such de facto leaders are unlikely to be held accountable either by denominational structures or by congregational procedures for evaluation. They hold themselves accountable to no standards other than their own. The number-one pattern of congregational ill health is that the congregation turns inward and becomes a cozy, members-only club; a close second is that the congregation's authorized leadership is either absent or ineffective, and unauthorized and unaccountable people have stepped into the vacuum. The obvious inverse and healthy pattern is that effective, authorized, and accountable leaders are in place, and the appropriate role and authority of such duly chosen leaders is understood, respected, and valued. There are, thus, two sides to this matter of leadership: effective leaders who are trustworthy and congregations who value and support effective leaders. Both are present, in significant measure, in the healthy congregation.

The Church Where Nothing Is at Stake

Several years ago, biblical scholar Fred Craddock noted that the most common problem he finds in contemporary preaching is that it seems, entirely too often, as if nothing much is at stake, that preaching proceeds as if it doesn't much matter. This critique can be extended beyond the pulpit to the whole life of the church. One chronic form of ill health today is what we might call the trivialization of the church. It is nice, it is friendly, it may be cute, and on occasion it is even touching. But, in the end, nothing much is at stake. Nothing of ultimate significance is evident in the church's proclamation, sacraments, faith, and life. If a congregation's life has something to do with the one who said, "I am the way, the truth, and the life," (John 14:6) it is no longer apparent. Conversely, a healthy congregation is one where something is at stake; where the words and the actions do matter; and where lives are being changed, healed, redirected to positive paths, and made new. Healthy congregations possess a sense of confidence in the gospel message and faith. This confidence is not arrogant, but members have a steady, humble confidence that what they are doing in and as the church matters and, in fact, matters a great deal. Otherwise, why bother?

Unity Sacrificed to Diversity or Diversity Lost to Uniformity

The unhealthy church fails to maintain a lively tension between two goods, or two values: unity and diversity. Perhaps diversity, along with individual freedom and autonomy, is so prized that the church loses any sense of coherence, center, or purpose. Alternately, unity and presenting a unified front to the world are so esteemed that difference and diversity are ruled out. The apostle Paul, especially, struggled to keep unity and diversity in a healthy and lively tension with his metaphor of the church as the body of Christ, where there are many different parts but one body. Healthy congregations work at honoring both unity and diversity. There is room for individual difference; indeed, it is valued as the gift of God. But welcoming difference does not become a warrant for everyone doing his or her own thing. Difference, expressed in different gifts, is put in service of a common good and shared ministry.

The Church That Is Not Able to Deal with Conflict

Congregations that neither recognize nor accurately name and then deal with and resolve conflicts tend to be unhealthy. Old issues and conflicts never seem to be resolved. They linger like festering sores. Decisions are avoided rather than made. No useful pattern or protocol for working through tough issues exists. Issues and disagreements are not surfaced in open and appropriate settings but become the material of parking-lot, after-meeting conversations and gossip sessions. People in such congregations avoid talking with the person or people with whom they have an issue. Instead, they talk to others about such people. The truth is not spoken for fear it will lead to more unresolved conflict. These are all common enough human problems and will never be completely solved or eradicated in any human group or institution. But in the unhealthy congregation, such patterns and practices have become the norm rather than the exception. Vital congregations, however, are ones where conflict is recognized, helpfully and accurately named and framed, then dealt with according to fair, reasonable, and understood protocols or practices. And once decisions have been fairly reached, those decisions are accepted and respected. Note, as indicated above, a healthy congregation, like a healthy family or marriage, has disagreements, even conflicts, at times. But a healthy congregation is able to face and resolve conflicts and move on.

The Church Out of Balance

Recently, a physical therapist explained to me that my shoulders were sore because I was overusing my upper trapezius muscles but under-using my middle and lower "traps." Congregations can also play too much to certain parts of Christian faith, liturgy, or ministry and underutilize others, with the result that they are out of balance. For example, some congregations seem to do Good Friday every Sunday of the year, as Christ on the cross is always and only the focus of preaching and worship. Other congregations may emphasize Christ the teacher or moral example and never have a word to say about Calvary and the depths of human sin. Some congregations talk only about individual change and conversion, while others have nothing to say of that but put all their eggs in the basket of changing systems and social structures. For some congregations, the sacrament of the Lord's Supper or Eucharist is always and only the Last Supper and never the victory table of the risen Lord. You get the idea. The Christian faith is complex and many faceted. It cannot and should not be reduced to a one-note song or a one-theme story. When that happens, a congregation gets out of balance and unhealthy. Healthy congregations have a lively respect for the whole gospel in its variety of textures and colors, stories and themes.

Where Spirit Eclipses Structure or (More Likely) Structure Quenches Spirit

Sociologist Max Weber noted the tendency of organizations to snuff out charisma or spirit, to make routine the founding gift or *charism*. By their nature organizations strive for internal efficiency, rationality, and consistency. These are not bad things, but if they are the only things going in a congregation, they succeed in snuffing out or arresting the free movement of the Spirit of God, which neither institutions nor individuals can or ought to control. On the other hand, structures and organization exist for a reason. They protect people from charismatic individuals and leaders who need to be kept honest and accountable. They protect people and groups from excess enthusiasm or from spirits that are not of the Holy Spirit. Once again, health lies in the creative tension between two goods or truths, that is, in the managing of the polarity of Spirit and structure and not the triumph of one or the other. Healthy congregations have reliable and respected systems and ways of doing things. But they also have experiences that open the doors and windows to allow fresh gusts of life and

Spirit to enter. They have people who lead beyond their authority and open new ways. Healthy congregations are capable of
creating new structures as new occasions and fresh movements
of the Spirit require them.

To be sure, other forms of congregational health and illness
exist. This listing is not intended to be exhaustive but rather il-
lustrative. But in my experience as pastor, teacher, and consultant, I believe these maladies and vitalities are the most common.
Does theology have something to say to these unhealthy patterns? Can theology contribute to greater vitality? I believe the
answer to these questions is yes. So now, let's turn to theology
and what it has to do with healthy congregations.

Questions for Reflection and Discussion

1. On your own or in a group, do a free association with the
   word *theology*. What does your word association suggest?
2. What would you describe as your most significant experience of theological learning or education? What made it
   significant for you?
3. What theological theme or conviction is most important
   to you in living your life today? Describe the role it plays.
4. This chapter lists several forms of congregational ill health.
   Is there one that particularly jumps out at you and gets
   your attention? If so, what makes it stand out?
5. List some of the attributes of a vital, or healthy, congregation from your viewpoint.

Chapter 2

The Missing Center

The Identity Crisis

Not long ago, I was leading a leadership and planning retreat for a large metropolitan congregation of my denomination (United Church of Christ). We had been working on identifying and responding to some of the congregation's particular organizational challenges when one leader blurted out, "But what do we believe? That's what I want to know!"

As if some dam had been opened, another person jumped in, saying, "Yes, I just feel that we're not sure who we are or what we believe." A startled and an awkward silence fell over the group, as if no one quite knew how to respond or even if such questions were acceptable or legitimate.

Had these two lay leaders, both of whom happened to be women and both on the younger side (say, under 40), named the elephant in the room? Were a clear identity and a discernible center of faith and conviction lacking? At least one person was sure they had not named the elephant in the room. This older man gruffly interrupted the silence: "Attempts to define what we believe make me nervous!" This seemed to elicit several nods of agreement, as if some voice of authority had spoken.

At this point one of the church's pastors intervened to say, "These are important questions, but perhaps not within the scope of the current event or discussion." The exchange was interesting, with revealing dynamics.

The two who raised the questions were of one generation and, it turned out, newer to the congregation. The man who put a lid of sorts on the conversation was a long-time member. Moreover, the pastor played a role pastors often play, that of attending to the process and quelling conflict. Sometimes that role is necessary and helpful, but I wondered if the pastor had stilled a potentially useful, if uncomfortable, conversation. Judging from the energy and the urgency of the remarks as well as the nature of the ensuing silence, I concluded a real and important, if difficult, question had been raised. Perhaps more than one difficult matter had been raised.

In fact, in this brief exchange several related concerns are discernible. One concern might be described as a *question of identity*. "Who are we and what do we believe?" asked one of the first speakers. She went on to say that she didn't think this was clear or that it was addressed in the church's ongoing life. Questions of identity are important to a healthy congregation: Who are we? and, What beliefs, values and convictions give shape and direction to our life and mission?

Another closely related question, to which the older man and perhaps the pastor seemed to respond, is about *boundaries*. If we define our identity, will we create boundaries with which we can or cannot live? What boundaries currently exist, whether named and acknowledged or unnamed and unacknowledged? A third, less prominent but still evident thread in the exchange may deal with not only how that particular congregation defines its identity and boundaries, but also *the process of communicating and discussing* these issues. Are these matters open to discussion or are they not? In an odd way, the apparently open-minded perspective of the older man ("Attempts to define what we believe make me nervous!") actually had a closing, not opening, effect on the discussion. He signaled for himself, and seemingly for others, discomfort with such a conversation. When such topics are outside the bounds of permissible conversation, one danger is that a congregation becomes clan or clublike, with authority given to longest standing members and to unwritten rules. Attempts to openly and theologically address identity and boundaries may, paradoxically, have the effect of opening up the congregation and leveling the playing field between newer and long-time members.

Congregational identity and boundaries, and the capacity to speak of such challenging matters, all bubbled up in short order and with energy and urgency. These questions are important for any congregation and vital to congregational health. My proposal in this chapter and the next is that Christian theological convictions regarding revelation and Scripture help congregations engage these issues and address the questions of identity and boundaries in fruitful ways. Some degree of clarity regarding identity may also help congregations to avoid the "Pecos River syndrome"—that is, being spread a mile wide but only a foot deep. When congregations lack clarity about identity and purpose, they tend to have a difficult time sorting out priorities and saying no to much of anything. In fact, the wide-but-shallow characteristic did afflict this particular congregation and was at the root of some of the organizational issues we had been working on. Thus, many matters of congregational health and disease clustered in this relatively brief exchange: identity, boundaries, openness and transparency of congregational process, and setting priorities.

A Brief Side Trip

Before turning in this chapter to the category of revelation and its relevance to these several aspects of identity, I want to make a brief side trip into what is known as "set theory." Set theory enables us to name and differentiate three different kinds of "sets" or social groups or congregations: the open, the bounded, and the centered. It is both my hunch and experience that many congregations get stuck and are unable to have this conversation because they think the alternatives are limited to either open or bounded sets. Many congregations will welcome a third option, the centered set.

An open-set congregation is one where you hear things like, "Everyone is welcome here." "We're an open congregation— people have all sorts of beliefs." "You can believe whatever you want here." This type of congregation can be visually represented as a random bunch of dots on a page representing different individuals or subgroups. There are no boundaries, that is, lines between who is in and who is out. But neither is there any center. Initially, such an open set may appear quite thrilling, especially to those who have come from a system that has clear, hard boundaries, and where they have felt they did not fit in or were subjected to pressures to conform that were uncomfortable. "Isn't it great? Everyone is welcome, no matter what," such an enthusiast might say. "Here, we can think and say what we want." But another, who has perhaps been around longer, might answer, "Like you, I found it great initially. But as time has gone on it has proven frustrating too. It's difficult to actually do anything together. And when it comes right down to it, I'm not even sure if we are together or if there is anything we belong to. We just seem to be a collection of individuals, each with his own viewpoint, ideas, and agendas!" Such are the strengths, and weaknesses, of the open set.

The bounded set is the opposite. Visually, the bounded set has very clear, dark, heavy boundaries. You might visualize a square, rectangle, or circle with some dots (representing individuals or groups) inside and others outside of the line defining the shape and set. You can tell who is in and who is out. The strengths and weaknesses of the bounded set are just the opposite of the open set. Where the latter proclaims "All are welcome here," but some people feel frustrated that there is no real "here" to be a part of or a unified group that can work together on shared goals, the bounded set has a clear but possibly confining sense of identity. Such a group does have a clear identity and can pursue common objectives, but there is little openness to difference or questions. If the open set seems inclusive, the bounded set appears exclusive. Often in congregations, conversation about identity, such as the one with which this chapter began, seem to pit the open and bounded set options against one another as if no alternative exists.

For many congregations a better choice is to think about their church as, and work toward becoming, a centered set. The centered set may be pictured as having a clear center, say, a large dot or small circle at the center but no boundaries; or if there are boundaries, they are highly permeable, perhaps a broken line defining inside and outside. Now, the identity questions are less about who is inside and who outside and more about direction. Are people moving away from or toward the center? In the centered set the congregation's task is not so much to police the boundaries as it is to define and articulate its center. "This is who we are and what we are about. You decide if this is right for you," is the message of such a centered-set congregation. In contrast to the open set, the centered set has an identity, a coherent core that gives definition and content. In contrast to the bounded set, the focus is not so much on the boundaries, which are permeable, but on the center. The centered-set understanding of a congregation allows for both identity and openness. Many congregations find the centered set concept to be helpful in a world where the extremes of the open and bounded sets are both common and, each in its way, inadequate.

Identity, Center, and Revelation

Reasonable clarity about congregational identity is important to the vitality of a congregation, just as it is to an individual. "Who are you?" while not an easy question, is an important one. In congregations and other organizations, the question "Who are you?" is equally tough and equally important. My observation is that many mainline Protestant congregations, like the one described above, are reluctant to pose such questions or to allow others to pose them. This discomfort suggests uncertainty about our identity and core convictions, which tends to make discussion of these matters difficult. Like many parents contemplating talking with their children about sex, we tend to be unsure of what we think or whether we can handle the questions, so we either avoid them, pretend everyone already knows the answers, or try to foist the responsibility for dealing with them onto others. "Isn't this covered at the church youth group?"

Congregations wrestling with such questions need to be reminded of a basic distinction about religions, one that helps us to
define and speak about our own. This distinction is between what
theologians and philosophers call "natural religion" and "revealed
religion." Christianity falls into the latter category, but also has
room for the former. What's the difference between the two, and
what difference does it make? Pastor and author, Martin
Copenhaver, in his book *To Begin at the Beginning,* describes the
two:

> Natural religion begins with the affirmation that God is ev-
> erywhere and in all things and goes on to contend that God
> can be perceived in all things without any special aid or rev-
> elation. Some who represent this view go so far as to say that,
> if our perception is properly developed, the presence of God
> can be discerned in all things with equal immediacy and accu-
> racy. We can learn as much about God from a blade of grass as
> we can from the most extraordinary human life. We can ex-
> pect to encounter God no more fully in the life of Jesus than
> in any other life.
>
> Revealed religion, which includes both Hebrew and Chris-
> tian traditions, also begins with an affirmation that God is ev-
> erywhere and in all things. But those who hold this view go
> on to stipulate that God is not equally perceptible in all things.
> Instead, God chooses to reveal God's own self more fully in
> some events than in others, more completely in some lives
> than others, and more clearly in some books than others. Jews
> affirm that God was more abundantly revealed in the Exodus
> than in their slavery in Egypt. Christians profess that we can
> learn more about God by studying the life of Jesus than we
> can learn from the life of our local butcher.
>
> To be sure, God is present and can be encountered in the
> blade of grass, in the butcher on the corner, and in many books
> that are not included in the Bible. But if we are to apprehend
> correctly how God is present in all things, we must view them
> through what God has revealed to us in special events, special
> people, and indeed a special book.[1]

The point for our purposes here is that Christianity is, quite apart from our individual preferences, a revealed religion. Christianity affirms that God has revealed the divine self and way to us in particular events, people, and books, particularly including God's work in creation, in the story of the people of Israel, and in the life, teaching, death, and resurrection of Jesus Christ. *Revelation* means "disclosure" or "unveiling." Rightly characterized as a revealed religion, Christian faith asserts that God's will and way have been disclosed to us, unveiled before us, in these particular events and people.

In other words, Christianity is not whatever you or I want it to be. There is a "there" there. A nonnegotiable core of revealed truth defines Christian faith and belief. True, in the various churches and traditions great diversity exists in interpretation and great latitude in application, but a specific core of content cannot be gainsaid, eliminated, overlooked, forgotten, or added to without Christian faith and the Christian church becoming something other than what they are. Moreover, Christians affirm that this core of revelation or revealed truth about God and God's will and way is not something we invented, but was given to us, revealed to us by God.

Let me be autobiographical for a moment. I grew up in a wonderful Congregational/United Church of Christ congregation in the 1950s and 1960s, arguably the heyday of mainline Protestantism, a period when churches like my home church were at the center of the culture and had great influence in American society. Perhaps because our influence was so broad, we tended to emphasize common human experience and moral values but not theological beliefs. I grew up with little knowledge of the Bible or theology (of course, it could be I just wasn't paying attention!) but hearing a great deal of emphasis on loving my neighbor as myself, working for justice, and being a responsible citizen and member of the community. Of course, nothing is wrong with any of that, except that today, in a very different time, this understanding of what Christian faith and Christian identity mean, while still necessary, is no longer sufficient. Moreover, the minimalist understanding of my childhood lacked adequate content. Christianity is and must be more than simply being a nice person or a better sort of American.

And it is! It is much more. Christianity is a set of convictions, and a story, and a relationship with God. It is grounded in God's work in creation, God's presence with the people of Israel, and God's revealing of God's self in the life, teaching, death, and resurrection of Jesus. Moreover, among these several major events, people, and experiences, Christians affirm that God's will and way has been definitively disclosed to us in Jesus Christ. For Christians, the life, teaching, acts, crucifixion, and resurrection of Jesus are the core "revealing" of God. It is for this reason that the church returns again and again to these stories.

A couple of caveats about revelation and about what Christians mean and do not mean when we speak of revelation are important to mention. The affirmation that God has revealed God's will and way to us does not mean that we completely or finally know God. As theologian Daniel Migliore puts it, "God does not cease to be a mystery in the event of revelation."[2] Christians err in acting as if we possess the whole and absolute truth, and that it is somehow our possession. No, God remains God, beyond our full or complete knowing and surely beyond our control. Revelation properly gives rise not to arrogance but to humility.

A second and related caveat has to do with God's revealing in Jesus Christ. For Christians, by definition, Jesus is the definitive revealing, disclosure, or unveiling. In Jesus Christ we see God revealed most fully and most clearly. As we test our claims to truth, as we weigh our decisions, as we struggle to understand what and how God is active today, this revealing functions as a kind of checkpoint: "Checkpoint Jesus." Having said that for Christians God is definitively revealed in Jesus Christ, we also affirm that God's revealing is not exhausted there. In other words, God continues to reveal God's presence, will, and way among us and to us. God is still speaking, but God always speaks in a way consistent with the God revealed in Jesus Christ. In Jesus we encounter a God who, let's admit it, often acts in surprising and disturbing ways, keeping company with the outcast and sinful, choosing the least and least likely, and revealing God's self ultimately, as Migliore puts it, "in the deep hiddenness of the cross."[3]

When someone asks, "What do we believe?" or says, "We don't know who we are or what we believe," it may prove useful to remind ourselves that in the Christian church, we have not been left entirely to our own devices. Ours is a revealed faith with a particular content. We affirm that God has revealed the divine will and way, definitively though not exhaustively, in God's self-disclosure in creation, in God's history with the people of Israel, in the person of Jesus Christ. To then engage these disclosures, or "revealings," of God in greater depth and with growing understanding is no small task. It is the work of a lifetime. But the point here is, we can respond to the questions of identity. We do have something to work with as we seek to name our center. Most of the church's various creeds and statements of faith are attempts to put into a short and compressed form, usable in worship, the core of what we affirm has been revealed to us. Sometimes these creeds have been made into tests of faith or loyalty or even patriotism. That is a misuse. Proper use of the creeds is not unlike the spelunker tying himself to the stake anchored outside the cave, as mentioned in the introduction. The creeds give us a fixed point from which to explore. They define a center to our life and faith. True, the meaning of such creeds and statements of faith is not self-evident. They require long-term engagement— study, dialogue, interpretation, and embodiment in our lives. This is how it should be. We ought to want a faith that asks something of us, and ours does.

Still, there is a "there" there. Christian faith is more than conventional morality and more, though never less, than a commitment to justice and compassion. Christian faith may have as a subplot the story of your particular congregation, but the stories of your particular church are not the content of Christian faith. Moreover, deciding on the core content of this faith is not up to us individually. As the order of worship for the service of evensong at Coventry Cathedral notes, "You are now entering a conversation that began long before you and will continue long after you are gone." Taking part in that conversation means that we too speak. We ask questions, seek understanding, and move either toward, or away from, the center. All this is necessary. God grants us the freedom to decide (and redecide) how we stand in relation to the Christian revelation. Some days we can affirm it all, and some days none of it. Most days, our response is more mixed. But the fact that some historical creeds (the Nicene Creed) and several contemporary creeds begin "We believe," reminds us that it's not all up to us. We are part of something bigger than just us alone. Some days, in our doubts, others carry us. Other days, our strong faith supports others. All of us are sustained by the revealed truth of our God and by the God who continues to reveal his grace, mystery, presence, and mercy.

Thus the creeds of the church are one attempt to describe the center of the centered set. They have sometimes been made into tests of faith that turned the church into a closed or bounded set. Other times such summaries of God's revelation have been treated so lightly as to create congregations of the open-set type, where everyone is welcome but it's not clear what we have been welcomed to. Different denominations have different ways of speaking of and using these short summary statements of the church's faith. My denomination, the United Church of Christ, avoids the word *creed* because of its historical associations with oppression and persecution. Nevertheless, we have a Statement of Faith, which plays a similar role in our denomination, while others turn to the historic creeds (Apostles' or Nicene) or more recent creedal statements. Our Statement of Faith is described among us as a testimony of faith, rather than a test of faith. It is the testimony of faithful witnesses who have gone before us. For those congregations that make use of it, the Statement can provide a center. It, and similar statements, can be the stake that anchors our exploration.

Revelation, Part 2

Revelation has two aspects: it is both the revealing of a particular content or message or story, but it is also an experience, an encounter, a gift, a grace. I have endeavored to show that our faith has actual content, something that God has revealed or disclosed to us. The content of the Christian revelation has three parts: God's self-disclosure in creation, in the history of the people of Israel, and in the person (life, teaching, actions, death, and resurrection) of Jesus Christ.

But revelation is not only this content and story; it is also an experience. Moreover, it is a particular kind of experience, one at odds with much of the rest of our experience, particularly as participants in the world of modernity. The nature of the experience of revelation also has implications for the health of churches. While the content of Christianity as a revealed religion helps us address questions of identity and center, the experience of revelation has the effect of decentering us. Almost by definition, the experience of revelation, while intensely personal, communicates, "It's not about you." There is an other before and unto whom we live, to whom we can turn, upon whom we may rely, and to whom we are accountable. Not to put too fine a point on it, but this quality of revelation as the experience of a greater reality beyond ourselves is at odds with much of the ethos of the modern world. Particularly, it is at odds with the modern notion of the sovereign and autonomous individual who is accountable to no one, who belongs to no one but him or her self. That's not the way Christians think or approach life. And if people hang around Christians long enough, they will find that they come to look at life and themselves and others in a way different from the dominant worldview, which does take the self with great, perhaps absolute, seriousness. Or, as some wag put it, the holy trinity for moderns seems to be "Me, Myself, and Mine." I am not simply talking about selfishness here, though that may be a part of this emphasis on the autonomous individual. Beyond that, is the notion—the mistaken notion, I believe—that the sovereign self, the individual, is the center of value and meaning.

Two stories may help to make the point. L. Gregory Jones, dean of the Divinity School at Duke University, related this telling anecdote about his son, Nathan. It seems that Nathan went off to a summer academic program for which his high school had nominated him. He called home to say, "You won't believe what they put on the official T-shirt we bought. I won't even wear it." On the front it said, "Accept nothing." On the back, "Question everything." Such slogans may sound edgy, but in a very real sense they are the conventional wisdom of our culture. Trust no one, accept nothing, question everything—everything, that is, but yourself. Declining to wear this T-shirt, Nathan put on another. The front of this black T-shirt read in white lettering,

"Loser." On the back, was a quote from Jesus: "Whoever loses his life for my sake will find it." Wearing such a shirt, he affirmed his life was not his own.[4] As an experience, revelation tends to move us in such a direction.

Here is a second story, from a theologian, Belden Lane, who fled from the precincts of high theology, the university where he teaches, for a few days of respite in the woods. Seeking renewal for his weary soul, Lane set off for a day of tramping among the hills and trees, hoping for an epiphany. "But this time," writes Lane in an ironic tone, "God would not be caught. I would drag the bag and snare back empty." Trudging back to his cabin, however, a small clearing beckoned, though the theologian was not sure why. He entered the clearing and sat on a fallen log. Suddenly he heard sounds, the sounds of something large and alive just outside the clearing amid the brush to the side. He waited, breathing softly, though his heart pounded. Into the clearing stepped a deer, which eyed him, stamped a hoof, snorted, stood, and finally exited. Meeting a wild thing was for Lane some kind of revealing, some encounter, and just the thing his soul needed. Here's the point: he did not find or choose it; "it" chose him. "It," whether the deer or the experience of wildness, came to him, revealed itself to him. He did not achieve it, figure it out, or attain it. It came to him as gift, as grace. That is the nature of the experience of revelation. We do not choose it; it chooses us.[5]

Moses did not suddenly decide to speak to a burning bush; it called to him. Abraham and Sarah did not take a notion to travel. They were called to set out. Jeremiah did not choose to be a prophet, nor did Mary choose to be the mother of the holy. Something, someone, some power not their own intruded upon them, revealing and disclosing itself.

This experience of gift is the dynamic, the quality of revelation. Thus, revelation is not only about content, the "there" that is there; it is also about the experience that decenters us. Revelation moves us off center and moves us toward a way of being in the world that finds its center in God, the holy, a power we cannot control but have experienced. As experience, revelation teaches us to take ourselves less seriously and to take God more seriously.

The experience of revelation is also crucial to the health of congregations. Too often individuals and congregations become preoccupied with themselves. Everything, or so it seems, is about "us." It is about how wonderful we are here at First Church or Second Church. What a proud history we have. What a marvelous record of giving. Or, alternately, it's about how unwonderful we are. What a fractious and sorry history we have. What lousy stewards we are. Either way, such an insistent focus upon ourselves is really beside the point. Revelation reminds us that the church, in a very basic and crucial sense, is not about us. It is about God, what God has done, what God is doing, and what God will do. "We have this treasure in clay jars," Paul reminds the Corinthians, "so that it may be made clear that this extraordinary power belongs to God and does not come from us" (2 Cor.4:7). Therein lies our center, our identity, and our hope. Revelation decenters us, and in the process restores us to our right minds. It gets the focus off us, whether we are swollen in pride or dejected in despair. It places the focus on the God of mystery, mercy, transformation, and grace.

When congregations forget or overlook either the content or the experience of revelation, and of Christian faith as a revealed religion, a loss of vitality is not far off. Forgetting the content of Christian faith as revelation, we become unclear about our center: our core story and convictions. We lack norms, and we become reluctant to talk openly about our faith and the difference it makes (or doesn't make!). And without the experience of revelation—of God's power and presence coming at us, of a reality external to us—we tend to become inward, preoccupied, and lacking in both confidence and energy. To affirm revelation is to affirm, "We are not our own; we belong to God." This is the source of our identity, our center, and our confidence.

Questions for Discussion

1. How do you react to the set theory discussed early in this chapter? Which kind of set (open, bounded, centered) describes your church as you currently experience it?

2. If you agree with the author that the centered set is a good model for congregations, name one step that you think would help your congregation toward becoming centered.
3. Consider the distinction between "natural religion" and "revealed religion" in this chapter. What do you find thought-provoking or helpful about that distinction? What questions do you have about it? What concerns?
4. Think of and share an experience you have had that is like what the author describes as the experience of revelation, that is, something that came to you as a gift or surprise, not something you achieved or figured out. Not something you found, but which found you or came to you. What impact did this experience have on you?
5. Share your reactions to the author's statement that, for Christians, Jesus Christ is the definitive, but not exhaustive, revelation. Is this helpful to you? How? If not, why not?

Chapter 3

Identity Questions (Continued) and Energy Shortages

The Role of Scripture

"What I don't understand," said a slight, gray-haired woman who spoke with just the trace of a New England accent, "is why, for worship, we have to read the Bible all the time? When I was a Unitarian," she continued, "we used to read from all sorts of things in our worship services. We read from the writings of Martin Luther King Jr., from Kahlil Gibran, and from various poets. Why, we even read the Koran! I think," she said with conviction, "that these days, with all the religious violence, it's important that we hear from other religious traditions!"

"Besides," chimed in a man who was standing on the edges of our conversation, "the truth is that, really, most any position can be supported by the Bible. You can be for or against capital punishment, the family, or nationalism. Whatever your position is, you can find support for it in the Bible!" The unspoken comment, which seemed to hang in the air after he finished speaking, was, "What good is the Bible—really?"

In other settings and congregations, one might hear sentiments that could be described as falling at the opposite end of the spectrum of beliefs about the Bible. Another person, one I heard on a recent radio program said, "God said it, the Bible records it, and I believe it!" Such a speaker seems to view the Bible as the result of God's direct dictation to secretaries named Ezekiel, Matthew, or James. "How can you doubt or question this?" wrote someone of a similar mind in response to a newspaper column I had written in support of the protection of civil rights for persons who are gay or lesbian. "How can you say this?" demanded my correspondent in horror. "The Bible says it so clearly. Look, it's right here in . . ." The fact that a particular statement or affirmation is made in the Bible is proof enough, apparently, that it is the truth for all times, places, and people. Then there is the pastor of a large, conservative congregation in our area who is fond of saying, on the radio, that "I never interpret the Bible. I only tell people what it says." The implication of such a statement is that interpretation of the Bible is not only not required, but also a hindrance to true faith and understanding.

Healthy congregations and capable pastors and lay leaders must respond to such challenges, questions, and assertions. Why this book? What's special about it? Where did it come from? How is it to be used and understood? What is the role of the Bible in the church? What is our theology of Scripture? These important and unavoidable questions demand a thoughtful and coherent response. In many ways, they have significant bearing on the issues of congregational health considered in the previous chapter: identity and boundaries. Like revelation and the nature of Christianity as a revealed religion, the Bible plays an important role when congregations have lost their sense of identity, their center, or their collective memory.

But these are not the only issues of congregational health that appropriate clarity about the Scriptures of the church and their role may address. Clarity about the Bible's role also bears significantly on a congregation's sense of vitality and its sense who God is and what God is up to in the world.

"I don't know quite what it is," she said. "It just seems that there's no energy here in our congregation. It feels as if we're going through the motions, but why? What's the point?" This not-uncommon lament may be framed in a variety of ways. People who experience their congregation, and particularly its life of worship, as "going through the motions" are diagnosing an energy shortage or an absence of passion. Or this might also be described as a loss of confidence. Or we might say that there seems to be a power outage. A congregation's life may be friendly, pleasant, moderately enjoyable, but we might not see much vitality or that much is really at stake. Does the church speak with any sense of authority or power? This is related to our convictions about the nature and authority of Scripture.

To be sure, a variety of theological themes address the issues of vitality, passion, confidence, and power. But a deep understanding of a theology of Scripture is among the most important of our core convictions in the Christian church. One biblical scholar makes the power of biblical texts evident in his comparison of the parables of Jesus to "verbal hand grenades."[1] Such an analogy clearly makes its point: the biblical stories and parables have an explosive force. Such passages of Scripture can "blow up" our conventional, fixed, and predictable worlds. And yet that very power is often depleted or hidden. Indeed, as I warn students in preaching classes, the tendency of many pastors when faced with the disturbing and explosive power of Scripture passages like the parables is to throw their own bodies on the grenade in order to protect the congregation from an explosion that might challenge it, disturb it, or blow things wide open! While the parables may be such small explosive charges, all of Scripture tends to challenge our assumptions and preconceptions.

Thus, our second theological theme, the role of Scripture in the church, relates significantly to two very different, broad issues of congregational vitality. On one hand, Scripture has what we might think of as a priestly role. That is, it helps us engage in questions of identity, norms, what is central, and what is peripheral. The Bible has a significant role to play in keeping congregations true to themselves as well as connected to the larger church and to the church's Jewish legacy.

But while the Bible has a priestly role in maintaining connection and identity, it also has a prophetic role by challenging us and the worlds we construct and inhabit. In this role, the Scriptures are not only a source of collective memory but also of passion and hope. Properly understood and interpreted, the

Scriptures have the capacity to mediate the transforming power, grace, and love of God. On many occasions, Jesus himself discloses this intention of the Scriptures of our faith. In his very first sermon, in his hometown synagogue at Nazareth, the congregation fit the text, from Isaiah, to their comfortable preconceptions. When Jesus began to preach on the text, the congregation found his sermon quite disturbing. It was so disturbing they tried to do to him what human beings often try to do to prophets, that is, kill them.

Although we can see the challenging nature of Scripture in many other stories from the Gospels, we recall another story nearer the end of Jesus' ministry when in his last week he taught in the Temple. Some Sadducees, a conservative religious group in first-century Judaism, tried to trap Jesus in an elaborate trick question about a woman who had been married to seven different men and asked whose wife she would be in the resurrection. (The Sadducees dismissed the resurrection and wished to discredit the concept.) Jesus answered them by saying, "You are wrong, because you know neither the scriptures nor the power of God" (Matt. 22:29). Jesus tied together the Scriptures and the power of God to transform our human categories and assumptions. Thus, the Scriptures and how we understand them theologically address two very different aspects of congregational health: identity and memory, on one hand; energy and transformation, on another.

Scripture and the Question of Identity

Why not read from inspirational writers like Kahlil Gibran, contemporary or classical poets, various social reformers, or even the texts of other religious traditions? In one sense, the answer to such a question is, "We do." We do read or hear from such sources, not always but often, as we interpret our own Scriptures in sermon and study. Many preachers and Bible study leaders bring in the words and insights of other sources, authors, faiths, and traditions as they interpret, proclaim, and teach from the church's own Scriptures. Preachers and teachers draw on movies, books, and contemporary events in their interpretation of the Scriptures, as they should. But the way these other texts are used and the role they have is different from the role and uses of the Scriptures of the Old and New Testaments. Such extra-biblical sources may be incorporated into a sermon or lesson, or quoted there, but they do not ordinarily fall under the category "Scripture" in an order of worship or in the life of the church. Nor should they be read as Scripture. The very designation "Scripture" is telling. When a congregation or religion describes a body of material as Scripture, it is, by definition, saying that these writings are authoritative for that faith and community. These writings and texts occupy a unique place. It is to these texts that we continually refer and defer, and, most important, from which we infer the nature and purposes of God. To speak of particular texts or the Bible as Scripture is to make a faith statement and confession, for the designation Scripture means that these texts are a congregation's normative witness to the acts, way, and will of the living God.

How might we think of Scripture to better understand its role and function in the church? What analogies can help us understand the particular function and place of Scripture in the life of a healthy congregation? I have sometimes found it helpful to suggest that the Bible is to the church as the United States Constitution, Bill of Rights, and Declaration of Independence are to the United States. That is, these particular texts are the ones that remind us of our particular origins, aspirations, and identity. Just as our nation and its citizens may find themselves interested in the founding documents of other nations, so we in the church may find the texts of other faiths instructive. But they are not our own. Just as the nation, its institutions, and its citizens have a special relationship and responsibility to the Constitution, the Bill of Rights, and the Declaration of Independence, so the church has a unique accountability to the collection of books that make up the Bible or the Scriptures of the church. They are our authorizing and living memory. When the Scriptures are forgotten or treated in a manner that is not serious, a congregation will tend to lose its way, its collective memory, and its sense of what is normative. Different congregations have different ways of suggesting their reverence for the Bible and that they take it with a unique seriousness. A friend recounts the story of giving a tour of his church's sanctuary to a group of foreign visitors who had attended worship there earlier in the day. He asked, "What seemed most strange about our worship to you?" "It was," said one young woman, "the parade at the beginning." "The procession?" asked my friend." "Yes, that, and the way someone carried in that huge book at the end of the parade."

"The Bible?"

"Yes, the Bible."

"What about it?"

"Well, the guy who carried it in set it down at the front, it was open, and then looked at the preacher as if to say, 'There, work from that!'"

"You know," said my friend, "she was right. That was the message."

Other congregations do other things, including standing for one of the readings, having the priest kiss the Bible, or speaking or singing special words before or after the reading of Scripture. All of these liturgical gestures are our attempt to say this book has a special place of honor, not unlike the place of honor the U.S. Constitution has in the National Archives.

The identity function of Scripture is signaled by use of the word *canon*, which is term that is sometimes also used in the same breath as Scripture. "The canonical Scriptures of our faith" is perhaps redundant but makes the point that this book has a special place and role. *Canon* is a Latin word meaning "measure," as in "measuring rod." The canon of Old and New Testaments provides a measure of and for the church as it seeks to evaluate its faithfulness, as well as the value of different teachings and interpretations of the Christian faith. In somewhat the same way, the Constitution of the United States plays a canonical role in the ongoing life of our nation. By it, we test and measure ourselves—our institutions, leaders, and laws. This means, of course, that interpretation is necessary and has a legitimate place in the church, for the Bible, and in the courts for the Constitution. In contrast to the pastor who claimed, "I never interpret the Bible, I only tell you what it says," a pastor who understands the nature and role of Scripture not only acknowledges there is room for interpretation but also a necessity for it. The meaning of various texts, stories, commandments, or parables is not self-evident in a new time and place. As federal judges and justices of the Supreme Court interpret the application of the Constitution to the ongoing life and laws of the government and nation, so pastors and teachers of the church have been given a primary responsibility for interpreting the meaning and application of the Scriptures for the church's life and the faith of Christian people.

Another useful analogy for the role of Scriptures in relation to questions of identity, norms, and center might be that of a library. The word *bible,* after all, literally means "book of books." And the Christian Bible is that, a book of books. The Bible, in the Protestant version, is made up of sixty-six different books, thirty-nine in the Old Testament and twenty-seven in the New. Within the sixty-six, some divisions and categories can be discerned and made, as in a library. Some books are historical, others are books of laws, some books of poetry and wisdom sayings, and there are letters. A diversity of literary types is present, as in most libraries. But the point of the library analogy is that the Bible is the library of the church, or at least its first and core library. Just as law firms, towns, medical practices, art museums, and individuals or families have libraries that relate to the identity, history, life, and ongoing practice of these various entities, so too the church has its own particular library, which houses our history, story, building specs, moral teachings, letters of past leaders, the teachings of the founders, and so on. This library reminds us who we are and whose we are.

The Scriptures of the church contribute to the identity formation and maintenance of the church in one other crucial, though frequently overlooked, way. In the second century, the church found itself facing the challenge of the teacher Marcion and the movement he authored, Marcionism. Marcion argued that there were two different Gods, the God of the Old Testament and the God of the newer writings, which would in time be recognized as the New Testament. Moreover, Marcion maintained that the God of the Old Testament was an inferior God and those writings should be dropped altogether by the church. Throughout the church's two-thousand-year history, versions of

Marcionism crop up every now and then. There is, in fact, a kind of incipient Marcionism in the common (and erroneous) description of the God of the Old Testament as a God of judgment and the God of the New Testament as a God of love. More than one Sunday school student has taken home the idea that God was grumpy and nasty once, in the Old Testament, but is full of sweetness and light now, in the New Testament. Not only does this require a very selective reading but also it makes life suspiciously fortunate for us!

In facing the challenge of Marcion in the second and third centuries, as well as subsequently, the church has affirmed the canonicity and indispensability of the Old Testament as Scripture. It has done so for several reasons that have bearing on the question of church identity and congregational health. First, the church has understood that Jesus cannot be severed or understood apart from the Old Testament, its story and its promises. These were the Scriptures for Jesus as for the authors of the New Testament. Apart from this context, his ministry cannot be understood. Second, when severed from the Jewish Scriptures and legacy, the church itself risks loss of memory and distortion of its witness. It may, for example, so tout Paul's (or Luther's) teachings about grace as to lose any sense of the ethical life grace requires of us. A particularly Old Testament emphasis on the church as a people called to be both unique and a blessing to other peoples may be jeopardized. Or, the church that cuts itself off from the Old Testament and its Jewish legacy may fall into anti-Semitic or anti-Jewish prejudices, which have stained the church's history many times in its history. Within the overall implications of Scripture for the church's proper identity and norms, this more specific aspect of Christian identity is important if the church is to address its record of anti-Semitism. The Scriptures taken as a whole and with proper reverence for the Old Testament as well as the New Testament keep the church connected to its Jewish legacy as a crucial aspect of its identity, without which the church is not itself and its witness is distorted.

One might respond to these assertions of the importance of Scripture for the identity, norms, and center of the church appreciatively but skeptically. "Well, that's great, but still there's a huge diversity here, even if these sixty-six books are bound up as one. How can we draw much in the way of guidance, direction, or identity from such a diverse collection?"

Acknowledging the diversity within the Scriptures is important. In addition to containing a variety of literary types, the Bible is a book, or book of books, that was written over a one-thousand-year period. Those one thousand years span a variety of historical eras and human cultures. Acknowledging the diversity within the Scriptures is important, but counting that diversity as a strength is also important. Diversity in the human experience of this God is reflected in the very diversity of the Scriptures. There are different perspectives and testimonies to the one God. Why, even in the New Testament, that there are four gospels and not just one is incredibly significant—or, to put it another way, that there is a four-fold gospel made up of Matthew, Mark, Luke, and John. Diversity exists in the church's understanding and witness to Jesus Christ in our founding documents and literature. Moreover, diversity and honest tension are present among the various texts of the Scriptures. Paul emphasizes faith, James works. Which is right? Both are, says the church, by including both within the canon. One is the word to hear at one time and the other at another. Our unity is not uniformity! In a time of cultural pluralism and diversity, an awareness of the diversity of the Scriptures is both important and a strength.

While this diversity of the Scriptures must be noted and honored, so too must their unity. The unity of the Scriptures can be described in two ways: a unity of focus and a unity of narrative. The unity of focus is suggested by the description of the Bible by the biblical scholar James A. Sanders. Sanders speaks of the Bible as God's story in his book *God Has a Story Too*. While God's story may contain the stories of biblical Israel, Jesus, Mary, and Paul and the early church, Sanders is right. The Bible is most of all *God's* story. God, whether revealed or hidden, speaking or silent, remains the central character throughout. All the various characters of the Bible point in their different ways toward the God revealed and proclaimed in the Scriptures. There is unity in this focus upon God.

The narrative of the Scriptures also has a unity. While the Bible contains many, many stories or narratives, a discernible and overarching master narrative encompasses the whole. This narrative begins in creation (Genesis) and ends in consummation (Revelation). Between these books are stories of the crisis of broken relations between God and humanity: the covenant between God and humankind, represented by Abraham and Sarah and their descendents; an ongoing conversation between God and humanity, carried out in the books of history, prophets, and wisdom literature and reaching a climax in Jesus Christ; the story of the church in the Book of Acts, then in the two collections of letters of the New Testament—the Pauline letters and the catholic epistles. This narrative unity can be summed up, as Brian McLaren writes in his series of books, *A New Kind of Christian*, with a series of *c* words: creation, crisis, call and covenant, conversation, Christ, church, and consummation. Others configure this overarching narrative unity in other ways. The point is, amid the diversity of stories, a larger story and a narrative unity exists. Part of the role of the pastors and teachers of the church is to help congregations and believers understand this narrative unity, or to see the forest for the trees.

In somewhat the same way that the early creeds provided a rule of faith for the early church and can continue to do so today, the Bible provides a canon, a measure of the normative faith and story of the church. Diverse enough to be a "big tent," the Bible has sufficient unity to provide identity and direction. Here, the vital congregation finds its founding, authorizing, and canonical texts and stories. Here, the healthy congregation finds a narrative that forms and transforms the church. Or to invoke another metaphor, the Bible functions as both roots and wings. Now that we have focused on the roots nature and role of the Scriptures, let's turn to the wings role.

The Scriptures and the Transforming Power of God

While the Scriptures have a role in helping healthy congregations locate and articulate the identity, norms, and center of the church, the role of Scriptures goes beyond such a roots function. The disease of some congregations is that they have lost a sense of identity or focus, but the disease of others (or the same con-gregations) can be a loss of vitality, energy, and passion. Congre-gations need to ask, Is there some sense of urgency, of something at stake, or are we simply going through the motions? In healthy congregations, one senses a certain vitality or aliveness. What role do the Scriptures have in these aspects of congregational health?

As I noted earlier, Jesus, in his reply to the Sadducees when they attempted to entrap him, connected the Scriptures with the power of God. "You are wrong, because you know neither the scriptures nor the power of God" (Matt. 22:29). The Scriptures of the church not only serve to keep the church connected to its memory and identity, the same Scriptures also mediate the trans-forming power of God. Another witness to this transformative capacity of Scripture is the Protestant reformer John Calvin. Calvin spoke of the Scriptures as the Word of God in several senses. Calvin's central understanding of the Word of God was not the Bible itself, that is, the words on the printed page, but more properly, as an event, a dynamic experience. The Word of God, said Calvin, occurs when the same Spirit that was present to the one who wrote is present to the one who reads. In other words, the Word of God is something that occurs when the Spirit and the Scriptures connect in listening and speaking.

Most Christians know this experientially, even if we may not consciously have thought about it. That is, most Christians have had the experience of reading a passage of Scripture without finding any particular meaning or life in it. But on another occa-sion that same passage may come to life for us, whether in pri-vate reading and reflection or in worship. It speaks to us and does so powerfully. For Calvin, this coming alive of the words on the page is the work of the Spirit. The Spirit brings the Scripture to life in ways that are vivid, memorable, and telling. What one day is just words on the page becomes at another time the Word of God. Hence, Calvin describes the Word of God as an event or an occurrence.

But the Scriptures as source of energy and passion in the life of the church offer even more than bringing words to life. Count-less believers through the generations as well as across the world testify that the Scriptures have the power to mediate the presence and power of God. Not always, to be sure, but often enough, these texts function like the wardrobe door of C. S. Lewis's Narnia stories. That is, they open onto another world and another dimension. They reveal God to us. Moreover, they reveal us to ourselves. They give us a new world and a new understanding of the present world.

We may be reading and studying a parable, for example, the parable of the workers in the vineyard (Matt. 20:1-16). Our initial reactions may be puzzlement or even to take offense. I recall leading a study on this text and, after a couple of readings both aloud and silently, one person blurted out, "I don't know what this means, but I know I don't like it!" Fair enough, it is a difficult parable. What's more, the parable may very well intend, or Jesus may intend, to offend those who hear it. We may gather ourselves up and say with indignation, "I don't think this is right. I don't think this is fair that the vineyard owner should pay everyone exactly the same, even though some have worked one hour and some have worked the entire day!" "What's such a story doing in the Bible, anyway?" someone else may chime in. "I thought God cared about justice!"

Patient exposition and discussion, honest questions and exploration may lead beyond our initial frustration and offense. We are offended when we identify, as the parable may well wish us to do, with the workers who have put in an entire day. Many of us tend to feel we have played by the rules and deserve what we have received. Some of us feel we deserve better than we have received. The parable probes this human capacity for self-justification and resentment like a doctor probes an infected wound. Perhaps then, another person in the group or the teacher asks, "What if we're not the workers who have put in the whole long day? What if we were to identify with those who came late?" Suddenly, the whole thing changes. Suddenly, we may see ourselves not as the deserving but rather as recipients of grace, unexpected blessings of mercy and care. True, such a move may be too much for some, who turn away puzzled or frustrated. But others may feel the world shift as they release their self-justifications, resentment, or feelings of not having gotten all that they deserve and instead see themselves as recipients of incredible, incomprehensible, and surprising generosity. A participant in one group studying this parable said, "I had thought of God as fair. But maybe that's not who or how God is. Maybe God is not fair, but gracious. Wow, that changes things!" Indeed, it does.

Scripture too has the capacity to change things, including us. It has the capacity to call into question our assumptions, "I deserve what I have" being one such assumption. A sense of entitlement often leads to distance, resentment, and division within communities. Assuming "God has been gracious to me, giving me more than I could ever deserve" tends to have different effects. "The final work of grace," said one wise pastor, "is to make us gracious." So the Scriptures not only have the capacity to strengthen identity, they also have the power to transform, to give us a new world as they reveal us to ourselves and reveal God to us. The Scriptures mediate God, the strange God whose ways said the prophet Isaiah, are not our ways, whose thoughts are not our thoughts (Is. 55:8).

In this way the Scriptures are a source of energy, passion, life, and new life for the weary Christian and congregation. My best preaching has not happened when I have a clear concept. On the contrary, the best preaching feels as if I have caught some slippery, living fish and can't wait to get back to congregation to say, "Wow, look at this!" or "Let me tell you what happened to me!" We may come to worship dragging but leave renewed and inspired. It happens. And it happens regularly when we understand the Scriptures, as did Jesus himself, not as merely an ancient collection of odd texts, but also as narratives that mediate and convey the transforming and life-changing power of God.

In a somewhat similar way, the Scriptures of the Bible can be a source of energy and power by correcting the tendency of congregations and their leaders or members to become moralistic. While the Christian faith certainly includes moral implications, it is imperiled when it becomes moralistic. Why, what's the difference, and what does this all have to do with the Bible?

For Christians, morality is an expression of our response to God's grace and love. The biblical book of 1 John states this priority and order simply: "We love because he first loved us"

(4:19). Our love for God, our neighbors, God's world, and our-selves is in response to God, who first loved us. Or in another aphorism, "Salvation is all about grace; ethics is all about grati-tude." When ethics is not about gratitude, a response to the grace and love of God, but rather a way of gaining the acceptance or attention of God or our fellow human beings, then morality tends to become moralistic, and Christian faith tends to become a religion of good works and achievement. Then we love, or seem to love, not because of God's love for us and our experi-ence of this love but to show God or other people what fine folks we are. We do deeds of mercy not because we have known mercy for our sins, but because they show others what noble people we are. Therein lurks the demon of moralistic versions of Christian faith, which tend to be less about the amazing grace of God and more about how we should think, feel, and act. As I say, there is a place and time for morality. It's just that we don't start there. We start with God.

What does the Bible have to do with this focus on God's initiative? The Scriptures, properly read and interpreted, also start with God. The Scriptures teach us to think theologically rather than anthropologically. They do not start with us or with how we are to behave. They start with God. I recall the dear gentle-man who attended a Bible study I led for several years. If he found the opportunity, he would always tell us, "If people would just follow the Ten Commandments, everything would be fine. They are the most important part of the Bible, don't you agree?" For him, it all seemed to come down to these simple rules. Only later did I get to know some of this man's grown children, who had little to do with church. "It was always just rules, rules, rules when we were growing up," said one, "and you know what? We never measured up to the rules!" The word of grace had been supplanted for this father by the word of law.

In fact, I have found that it comes as a surprise to some people when they discover the Bible does not start with the Ten Com-mandments, as if God said, "Hello, here are the rules." But the Ten Commandments come later, after God has brought the people of Israel up out of slavery in Egypt. First comes this act of libera-tion, this act of grace; only second the law and how we are to act.

When we forget this, which the Bible does not do, we tend to turn our faith into something moralistic and not life-giving. Somehow, the word and experience of grace are energy giving, while "rules, rules, rules" can deplete our energy and joy. Our confidence, to put it another way, is not in ourselves; it is in God. When congregations lose passion, energy, a sense of urgency, and confidence, the remedy does not lie in moralistic scolding. Such a scolding may have a short-term effect, but in the long term it wears off. Neither does real renewal lie in artificial infusions of energy, whether through blowing up balloons or turning up the volume on the music. Real renewal lies in God and God's story found in the Scriptures.

James A. Sanders, the aforementioned biblical scholar, makes this point by urging the preachers and interpreters of Scripture, "Theologize before you moralize." If Scripture is God's story and God is the central character, ask first, What is God doing? How does God act? What does God care about? How does God surprise us? What is God up to here? How is God different from what you expect? Only after exploring such questions do we ask the next questions: How then are we to act, and what are we to do? That is, in light of the nature of our God, how are we to live and behave in the world? Theologize before you moralize, because that is the way Scripture itself works. When congregations lose passion, confidence, or power to change lives, it is often because they have substituted conventional morality and a religion of good works and achievement for gospel and the power of God.

Here in these stories and parables and letters and laws we encounter the transforming power of God who has the capacity to do a "new thing," to bring life out of death, to create something out of nothing, to call "into existence the things that do not exist" (Rom. 4:17). This is the power of God, which the Scriptures mediate and disclose. In this encounter, the church finds passion, confidence, and hope. What could be more important to a healthy congregation?

Scripture is relentless in its effort to wrest our anxious attention from ourselves—from our needs, wants, achievements, shortcomings, failures, fears, or success. Scripture tries to refocus our attention on God, the unexpected merciful, majestic, hidden, and revealed God of the Old and New Testaments. Congregations that focus on themselves, either in pride (Aren't we something special? We're the best church in town!) or in despair (Who could possibly love us? We can't do anything important.), have lost their proper focus. They lose the capacity to be communities of transformation. They lose health. Worship informed by a lively understanding of, appreciation of, and attention to the Scriptures places us in the presence of the living God. Unlike the rather staid and boring Sadducees of the New Testament, we experience life because we know the power of God to redeem, to change, and to heal. A proper understanding and interpretation of the Scriptures is absolutely crucial for the health of the church. The Scriptures are a source of both identity and transforming power.

Questions for Reflection and Discussion

1. As a source of the church's identity, the author compares the Scriptures to the U.S. Constitution and to the library of a town or business. Do you find these analogies helpful? Why or why not?

2. The Scriptures have both diversity and unity. In what ways do you see the Scriptures as diverse? Is their diversity a strength or weakness in your view?

3. Identify one biblical story that has been transformative for you personally or in the life of your congregation. Describe how it has been important in your life.

4. The Scriptures address questions of identity and matters of passion and confidence. Which seems most urgent for congregational health and vitality as you consider your congregation and the wider church?

5. After reviewing the outline of the biblical story through the series of c words, (creation, crisis, call and covenant, conversation, Christ, church, and consummation), try telling the biblical story aloud in your words to another person or group.

Chapter 4

Keeping Your Balance

The Trinity

T heologian Daniel Migliore says that theologians ask four basic questions on behalf of the church, as well as asking these questions of congregations. The first is, Are the proclamation and practice of the church *true* to the revelation of God in Jesus Christ as attested in Scripture? In short form, that might be, Is the church's proclamation and practice the true gospel? There are, as Paul notes, different gospels (Gal. 1:6) that are not the gospel at all. They are distortions of the truth of the gospel. Migliore's second question is, Do the proclamation and practice of the community of faith give adequate expression to the *whole* truth of God in Jesus Christ? Is our proclamation and practice inclusive of the whole gospel? There is a breadth to the gospel that resists reductionism.

The third key question is, Do the proclamation and practice of the community of faith represent the God of Jesus Christ as a living reality in the *present* context? Or to paraphrase again, Is it the present gospel, that is, does it connect with the present time and place and speak meaningfully to it? Fourth and finally, Does the proclamation of the community of faith lead to transforming *praxis* in personal and social life? In other words, what difference does it make?[1] To reframe these four questions of theology just slightly in order to connect them to the life of congregations, we can ask the following questions:

- Does the congregation embody the true gospel?
- Does the congregation embody the whole gospel?
- Does the congregation embody the gospel for today?
- Does the congregation's life and practice make a difference?

These four questions about the faith and practice of churches might serve as insightful guides for congregations' theological self-evaluation. Posing these four questions regarding a congregation's life and teaching would make a great exercise, study group, or sermon series: Is our congregation's life and teaching the true gospel? Is it the whole gospel? Is it the present gospel? And what difference does it make? In a time when congregations and clergy employ a wide variety of diagnostic and evaluative tools that are derived from other disciplines, these four basic questions suggest a foundation for theological evaluation of the church. I encourage you to approach them, if you do, not so much in search of conclusive or simple yes-or-no answers. Take them as suggestive and as provocative. Pose them as open-ended inquiries.

The Congregation and the Whole Gospel

This chapter is guided by the second of the four questions: Is it the whole gospel? Or, does the congregation embody the breadth of the gospel? The question, is it the whole gospel? points to a particular manifestation of ill health in the church, a partial gospel or emphasis in which some elements of Christian faith and practice so predominate that others are effectively diminished, if not altogether lost. Too many congregations, parachurch groups, movements, and pastoral leaders have a complete grasp of only a partial truth. In this connection, we do well to keep in mind the classical definition of a heresy. A heresy is not a complete lie; it is a partial truth that is elevated to the status of the whole truth. It is a relative truth posing as ultimate truth.

Thus, as the Letter of James argues famously, faith without works is dead (2:17). In the hands of the fourth-century British teacher Pelagius, this statement became a partial truth that was elevated to the status of the whole truth. Pelagianism was deemed a heresy for its implication that Christians might earn God's blessing or our salvation by our works. Or, for a different example of another type of partial truth or value made into the absolute or complete truth, consider patriotism or the love of country. Patriotism is a value that can be applauded. But when patriotism is elevated to the complete and final truth, it becomes heretical.

In a religious climate marked by competing denominations and churches and a market economy that prizes developing a market niche and being "on message," we face manifold temptations to elevate one partial truth, or one kind of faith experience, to the whole truth. Congregations and pastors are tempted to identify what makes them different or unique and stress that identity. The result is churches and ministries that are out of balance. They are less than the whole gospel.

Moreover, a psychological dynamic is at work that is as true of congregations and other organizations as it is of individuals. We tend to play to our strengths, to do and keep on doing what we have found we do well. Inheritors of the pietistic traditions continue to turn to spirituality, prayer, and devotion. Social activists tend to turn to organizing and political process as their default option. We develop a so-called muscle memory for our strengths and repeat those, though the repetition may mean, as I mentioned in chapter 2, that certain muscles are overworked, while others are underutilized and may atrophy as a consequence. The result can be a painful shoulder impingement!

The church has a variety of resources for keeping its balance, for holding truths in tension, which Danish philosopher and theologian Søren Kierkegaard claimed is the nature of faith itself. The emphasis in the Letter of James on works and deeds is held, for example, in tension with Paul's emphasis on grace in Romans and Galatians. Without a Pauline emphasis on grace, works becomes works righteousness. But without works, faith has no concrete response or expression.

Or to turn to the Old Testament for another example of truths in tension, in the Book of Exodus we read that the sins of the fathers will be visited on the children to the fourth generation, an insight into the social nature and unforeseen consequences of sinful choices. But centuries later the prophet Ezekiel rejected the very same teaching, citing with contempt the proverb, "The parents have eaten sour grapes, and the children's teeth are set on edge." (Ezek. 18:2). The prophet told Israel to stop repeating what had become a noxious excuse for its own irresponsibility. ("It's my parents' fault!") Each person, asserted Ezekiel, is responsible for his or her own choices. One could enumerate many examples of ways in which Scripture itself works to keep the church in balance, by doing justice to the complexity of life and faith.

Another resource for keeping our theological balance, as well as doing justice to the complexity of life and of our faith, is the church or liturgical year with its seasons of Advent, Christmas, Epiphany, Lent, Eastertide, Pentecost, and Ordinary Time. Each season of the year has particular themes, colors, and accents. Congregations and pastors that are guided by the church year find it a helpful reminder of the whole gospel. We see Jesus as teacher and healer during Epiphany, but as suffering servant during Lent. During Eastertide we witness Jesus as the risen Lord. Within the framework of the church year, we see that not every Eucharist is a remembrance of the Last Supper. Some are remembrances of the victory meal of the risen Lord. Or even better, meals of both betrayal and the victory of new life are held in creative tension.

A Whole Gospel and the Trinity

With such themes in mind, we turn to the Trinity as one of the primary theological resources that help congregations and their leaders keep their balance and bear witness to the whole gospel.

What is the doctrine of the Trinity and where did it come from? While there are formulations in the Scriptures that can be called trinitarian (for example, Matt. 28:19, 2 Cor. 13:13), the Trinity as a doctrine, or teaching, is not to be found in Scripture itself, as least not as a developed concept. The doctrine of the

Trinity is a postbiblical teaching of the church, part of its tradition. Its earliest use is attributed to the second-century teacher and theologian Tertullian, who coined the word *trinitas* to speak of "three persons of one substance."[2] Full development of the doctrine of the Trinity came with the Council of Nicea in the fourth century.

Many teachers have reached for different words and images to interpret the Trinity and its meaning. For example, Presbyterian minister David H. C. Read interpreted the Trinity as "God everywhere and always, God there and then, and God here and now."[3]

In my own ministry, I have sought to explain the Trinity through the metaphor of water. God the Creator or Father might be thought of as similar to groundwater. Such water is not ordinarily visible to us, yet it is always present. These deep waters move and flow beneath the earth. Life itself depends upon these unseen groundwaters. At a particular location on the earth's surface and at a point in time, a spring appears, a site where the groundwater wells up to become visible. Jesus Christ, to continue the analogy, is like that spring. He is the visible revealing— the manifestation of God in a particular life, at a particular point in time, and at a particular place. But the water that bubbles to the surface in this spring does not remain there. This water flows forth in a river or stream and divides into other streams, which convey the waters of grace to different places and at different times. Such is the Holy Spirit, God's presence throughout the world and across history.

Like all metaphors, this one has its limitations and breaks down if pushed too far. However, the water metaphor may suggest a way of understanding the Trinity. It does manage to convey the truth that the Trinity itself seeks to convey: that Christians know the one God in different ways. We experience the same God but in varied forms. God is the Mysterious and Unnameable One whom we trust but cannot see, like the groundwater. "I am who I am," God answered when Moses asked God's name; "my name is 'Unnameable,'" so to speak (Ex. 3:14). God is revealed uniquely in the particular life of Jesus, in his words and deeds, and in his life and death and resurrection. "Who do you say that I am?" Jesus asked his disciples. "You are the Messiah, the Son of the living God," answered Peter (Matt. 16:16). We name the Name. And God continues to guide the lives of the faithful, the life of the church, and of all creation in and through the Holy Spirit. Like the wind, the Spirit blows where it wills, Jesus said (John 3:8). We live the Name that lives in us. The three are one, and the one is three. The Trinity seeks to describe what cannot be fully or finally described.

The Trinity as Resource for Healthy Congregations

What has the Trinity to do with healthy congregations? Not long ago I was invited to preach at a conference for college students who were considering theological education and ordained ministry. Among the group were students who understood and identified themselves as evangelical Christians, Pentecostal Christians, and mainline Christians. As the four-day event wound to a conclusion, I happened upon the lead organizer, who sighed the sigh of people in such a position when they have found that they have not, and perhaps could not, please all the various groups or factions. "The evangelical students," she said with a roll of her eyes, "are complaining that they have not had enough space." By this she meant that evangelical students had felt the event out-of-balance, leaning toward a more mainline theology. "I wonder what we can do differently?" she asked, not so much expecting an answer as frustrated by the difficulty.

As I listened to the conference organizer lament the divisions and dissatisfactions within the group of 150 students, I thought about an observation made years ago by the theologian H. Richard Niebuhr. He remarked that churches tend to be churches of one person of the Trinity or another; one, but not all three. I suggested to my colleague that it might be interesting, for a future conference, to have a discussion with panelists talking about Christianity from the three perspectives: evangelical, Pentecostal, and mainline. My hunch is that we might find Niebuhr's observation pertinent. That is, I suspect the mainline group might be characterized by a theology and piety that is focused on the first person of the Trinity, the sovereign and mysterious God the Creator. For them, God is the God of history and of nature. Perhaps the evangelical students would turn out to emphasize the second person of the Trinity, Jesus Christ the Son and Redeemer. For them God is Jesus and what God has done in and through Jesus. Certainly, the language of the evangelical students with whom I spoke seemed to focus almost exclusively on Jesus. Likewise, the Pentecostal students in the group seemed to be drawn toward the third person of the Trinity and to exhibit a piety shaped by the Holy Spirit. They spoke readily of the Spirit's guidance and activity in their personal lives.

My further hunch is that the growing edges of each group's faith might lie in further exploration of one of the persons of the Trinity that was not their default option or strong suit. Pentecostals might need and benefit from greater attention to the teachings of Jesus. Mainline and liberal types might be instructed by a stronger doctrine of the Holy Spirit as God's living presence and power. Evangelicals might give greater attention to God, Father and Creator. Often we grow by being pushed out of our comfort zone. If Niebuhr was right, we tend not only as individuals but also as congregations to find a comfort zone in one person of the Trinity or another and then to stay there. Growth may lie in venturing away from our comfort zones. Moreover, congregations may enhance their health and find their theological balance through the Trinity. The Trinity is one way to proclaim and live the whole gospel.

The Trinity and Various Unitarianisms

Another way to state the significance of the doctrine of the Trinity is to point out that the Trinity is an attempt to guard against various "unitarianisms," whether it is a unitarianism of the first person or the second person or the third person of the Trinity. The Trinity is a kind of theological system of checks and balances, curbing excesses and providing accents or emphases that complete or improve our partial truths and limited insight.

In some congregations, there tends to be a unitarianism of the Creator. God is the Ground of all being (in theologian Paul Tillich's phrase) or the source of inalienable human rights or the deist's watchmaker who created the world but then left it to be governed by natural laws and human powers. When God is only understood as Creator or Father there are certain dangers. Such conceptions of God tend to become vague and abstract. Lacking definite content, such understandings of God may prove so vague as to be susceptible to manipulation by those who would invoke God for their own purposes. Of course, attempts to use God for our own agendas can happen no matter which person of the Trinity is given emphasis, but a unitarianism of the first person of the Trinity has, in my experience, contributed to what I have come to describe for myself as "civic-faith" versions of Christianity. Later in this chapter I explore civic faith in more detail, as one illustration of a loss of balance and a form of ill health.

The Trinity's affirmation of God as creator and God of history protects against dangers of a unitarianism of the second person of the Trinity, where Jesus is the exclusive object of trust and devotion. "I have Jesus in my heart, and that's all I need" or "Honk if you love Jesus" are some of the more dubious expressions of a narrowing of faith to the second person of the Trinity. When this happens, Jesus becomes a kind of cult figure. He is "our guy," almost a tribal deity for those who know him and call on his name (and to hell with everyone else!).

The risk here is "Jesus-olatry," forgetting that Jesus himself lived a God-centered and God-empowered life. Too often in congregations where there is a unitarianism of the second person of the Trinity, God the Father or Creator is actually described in a way that pits God the Father against God the Son. For example, "God's righteous anger required the sacrifice of the Son for its appeasement," whereas the plain teaching of Scripture is that "in Christ God was reconciling the world to himself" (2 Cor. 5:19). God the Creator and Redeemer are one and not at odds with one another. Moreover, the reduction of the Trinity to the second person alone tends to reduce Christian faith to something quite individual, concern with my personal salvation and not with the salvation and redemption of the world God loves, has created, and continues to create each new day.

Later in this chapter, I look in more detail at the danger posed by a particular form of preoccupation with the second person of the Trinity. What happens when so much emphasis is placed on the second person of the Trinity that all else pales? To this question we shall return under the theme, "A Too Personal Savior."

Then the third possibility is a unitarianism of the Spirit. When this happens experiences of the Spirit or the gifts of the Spirit tend to become the be-all and end-all. In the Bible, both Paul and the Gospel of John recognized the challenges of a spirit-filled Christianity that eclipsed the second and first persons of the Trinity. Paul sought to provide pastoral counsel and care to the congregation at Corinth and noted their many spiritual gifts and experiences. But he also noted that these very gifts and experiences tended to become fuel for the fires of spiritual arrogance and factionalism. "Knowledge [great spiritual knowledge and experiences] puffs up," wrote Paul, "but love builds up" (1 Cor. 8:1). We also shall return to this matter of overemphasis on spiritual experiences later in this chapter under the theme, "A Downside to Spiritual Highs?"

For now, we note that in the Gospel of John's extensive teaching on the Spirit, John is at pains to keep the Spirit connected to Jesus himself. The Spirit does not speak on its own, says John, but reminds the church of what Jesus taught. The Spirit, says John, does not sing solos, but reveals the things of Jesus (John 14:25-26). Moreover, there is for John no avoiding the way of costly, cross-shaped discipleship in preference for spirit-filled ecstasy. Some scholars claim that such a charismatic distortion is behind John 14:6, in which Jesus said, "I am the way, and the truth, and the life. No one comes to the Father except through me." In other words, Jesus, through John, here reminds early charismatics that the gift of the Spirit does not make the way, the truth, and the life of Jesus, including costly discipleship, irrelevant. Jesus remains the way for which the Spirit strengthens and guides the followers of Jesus and the children of God.

Christians know God as three in one: God as Father, Son, and Holy Spirit, or in another formulation, God as Creator, Redeemer, and Sustainer. As creator, God is God of history, nature, and cosmos. This God is vast and not to be identified with any one nation, religion, race, epoch, class, or culture. God can be revealed through various cultures and religions. If Scripture is the first book of the church, nature is the second book revealing God to us. And yet this vast, often hidden God is made particular in the life and person of Jesus of Nazareth. Our claims about God and for God are illuminated and tested by God's decisive revealing in Jesus Christ, in his life, teaching, death, and resurrection. Nor is our cosmic God, while revealed in a particular time, place, and life, stuck there. The Holy Spirit, as the active presence of God, continues to act in the world, in the life of the church, and in the lives of believers.

When we imagine we have figured out God or adjusted God to fit our favorite category, God turns out to be not so simple. During the 1930s, when God became so vast, vague, and ill-defined as to be easily identified with nation and race in Nazi Germany, the Confessing Church protested and resisted the Nazis by pointing to Jesus who alone is the way, the truth, and the life. As early Christians had professed, "Jesus is Lord" and "Caesar is not," so the Confessing Church said, "Jesus is Lord" and "Hitler is not." But when a kind of Jesus-olatry sets in, and Jesus becomes "our special guy" and the exclusive property of our group or church, God the Creator and God the Holy Spirit broaden and correct our understandings. When it's all about being filled with the Spirit, the second person of the Trinity reminds us of the cost of discipleship, and the first person of the Trinity speaks to us of a consummation that is not yet. In short, the doctrine of the Trinity keeps us from settling for a God who is on one hand too small, or on the other so big or so vague that God becomes a "sacred blur."

The Problem of Civic Faith

As a young person I frequently heard the question, "Do you believe in God?" I asked it of myself. Friends asked it of one another. It floated in the culture as *the* religious question. I was always somewhat uncomfortable with the question, and not just because it put me on the spot, though it did. I was uncomfortable because the question seemed to me altogether too vague and too broad. "God? What do you mean?" I wanted to ask. People seemed to attach so many meanings, or no real meaning so far as I could tell, to that little three-letter word.

I was helped when someone suggested to me that the vague, "Do you believe in God?" while a meaningful question to some, may not be the only or even the best question with regard to religious faith and belief. A more biblically shaped question may be, "*Which* god do you believe in?" In other words, the Scriptures understand that there are many possible contenders for what Tillich called our "ultimate concern."[4] While the Bible does insist on one, true God, the stories, history, letters, and teachings included in the Bible reveal that we can also create our own gods or idols. We may say, "I believe in God" and mean that I believe in my Self, writ large. Or we may mean that we believe in some sort of nationalistic deity that is devoted to our nation's welfare and preeminence. Martin Luther said, "A man's god is whatever his heart clings to and confides in." He understood that simply saying or feeling, "I believe in God" may not say enough.

Martin Copenhaver describes this phenomenon in the following way:

> A recent survey revealed that ninety-six percent of Americans believe in God. We can explain this finding only when we grant that believing in God is rather easy. (Can anything that ninety-six percent of Americans can do be anything but easy?) Without Jesus, the concept of God can remain just that—a concept. Such a view of God becomes little more than what someone described as 'a sacred blur.' We can refer to God and still sound merely theological, without severely compromising our worldliness or sophistication. But more, such a comfortably vague concept of God does not require much from us. We not only have little sense of what this God is like, but also few clues about what this God might expect of us.[5]

Copenhaver names, for me, the problem of civic faith, that is, a faith that keeps God so vague as to be almost anything from sheer sentiment, to a love of nature, to personal conscience, or to seemingly noble ideals. There is not enough "there" there, to recall the phrase I used in an earlier chapter when speaking of the doctrine of revelation's significance. Moreover, Copenhaver is right: Jesus does give content to the term *God*, as well as asking something more specific of us. That can be uncomfortable!

Sometimes dealing with a vague God or concept of God is much easier than with a particular life and way of living.

Congregations that tend to be most comfortable with the first person of the Trinity—the God of creation, nature, and history—often run the risk of such generic faith. God is only the one who cannot be named and not also the one who is named Jesus Christ. God is distant and transcendent, but somehow never gets down to earth in a way that is palpable and that asks something definite of us. Of course, this fuzziness is not true of all people or churches that give a primary emphasis to the first person of the Trinity, but it is a risk in such settings. When there is such a unitarianism of God the Creator, God may remain too vague and our faith too comfortable with the culture that surrounds us. The Trinity, or greater emphasis on the other persons of the Trinity, can be an antidote to such generic versions of faith and to civic faith.

In congregations that seem most comfortable with God as first person of the Trinity, I sometimes note a tendency to think and speak of God as an intellectual concept, but hardly one with whom we have a living relationship. "God," as the theologian Eugene Wehrli once commented, "is a concept to be discussed, but not a relationship to be confessed."[6] With too little sense of God's active presence in the world, a congregation can seem more like a seminar about God than a community where God's transformative presence is changing lives.

What is wrong when this happens? It is this: we may speak of God but behave as if God does not exist or make any real difference. For example, beginning denominational meetings with Bible study is quite common, in my experience. We devote half an hour to Bible study and God talk. But then we move to the business meeting, as if God has gone to sit by the pool and has nothing whatsoever to do with our—that is, the church's—business. Business turns on budget shortages, interest group advocacy, and various institutional anxieties. We go about our business, whether strategies for church growth or administration of pension funds, as if God does not exist. This is what I mean by civic faith. We pay lip service but not life service to God. God remains distant, vague, and unrelated to our business as the church.

When this happens, people can be heard as they stagger away from such meetings saying such things as "That was more like a corporate stockholders meeting than a church meeting!" The disconnect between our expressed values and our actual practice saps vitality.

A Too Personal Savior?

Not long ago I got an email from a reader asking if she might pose some questions about my faith. "Yes of course," I responded, "providing I can also pose some questions to you about yours!" Before long she asked a question I had been asked before, "Is Jesus Christ your personal Lord and Savior?" I answered, "Yes, but I must add this note: when I hear those words, 'personal Lord and Savior' they often seem to be some kind of code language. They signal to some people that one belongs in their group, while others who don't use that language as readily, or who decline to us it, are considered not in the group. This kind of thing—code language and code words—makes me nervous."

My dis-ease is not merely social or psychological, it is theological. Our code language seems to be an attempt to capture and control the living God, to reduce God to our limited understandings and experience. In this sense, Jesus can become too personal. Jesus, and thus God, is reduced to the dimensions of my heart, my personal experience, and my salvation. The God of the vast cosmos, the grand sweep of history, and the complexity of nature somehow seems to disappear in favor of my very personal and often quite individual God. Moreover, without adequate emphasis on the Spirit, this type of faith seems to reduce Christianity to a once-and-forever salvation experience, not an ongoing life of faith.

Not only does God, when reduced to my personal Savior, seem too limited, but also the work and concern of God in such conceptions seems cut down to individual salvation and personal life after death. The believer is preoccupied with salvation as eternal life, meaning a quantity of life rather than a quality of life. Moreover, this understanding of salvation seems to take on quite individual tones, without much concern for the new creation or a new humanity witnessed to in Revelation: "Then I saw a new heaven and a new earth. . . . And I saw the holy city, the new Jerusalem. . . . And the one who was seated on the throne said, 'See, I am making all things new'" (Rev. 21:1-5).

Dangers to congregational health appear in such a reduced rendering of God. One is captured in the quip that some Christians (and congregations) are so "focused on heaven that they are no earthly good." God's redemptive presence and work seems to have very little implication for present life. Congregations become unhealthy when salvation is reduced to the merely individual. There is too little sense of church as a *people* of God and a new *community*. Individuals and souls are saved, but what of the redemption of communities, cities, and the creation itself? That seems to fade from view, though they are a major theme of the Scriptures. In some ways, this reductionism even betrays Christian faith, for it can begin to seem quite self-preoccupied. According to theologian John Leith:

> Calvin insisted that the glory of God is more important than the salvation of one's own soul. Hence Calvinists were always skeptical of those who become preoccupied with the salvation of their own souls or the preciousness of their own holiness. . . . Nicholas Berdyaev gives a horrible account of saints who are ready to trample over each other getting through the narrow gate of heaven. Sanctification has to do with personal life, but it always directs personal life away from self, away even from its own holiness, to the fulfillment of the purpose of God in history and society.[7]

What shape does this distortion take today? Of late, an odd development is taking place among some more conservative Christian congregations and organizations, those that tend to be Jesus focused. While such groups have for years deplored "identity politics," that is, political action organized around ethnic, gender, or sexual orientation identities, increasingly these same groups seem to be employing that strategy themselves. So, for example, such congregations advocate teaching "creationism" and "intelligent design" in public schools as simply another perspective that deserves to be considered and included. The implication is that teaching evolutionary biology is exclusive.

But turning Christianity into identity politics belies the very content and nature of Christian faith. It turns the gospel upside down, making the Christian faith the servant of a particular group's interests and agendas, rather than making a congregation or Christian organization a servant of the God of the Great Commandment, "'You shall love the Lord your God with all your heart, and with all your soul, and with all your mind. . . . And . . . 'You shall love your neighbor as yourself'" (Matt. 22:36-39). This morphs faith into ideology and forgets that God sent his Son not to save Christians but to save the world. Such Christianity turns Jesus into "our guy" and forgets that God calls those whom God has chosen to be a blessing to all the peoples of the earth. More is at work than a deficient trinitarianism, but that is a part of it. And a more robust trinitarianism is an antidote to reducing Christianity to another entrant in the world of identity politics.

The Downside of Spiritual Highs

In Paul's letters to the congregation at Corinth, two topics predominate and are woven together: spiritual gifts and experiences are one, and factionalism and conflict within the congregation are the other. At least for some in that first-century church, their experience of the Spirit's presence and of the gifts of the Spirit was not only powerful but also quite heady. In other words, it had gone to their heads. Rather than leading them to a proper sense of self, these experiences and gifts of the Spirit had led some at Corinth to inflated self-estimates and swollen egos. "We are the enlightened," some claimed. "We are in the know. We've been lifted up to a new dimension." And "We possess gifts, like the gift of speaking in tongues, that others haven't got." Experiences of the Spirit led to spiritual boasting and arrogance that in turn resulted in a congregation so divided that when it gathered for the sacrament, "It is not really to eat the Lord's supper," said Paul (1 Cor. 11:20).

Some members of First Church Corinth were so focused on their own spiritual experience that they ignored or overlooked

others, especially the needy. Congregations are unhealthy when
people so prize their own spirituality that they grow blind or
indifferent to the presence and the needs of others, particularly
those whose experience may be different than their own. Factionalism and dissension are often the result.

I recall, for example, the first congregation I served as a pastor. Some in the congregation understood themselves as "born-
again Christians" who had been born anew by the Spirit. They
devoted much of their energy, though not in particularly positive
ways, to others in the congregation who were not, in their view,
"real Christians," for these had not been born anew by the Spirit.
The born-again group invited me to one of its prayer meetings
where they prayed, by name, for those they saw as the unsaved in
the congregation. (I wondered, would I have been on their prayer
list had I not been there?) They also invited to their prayer meetings members of the church who, though not of their group,
were susceptible to their persuasions. The net effect of these semi-
secret meetings was painful dissension in the congregation, hardly
a witness to the renewing power of the Spirit.

Certainly, a focus on the third person of the Trinity and the
gifts of the Spirit need not necessarily lead to such divisions or
to spiritual arrogance. Nevertheless, it seems to have happened
often in the history of the church beginning in Corinth and
continuing to the present day. I recall the sermon at seminary
where James A. Forbes, then a professor at Union Seminary and
now senior minister at The Riverside Church, confessed that he
had never spoken in tongues though he had been raised in his
father's Pentecostal Church. Because he had never spoken in
tongues or received this particular gift, Jim felt a deep sense of
inadequacy as a Christian. In that community, as in many Pentecostal churches, tongues had become *the* gift and the mark of a
real Christian. Just as in some other communities use of the words
"my personal Lord and Savior" is an admittance card, so in the
Pentecostal church of Forbes's boyhood, speaking in tongues was
required. When this happens, the church begins to resemble an
exclusive club more than a church, for God's grace has been
supplanted by our own experiences and attainments.

One can value the gift of tongues, or any other gift of the Spirit, without making it *the* normative gift or spiritual experience. When particular spiritual experiences and gifts become the focus of a congregation, turning these into merit badges or personal validations becomes all too easy. Perhaps this is why Jesus, following the visionary experience of the transfiguration, warned the three disciples who had been to the mountaintop with him not to speak of what they had seen or experienced. It would move the focus off obedient discipleship and onto the disciples themselves: "Wow, guess what happened to me up there on the mountain? Aren't I special! Too bad you didn't get to go!"

Faced with such spiritual arrogance, Paul deliberately directed the Corinthians back to Jesus and to the cross. "God chose what is foolish in the world to shame the wise; God chose what is weak in the world to shame the strong; God chose what is low and despised in the world, things that are not, to reduce to nothing things that are, so that no one might boast in the presence of God" (1 Cor. 1:27-29). The Corinthians needed to refocus on the second person of the Trinity and the cross of Christ to cure the illness of spiritual arrogance. Note, please, that Paul is not at all against spiritual gifts. They simply must be guided and formed by the greatest gift of all, love. Without that gift and the concern for others that it entails, the other gifts count for less than nothing (1 Cor. 13). A unitarianism of the Holy Spirit was balanced and corrected by the second person of the Trinity. Likewise, an emphasis on the first person of the Trinity encourages us to remember that God cannot be captured in or controlled by our own limited experience.

This, in the end, may be the great contribution of the Trinity. The Trinity resists reductionism by which God is conformed to our group, ways, or agendas. The triune God, who is three in one and one in three, is more than our vague civic faith pieties, more than Jesus as our tribal deity, and more than my spiritual gifts and experiences.

How might this look in a healthy congregation shaped by a robust faith in the triune God? A crucial element in such a congregation's ethos is spiritual humility. God does not belong to us, we belong to God. In mission and outreach, this might mean that congregations do not understand themselves as "taking" God or Jesus or the Spirit to others. Rather, such congregations follow the leading of the triune God as they participate in God's mission in and for the world. We do not own God, God owns us.

And because the Trinity describes God as relational in God's very being (three persons in one), the life of a healthy congregation informed by a robust trinitarian faith prizes relationships and takes them very seriously. This includes relationships within the community of faith as well as seeking and forming relationships with others beyond the congregation. "Being in relationship" defines the triune God and characterizes healthy congregations. To be made in the image of this God and to live in that image is to live in genuine and respectful relationships with others. Christianity is not a solo act. Those who trust in the triune, three in one, God seek real relationship with others, even as the triune God seeks relationship with us.

Questions for Reflection and Discussion

1. Collect the orders of worship for the last month of services at your church, and look at the hymns you have sung together. What do the hymns suggest to you about your church and its comfort or discomfort with different persons of the Trinity?

2. Does H. Richard Niebuhr's assertion that most churches are churches of one person of the Trinity or the other make sense in your experience? If so, what would you say was the emphasis of the church that nurtured you?

3. Which person of the Trinity promises the greatest challenge and opportunity for growth in your congregation or in you personally?

4. Review the four questions of theology from the beginning of the chapter. Which one seems most urgent for your congregation today? Why?

5. If the Trinity tells us that in God's very being God is relational, what implications might this have for the ministry of hospitality in your congregation?

Chapter 5

Beginning at the Beginning

God the Creator

"The earth is the LORD's and all that is in it; the world, and those who live in it." So begins Psalm 24, summarizing a basic conviction of Christian faith: the triune God is our creator and the creator of all that is. The Bible's first words put it as succinctly, "In the beginning when God created the heavens and the earth" (Gen. 1:1).

Framed in these core affirmations are a series of deeper convictions. God is creator, and we are creature. There is a difference between the two. God is primary; we are secondary. "In the beginning—God"; all that exists has its life and being at the hand of a gracious and welcoming God. We are not the authors of our own existence, God is. Moreover, we do not need to wait for God's act in Jesus Christ to speak of grace. Creation itself is an act of grace. There's more: creation, while not God, is good—indeed, very good. This majestic affirmation embraces not just some of life, what happens to be useful and delightful to me or you, but everything from rattlesnakes to rhododendrons. Human beings are assigned a stewardship role in relation to creation, not an ownership one.

From these basic convictions flow a number of implications for congregations and their members. First, our lives make sense in relationship to God. "We do not live," as the apostle Paul put it, "to ourselves" (Rom. 14:7). Getting this straight has a lot to do with congregational health. So too does a basic sense of confidence, born of faith in God our creator, which keeps congregations from being haunted by timidity or despair. Furthermore, congregations that take seriously the conviction that God is our creator avoid damaging dualisms of spirit and flesh, body and soul. Congregations grounded in the majestic words of the creator that God's world is "very good" do not withdraw from the world God loves, but are engaged in that world. Finally, the order of creation confers the blessing of rest—sabbath—for the world is not ultimately in our hands. We take, in turn, these five implications of the doctrine of creation: (1) we belong to God, (2) we are grounded in basic hope (not despair), (3) dualism is misleading, (4) withdrawal is not an option, and (5) sabbath rest is possible—indeed, commanded.

We Belong to God

"Know that the LORD is God. It is he that made us, and we are his; we are his people, and the sheep of his pasture" (Ps. 100:3). This affirmation of the psalmist sounds innocuous, but it is not. Not when it is put up against the alternate claims of modernity and its doctrine of the autonomous individual who depends upon nothing but his or her inner resources. Elsewhere I have traced the philosophical origins of this doctrine in the philosophers of modernity, Descartes, Rousseau, and Kant.[1] They promoted the idea that the individual is by nature complete, competent, and good. While one can understand and even appreciate this emphasis as an antidote to medieval thought, it has a serious downside, one that is manifest in congregations. When people make Does this work for me? the basic question, the life of congregations is distorted. In the church we teach people to ask different questions, such as, What does God, to whom I am accountable, ask of me? Modernity, especially in its consumerist iterations, has taught us, "It's about me." Christian faith, grounded in the conviction that God is our creator, teaches us something different: "It's not about you." Not ultimately. It is about living in relationship to God our creator and in ways that are pleasing to God.

Today's congregations are often in danger of becoming congregations of all consumers, rather than, as the reformers taught, a priesthood of all believers. Instead of seeing ourselves as derived and contingent, and therefore accountable to a gracious God, we are taught by modernity and as consumers to consider our own satisfaction the central value. Thus, we come to worship asking the wrong question. We ask, was I pleased, touched, entertained, moved, or helped? These are not bad questions, but they are not the first question. The first question is: did we, did I, worship God; did I praise God? "What is the chief end and purpose of man?" asks the Westminster Catechism. "To glorify and enjoy God forever," it answers. Congregations tend to be healthy when this core conviction is clear and honored, and when we avoid reducing everything to "what works for me." The twentieth-century Trappist brother and writer Thomas Merton captured the basic implication wonderfully when he wrote, "The fact remains that we are invited to forget ourselves on purpose, cast our awful solemnity to the wind and join in the general Dance."[2]

Despair or Timidity

The health of congregations is strengthened by hope. Hope derives, at least in part, from trust in God our creator and in the confidence that God's creation is very good. While the next chapter devotes more attention to human sin, these words of the contemporary theologian Jürgen Moltmann in his *Theology of Hope* are instructive:

> Among the sinners whose future is eternal death in Rev. 21:8, the "fearful" are mentioned before unbelievers, idolaters, murderers and the rest. For the Epistle to the Hebrews, falling away from the living hope, in the sense of being disobedient to the promise in time of oppression, or being carried away from God's pilgrim people as by a flood, is the great sin which threatens the hopeful on their way. Temptation then consists

not so much in the titanic desire to be as God, but in weakness, timidity, weariness, not wanting to be what God requires of us.[3]

Western theology is more accustomed to locating sin in the realms of false pride and arrogance—"the titanic desire to be as God"—than in timidity, weariness, and despair. And yet, as many feminist theologians have noted, this is but half the story. Timidity and despair, and not only overweening pride, are also forms of sin prominent among us today. As a popular song put it not so long ago, "All we are is dust in the wind." Resignation may be more a threat today than false confidence.

Let's be honest. Few among us have not had such a thought or experienced days, even seasons of life, when we have not felt as if we were simply blown about on the winds of chance and change in a basically random universe. Shakespeare puts such words in the mouth of Macbeth: "What is life? A tale told by an idiot, full of sound and fury, signifying nothing."[4] Moreover, the Scripture's own book of Ecclesiastes is not far from such a perspective, when the author writes, "Then I considered all that my hands had done and the toil I had spent in doing it, and again, all was vanity and a chasing after wind, and there was nothing to be gained under the sun" (Ecc. 2:11). Such thoughts may, on occasion, have a place and be a salutary antidote to overbearing confidence and arrogance. But they may also be a resignation, a passivity in the face of life that betrays the spirit and faith of the first words of the Apostles' Creed, "I believe in God the Father almighty, creator of heaven and earth." These bold words of hope assert that life has meaning and purpose, however difficult it is to discern at times, especially when we are in the muddled middle of life.

Despair and timidity seem strong in many congregations these days, and not entirely without reason. Recently I was a guest preacher at a downtown "First Church" of a mainline denomination. Their sanctuary seated 1,200, but their regular congregation was 60 people. I made the observation as I began my sermon that they seemed like David trying to wage the good fight while clad in Saul's bulky and confining armor. I wondered if their sanctuary were not a beautiful death trap, one that reminded them each time they gathered of what they were not rather than what they were. And yet, like many congregations in such a predicament, they clung to the old space with its memories of another time, a golden era of power and prominence. Of course, the challenges facing such a congregation are hardly a matter of the building alone, but in the face of their challenges they seemed hunkered down, unable to move, unable to see God in the present and future as well as in the past.

A different story comes from a 150-member, small-town congregation in the late 1970s. That congregation weighed sponsoring a refugee family, one of the many rendered homeless by the war in Vietnam. Some argued, "God is calling us to this; we can do it." Others countered, "We are too small to be doing such a thing. We don't have enough resources." To be sure, caution and asking hard questions has a place, but sometimes such questions proceed less from due diligence than undue despair or timidity. Not this time: the congregation voted to sponsor a Hmong family from Laos. It was a challenge to welcome a family who spoke no English and who came from the premodern world of a hill-country village. The congregation, nevertheless, rose to the occasion, as did the members of the family themselves. While the challenges were many, in time the Cha family flourished. They helped other members of their clan settle in this small logging and farming community in the Pacific Northwest. Twenty years later they owned homes, their children were star athletes at the town high school, and others were going on to college. The parents owned successful truck farms that supplied nearby markets. Some of the people most affected in that small town were Vietnam veterans who found in the sponsorship a chance to confront and heal some of their wounds. The hopeful orientation of a small congregation proved to be like Jesus' mustard seed image of the kingdom, which became a large tree sheltering many birds of the field.

I suppose one might respond, "This is interesting, but what bearing does our conviction that God is creator have here? The creation happened long ago." Wrong. The biblical doctrine of creation is not that God created the world, set things in motion,

then departed. Rather, that doctrine is that God the creator, the
maker of the heavens and the earth, is still creating in each new
day. Pastor and author Martin Copenhaver suggests a helpful analogy for understanding this point. "God did not create us as a
painter creates a painting, hangs it on the wall, and goes on to
other endeavors. God creates more like a cellist 'creates' a sonata;
if the creator were ever to stop creating, so would creation end."[5]
For a congregation to cling desperately to its past is, in a sense, to
manifest indifference to the work of God the creator in the present
and the future.

A less than full sense of hope and confidence also undermines congregational health in mission and service to neighbors
in need. Both neighbors and needs change, and in this change
God is up to something. Creation is continuing. Are congregations able to ask the hard questions, What's going on? What is
God up to in the world and in our community? What is God
calling us to be and to do in this time? Such questions may mean
letting go of once valuable programs and ministries that served
God and neighbors well in one era but have become sacred cows
in another. Making such determinations is not easy. But if God is
the maker of heaven and earth, a hopeful orientation is at the
heart of congregational life.

Such an orientation is funded not only by Christian conviction that God is the creator but also by other teachings of our
faith. In the aftermath of the crucifixion, when the news of the
resurrection seemed to the disciples both foolish and frightening, they received the message from angels at the tomb, "He is
going ahead of you to Galilee; there you will see him" (Mark
16:7). I find in this message an affirmation of God's continuing
creation—when we, as represented by the disciples, thought it
was all at an end. What appears to us to be the end is not; it is a
new beginning. Moreover, this part of the Easter story is an affirmation that Christ, the living Jesus, goes ahead of us in the world.
Whether we "take the wings of the morning and settle at the
farthest limits of the sea," or "the light around me become night,"
it is still the heavens and earth that God has made and into which
Christ Jesus has gone ahead of us to meet us there (Ps. 139:9, 11).
Timidity, fear, and despair are for most people and congregations

parts of the human journey and their life experience. But for those formed by this story of creation and new creation, and for those who are able to affirm, "I believe in God, the Father almighty, creator of heaven and earth," hope and basic trust are powerful antidotes that can keep timidity and despair from becoming a chronic condition or stance in life.

Dualisms of Spirit and Flesh, Body and Soul

A particular form of this despair is seen in various expressions of dualism, which divide created life against itself. Such dualisms hold the body is evil, while the soul is good; or the spirit is of God, while the flesh is of the devil. These are the ancient heresies of Docetism and Gnosticism, both of which are alive and well among us today.

The Docetists did not believe that Jesus was truly human. Rather, they held he only seemed or appeared to be human. He could not be human, made of flesh and blood as we are, because the body was viewed as belonging to a lesser and evil realm. Were God to become human, were the Word to become flesh, as the Gospel of John puts it, God would be tarnished and degraded by association.

The Gnostics held a similar, if slightly different view. *Gnosis* means "secret knowledge," something that is available only to the special few, the enlightened, the spiritual elite. Like the Docetists, the Gnostics looked upon the realm of the body and the earth as a lesser dimension. Contemporary inheritors of such dualisms tend to speak of the spiritual realm as if it were elsewhere, another dimension or place, to which we must escape. We are to get free of this world with its hang-ups and decay in order to participate in something spiritual.

Christians too have embraced this dualism. Novelist Wendell Berry, in his moving tale *Jayber Crow*, incisively analyzes the way Christians have fallen into dualisms that lead to discounting of this world and that have much to do with our abuse and exploitation of nature. In the following, a young Jayber Crow, the main character and narrator, tries to make sense of a preacher's negative attitudes toward the body.

I took to studying the ones of my teachers who were also
preachers, and also the preachers who came to speak in chapel
and at various exercises. In most of them I saw the old division
of body and soul that I had known at The Good Shepherd. The
same rift ran through everything at Pigeonville College. . . .
Everything bad was laid on the body, and everything good was
credited to the soul. It scared me a little when I realized I saw
it the other way around. If the soul and body really were divided, then it seemed to me that all the worst sins—hatred and
anger and self-righteousness and even greed and lust—came
from the soul. But these preachers I'm talking about all thought
that the soul could do no wrong, but always had its face washed
and its pants on and was in agony over having to associate
with flesh and the world. And yet these same preachers believed in the resurrection of the body.[6]

Berry discerns the way Christianity has participated in this dualism, even as we affirm the doctrines of creation, incarnation, and
the resurrection of the body.

Such dualistic tendencies are evident in a number of ways in
the life of congregations. Sometimes I have heard people wonder why taking an offering, collecting money, is a part of worship. Worship, they seem to believe, is spiritual, while money is
worldly. Another expression of a dualistic tendency in the church
is the idea that the church has no role in politics and should stick
to so-called spiritual matters. Often too, congregations do not
include stewardship of the earth in their understanding of their
mission. In all three instances a dualism of spirit and body, heaven
and earth diminishes body and earth. Such a view is also implicit
in forms of church organization that divide the congregation's
"spiritual life" and "business life" into two separate compart-
ments or boards.

Perhaps the big one here is the church's frequent reticence or
ambivalence about sexuality. You don't hear all that many sermons on the Song of Songs, with its celebration of sensuality and
sexuality. Sex is seldom addressed frankly as a part of the life of
faith, except perhaps in the youth group. Too often it seems congregations and their leaders view topics that include sexuality as

inappropriate for church, thus participating in this ancient dualism that devalues the body and often contributes to the demeaning of women.

Finally, one sometimes hears pastors boast that they have no idea what anyone in the congregation gives or pledges in support of the mission of the church. This may have a valid basis in wanting to avoid prejudice or favoritism, but sometimes pastors who claim such ignorance sound as if such knowledge were beneath them. Rather, it seems to me, knowledge of giving patterns is pastorally important, though such knowledge should be treated with respect and not become a basis for favoritism.

Dualism finds expression in congregations not only in attitudes towards money, politics, sex, and mission but even in our inability to see God in the imperfect lives of a congregation's people. Over and over again in the Scriptures, we hear lofty designations for the church. We are called "the body of Christ," "a holy nation," "a chosen race." Then we look around the sanctuary. What do we see? Dr. Hermann, his mouth gaping open as he snores through the sermon. There's Billy and his younger brother Kenny fighting over a toy and the couple whose marriage is a mess. Of course, not everything looks that way. We see exemplary people, kind and generous people too. But it's not hard to feel there's a mismatch, a gap, between our lofty theological names for the gathering at St. James by the Shopping Center and the actual people we are. The consequence, at least sometimes, is that while we claim to love God we turn away from God's actual and imperfect people. We could easily imagine, with the Gnostics, that the true church must be somewhere else. It can't be *this* bunch! To affirm that God made the heavens and the earth, that God takes on mortal flesh and works in the world through ordinary people, is to be able to affirm this people—these people— as the body of Christ.

The second-century creed of the church, the Apostles' Creed, was the church's attempt to resist the Gnostic and Docetist pulls toward dualism and denigration of the body, the earth, and the world. In the Apostles' Creed, the church declares its faith in God, "creator of heaven and earth." Both are God's good creation. Moreover, the humanity of Jesus Christ is stressed in the creed, as it speaks of his actual conception, birth, suffering, and death, all of which were inconceivable to those who posited a separation between the spiritual and material. Finally, note the church's declaration of faith in "the resurrection of the body." In contrast to the dualists who believed that salvation meant getting rid of the body, shucking it off like the leaves that enclose the ear of corn, Christians affirmed that the body participates in the resurrection.

Because God is the creator of the world, because God has become human, we Christians understand engagement in life, relationship, and history as an expression of our faith. Moreover, we know God as one born in a manger amid mud and straw, with the cry of a child and the mess of childbirth. Word and flesh are one.

Withdrawal from the World

I went to seminary in New York City. One bright September morning, just days before my first classes at Union Theological Seminary, I stood on the corner of Broadway and 110th on Manhattan's Upper West Side. Everywhere it seemed life swirled and surged around me. Vegetable sellers hawked their colorful wares. On the crowded sidewalks, people of all hues and many cultures pressed together. Some rushed along while others strolled. In the street, cabbies honked their horns and shouted as pedestrians crossed at will. I, a young man from the comparatively quiet Northwest, stood on the corner, simply taking it all in: the intense, colorful life of one of the largest cities in the world.

Suddenly someone whispered in my ear, "Where is God in all this?" Not a question one expects in such a setting, or maybe in any setting, so I was caught off guard. For a moment I considered playing dumb, as if I had not heard, or I might simply put on the experienced New Yorker's mask of glazed indifference. But because I was to start seminary in a few days, I felt some sort of odd duty to respond to such an overtly theological question. "Where is God in all this?" I repeated. Then, lifting my arms, as if in grand embrace, I said, "Why, God is here! God is in *all* of this!" The person who had posed the question seemed to disappear as if by magic. She or he, I can't remember which, was a Moonie, in town and working the streets in preparation for a Madison Square Garden rally with Rev. Sun Myung Moon. When the representative of Rev. Moon asked the question, "Where is God in all this?" the implied answer was not difficult to discern in the question itself, namely, "God is not to be found here. Not here in the dense swirl, color, and chaos of a large urban center. Not here amid the colliding worlds of commerce and education. Not here amid the drug sellers, panhandlers, and ne'er-do-wells." I am pretty sure that had I stammered something like, "Gosh, I'm not sure where God is?" I would have received an invitation to come with that person and find God amid the strictures and structures of Moonie life—in other words, in the claim that we can find God only by withdrawing from the world. But, no, I asserted (surprising myself in the process), "God is here, God is in all this!"

Such an affirmation proceeds, I believe, from the Bible's very first words, "In the beginning . . . God created the heavens and the earth" (Gen. 1:1). It flows from the Christian conviction that God is the creator and that the world God has made is good. Such a core conviction is reiterated time and again in Scripture as basic trust is linked to belief that God is the creator. "My help comes from the LORD," sings the psalmist, "who made heaven and earth" (Ps. 121:2). By way of contrast to the Moonie's conviction that God is not to be found in the midst of life (nor in the city), a core affirmation of Christian faith, and the basis of confidence and hope, is that "the earth . . . and all that is in it" belong to the Lord (Ps. 24:1).

Great health flows from the steadfast belief, often in the face of considerable evidence to the contrary, that life is God's good creation. Such a conviction is the ground of a basic self-regard, as witnessed in the once popular assertion, "God made me, and God don't make no junk!" The conviction that God created the world and pronounced it good is also the basis for a regard and respect for other human beings and human cultures, as well as all of what we call "nature." And, finally, this conviction is the basis of hope and a confident entry into and vigorous participation in the world, which is one manifestation of faith.

Lest this appear naïve, let me state here the connection between this chapter and the next. In this chapter we discern hope in the Christian conviction that God is the creator. In the next chapter, from the doctrine of sin and the Christian conviction regarding evil, we draw the basis for realism. Christian faith and life invite us to hold these two—hope and realism—in tension. I encourage you to consider this chapter and the next as parts of a whole, two sides of one coin. Our core convictions invite and encourage hope, but not a blind hope. It is not a Pollyanna-type optimism that fails to see or to take into account the brokenness of life.

Sometimes the impulse toward withdrawal is yoked to dualism in such a way that it gives the impression that the only thing that matters, the only thing God is concerned about or Christians need care about, is life after death and the fate of the eternal soul. "Where are you going to spend eternity?" ask preachers and evangelists, as if we may as well go there right now, having no need to think about where and how we are living at present. But this is a distortion of Christian faith, one that denigrates God's good creation and the gift of life. In a similar way, my New York encounter with the Moonie was the invitation to step away from this world, where God is not, to enter another world, the world of Rev. Sung Myung Moon, where God is to be found.

Of course, the temptation to withdraw need not be so dramatic. Holing up in our homes is pretty easy, cocooning ourselves in our little worlds, our lifestyle enclaves. We avoid certain parts of town, certain kinds of people, and particular experiences, in our own way withdrawing from the world God has created and that God loves. One of the blessings to my life as part of the church has been its challenge to my attempts at such withdrawal or isolation. When I was a child and the civil rights movement was beginning to sweep the nation, my church drew me to interracial youth groups and summer camps. When a visit to the jailhouse, and particularly the jailhouse that happened to be known as the Bronx House of Detention, was the last place I would have thought to go, it was the church that said to me, "'I was in prison and you visited me'" (Matt. 25:36). When the barrios of Nicaragua, the dying rooms of the sick, the haunts of the hungry were not on my itinerary, the church put them there, with the promise that Jesus had gone ahead of me and there I would find him. And the church was right. I did find Jesus already there and learned from him in settings and places that, were it not for the church and its faith that God created the heavens and the earth, I might never have gone. Healthy congregations are able to follow Jesus all sorts of places, trusting that what may seem to us to be places of desolation and death are places where God is present.

In important ways, our faith and its conviction that God is the creator is a very world-affirming, hopeful, and bold one. When the church embraces despair or timidity, when we drink at the wells of world-denying dualisms, when we withdraw into our privileged or like-minded enclaves, we become ill.

One of Scriptures greatest stories of suffering and the way that suffering challenges our sense that life is meaningful is the book of Job. And yet that same story is also, in the end, most affirming of creation and the gift of life. Nevertheless, for many years the ending bothered me. As you may recall, the book of Job has a "happy ending." In chapter 42, Job is restored. He gets it all back. He marries again. He farms again. He has a new family, and he owns livestock. He regains his health.

But I didn't like it. I just thought it too easy, too pat, and too comforting. I thought it would have been better to end the book a chapter before, with Job repenting before the vast and mysterious God, period. And I am not alone in my lack of appreciation for Job's Hollywood ending. Many scholars and commentators don't like the ending, which they claim is a later addition, any better than I did. But then I lived a few years of life and got a different take on Job and the happy ending. It began to occur to me that this ending was a pretty amazing thing and maybe not the simple payoff that I had thought. For, after all, if you and I had been through all that Job went through, including terrible illness, the death of his entire family, loss of land and livestock, and sinking to the bottom of the ladder of social status and esteem, would we have been eager to live again, to marry again, to father children again, or to farm and work again? Perhaps not.

Quite possibly our response to such disappointment and suffering would be bitterness. Remarkably, Job was willing to give it
all another try. After all that he had been through, he said yes to
life and to God again. Moreover, it is noteworthy that the God
Job encounters out of the whirlwind (Job 38) is the creator God,
the God who is in charge of the sea and who makes sure it stays
within bounds, who makes snow to fall, who presides over the
lion, and who sets the leviathan to swim in the ocean depths.
God the creator meets Job. And Job, in the end, responds to the
gift of life and the mystery of creation by embracing it again,
saying yes to God by saying yes to life. Though, as we shall consider in the next chapter, the world is also a fallen world, it is still
God's world and God's creation. Job's astonishing yes affirmed
this truth. This is the basis of a courageous engagement in life
and a trust that there is no place we can go that God has not
already gone—that is at the heart of Christian faith.

Many years ago when I graduated from high school, the man
who was then my minister sent me a quote attributed to a Christian teacher who lived as one era, the Middle Ages, was dying,
and as a new era, the Renaissance, was being born. The words of
Desiderius Erasmus capture the basis in creation of our hopeful
orientation. It is certainly no accident that these words reference
the Genesis creation story and God's pronouncement that the
world is very good. Now my practice is to send these words to
others on the occasion of their graduation from high school:

'Tis a brave world, my young doctor!
Do not be afraid of it; do not calculate your chances so closely
That you miss your chance;
Do not pretend to know what you do not know.
Work and laugh and give thanks for these three are one.
You did not make the world. You cannot remake it.
You cannot even spoil it.
You may, however, know the wonder of improving some small
  corner of it,
But (do not forget that) before you arrived
The world was pronounced "very good."
Go now and enter into its joy.

Creation and Sabbath

One final theme, drawn from the conviction that God as creator bears on congregational health, remains to be explored. While I have made much of the implications of this conviction for active engagement in life, even engagement can be taken to an extreme. We can take too much responsibility on ourselves with the result that we lose the capacity for rest and for sabbath. We feel that we must be busy and going all the time, "24/7." Our lives become driven and frenetic.

In modern culture, we tend to think of the day as beginning with the rising of the sun. In the Scriptures, the day begins at evening. The implication is that, as we go to our rest, God continues creation. When we get up in the morning, thrust the covers back, and get to our feet, the day has long been in progress. The day does not begin when we do. We join a work in progress.

Likewise, the biblical teaching of sabbath is part of the creation story. On the seventh day God rested and commanded that we too rest. The Sabbath reminds us that not everything depends upon us and our doing. Creation is the gift of the creator. Creation is sustained by God and not by us. We have our part to play and six days to work. But by resting, we also affirm the conviction that God is creator and that we are creatures. As a pastor, I have found that people respond to the notion of sabbath by saying, "I have too much work to do! How can I possibly take a full day off?" The rabbis had an answer to that question. "Rest as if your work were all done."[7]

Many congregations today encourage a kind of relentless busyness and activism. We do from meeting to meeting, project to project, task to task without rest or interruption. Sometimes people avoid worship because they fear being pressured to take on yet another job, yet another committee assignment. It may be, as author Eugene Peterson speculates in his book *Working the Angles*, that keeping the sabbath is the church's most countercultural practice. Whether that is true or not, a sabbath-keeping congregation is able to stop, to cease, to rest, and rejoice in the gift of life and creation. So we conclude as we began this chapter, by affirming our dependence upon God our creator. We do not belong to ourselves alone. We belong to God.

Questions for Reflection and Discussion

1. Describe someone you know whose life embodies hope. What are some of the factors you think contribute to that person's hopeful orientation? Can congregations, like individuals, embody a hopeful orientation? On a spectrum of hope and despair, where would you locate your congregation?

2. Reread the quotation from Wendell Berry's novel, *Jayber Crow*. What words or phrases speak to you? What touches you most deeply? Why?

3. Try putting what the author describes as "dualism" into your own words. Where and how have you experienced this dualism in church life?

4. How is sabbath practiced in your congregation and in your life? What helps you keep sabbath, and what hinders it?

Chapter 6

Why Nice Is Not Enough

Human Sin

"These prayers of confession," said a middle-aged woman, "they're just such a downer. I believe church should be upbeat, positive, inspirational. I don't come here to feel bad about myself."

"I don't see it that way," said another woman of about the same age. "I feel the prayers of confession are when we get honest, when we tell it like it is. They're like that aftershave commercial, you know the one with the slap and the guy says, 'Thanks, I needed that.'"

"Well, maybe you need to be slapped around," said the first woman, "but I certainly don't!"

Many pastors, at least those who follow a pattern of worship that includes an act of confession of sin and assurance of pardon, have heard and been a party to such conversations. Not only are prayers of confession in worship services often troubling and a matter for debate and discussion, but so too is the doctrine of sin.

"I don't buy that original sin stuff. I believe that people are good. When the church talks constantly about human beings as sinners, as depraved . . . well, it's just too much. I mean, get real," concluded this young man.

An older man, with a mischievous smile on his face, countered, "Oh, but sin is the most real doctrine of our faith! It is, as G. K. Chesterton said, the only empirically verifiable doctrine of the Christian faith." Then, as if to playfully provoke his younger friend, he added, "After all, anyone who believes in 'total depravity' can't be all bad!"

The Other Side of the Coin

In the preceding chapter about God the creator and hope, I noted that chapters 5 and 6 are two sides of one coin. The conviction that God has created the world and pronounced it good is the basis of a hopeful orientation. But the hope of Christians is not naïve hope. This life can be very difficult, even tragic. The world is a place of both extraordinary beauty and hideous brutality. Life is an amazing gift and it is also, at least at times, a heavy burden. To do justice to the complexity of reality, Christians seek to hold hope and realism in tension. They affirm life as God's good creation and as a marvelous gift. And they see the world as fallen, that is, disordered by human sin and by evil. Both views are true.

Christianity's vision about life is both informed and deepened by its teaching about human nature and sin. Many philosophers and theologians have written about human nature and what is distinctive about it. Some, for example, have defined human beings by their capacity to reason. Others have argued that the human capacity to conceive and project a future is distinctively human. Still others have claimed that the uniqueness of human beings lies in their mandate to exercise dominion over the world of nature. Christian understandings of human nature tend to emphasize that we are not simple beings. Rather, we are complex creatures whose nature is characterized by two qualities that easily come into conflict. We are simultaneously free and we are finite. We are free: capable of choice, change, and self-transcendence. We are able to explore the far reaches of space and the depths of the oceans. We create machines and technologies that have never before existed and that alter the environment. We build buildings that seem to defy gravity, and we develop cures for diseases that were thought to be incurable. And yet, we are finite. We will die. We are limited in our capacity to control life's variables and in our knowledge. We see, but not clearly. Moreover, our undeniable creativity and capacity for altering our environment has yielded mixed results. Explorations of space and oceans have led to the militarization of space and territorial disputes about the oceans. Our technologies for hydroelectric power have brought electricity to the most distant towns and lit up great cities, but the same dams have destroyed indigenous cultures and wild fish species. From the top floors of our gravity-defying buildings, we have seemingly lost sight of homeless men and women who nestle in the nooks and crannies of our large cities and whose needs we are either unable or unwilling to meet. Made in the image of God, we are creators with great power and freedom. But as creatures of the creator, we are limited and finite beings, made of dust. The great American novelist Nathaniel Hawthorne captured the strange mixed nature of our experience when he wrote: "Life is made up of marble and mud. And, without all the deeper trust in a comprehensive sympathy above us, we might hence be led to suspect the insult of a sneer, as well as an immitigable form, on the iron face of fate. What is called poetic insight is the gift of discerning, in this sphere of strangely mingled elements, the beauty and the majesty which are compelled to assume a garb so sordid."[1] For Hawthorne only a "comprehensive sympathy above us," that is a divine grace, can enable us to live with grace as this strange blend of marble and mud, free and finite.

Christian thought and teaching regarding the nature and forms of human sin flow from this understanding of our dual nature as free and finite, capable of self-transcendence and yet simultaneously limited in sight and insight. Sin is understood to take two basic forms, which are distortions of our dual nature. On one hand, we make too much of our freedom. We seek to dominate others. We presume ourselves to be so sufficiently wise or virtuous or strong that we have no need of God or of others. We take our freedom to such heights that we build personal or societal towers of Babel that defy our nature as limited creatures.

This distortion of our freedom has often been characterized as the sin of pride, that is, false pride and arrogance. We claim too much for ourselves. We are presumptuous. We are willful.

But such distortion of our freedom, which denies our relationship to God our creator or others, is hardly the only face or form of sin. Sin is not only, as noted earlier in this book, titanic and overweening presumption or willfulness; sin is also resignation and servility. It is will-lessness. It is the slide into powerlessness. Sin may take the form of making ourselves absolute and the center of all things. And it may take the form of hating ourselves, refusing to take our rightful place and the power that is ours as people created in the image of God. One form of sin exaggerates our freedom and power and fails to take account of our nature as limited beings and as creatures. But the other form of sin overestimates our limits and fails to accept the invitation of our freedom, our capacity to make choices and to act in ways that make a difference by participating in God's redemptive purpose. Theologian Daniel Migliore offers the insightful suggestion that on the night Jesus was betrayed, we see both forms of sin. "Judas's act of betrayal is sin in its aggressive form; the fear and cowardice of the other disciples is sin in its passive form."[2]

Before moving on to the implications and expressions of Christian teaching and conviction regarding sin for congregational health, I offer one further observation. Many pastors, theologians, and ethicists, both lay and ordained, have rightly been troubled by reductionist understandings of sin that whittle this complex matter of sin down to lists of "dos and don'ts," or to a seemingly simple moral code. A consensus exists, particularly in twentieth-century Christian theological thought and writing, that interpretations of sin that reduce the matter to moral codes have failed to do justice to sin's complexity and to its presence in social structures and systems. Sin, held many teachers and writers of this period, is more than individual behavior. Sin is more than personal infractions or violations of a moral code. Sin is systemic and includes such matters such as racism, sexism, poverty, and political oppression.

Certainly these theologians and preachers have been right in what they affirmed. But I wonder if they were wrong in what they rejected. In other words, in their efforts to help us see the social and systemic nature of sin, I wonder if we have lost sight of the personal dimension of sin. Thus, we have eyes to see systemic sin but seem blind to recurring individual or personal sin, such as lying, manipulation, abuse of power in personal relationships, or the failure to exercise appropriate responsibility. In recent decades, perhaps particularly in mainline Protestant congregations and denominations, we are very much aware of social and systemic sins like racism and sexism, but we seem less able to name and confront sin that takes a more personal form. We condemn, as we should, national aggression, sexism, and genocide. We seem, at least sometimes, blind to the ways people manipulate power to diminish others, to destroy the health of families or congregations, to pursue their personal security at the expense of others.

If there was a time when our understanding of sin was too confined to the personal and individual, now it seems our important efforts to redress the balance have perhaps gone too far. One consequence of this is that congregations and their pastors may speak with eloquence and frequency about social and systemic sin but lack words for failures of character that are marring the lives of individuals and congregations. Even as we lament genocide in Africa, economic exploitation in South America, or "glass ceilings" in corporate offices, we may fail to discern or name sin when a pastor is simply lazy and doesn't struggle with the text in preparation for next week's sermon. We seem not to have the words to name it when people play on guilt to manipulate other people or when individuals chronically fail to keep the promises they have made to others. An adequate understanding of sin requires that we are able to discern and name sin in both forms and arenas: the social and systemic and the personal and individual. To overlook the latter dimension of sin disables congregations and is a factor in their loss of health. In reality, the personal and the systemic nature of sin go together. Seldom does a person manage to behave like a bully in the life of a congregation unless the system of the congregation allows such behavior. Insightful understanding of human sin sees both the individual misbehavior and the role of social systems in supporting such behaviors. For example, we may identify a pastor who is a serial sexual abuser. But a church or denominational system that has failed to notice the behavior and respond is also at fault.

Congregations and their members are not well served when churches, pastors, and teachers do not teach and speak accurately about the reality of sin. Over the years many people have staggered into my office to pour out a story that includes the words: "I don't understand how people can be like this, how they can be so mean and devious and hurtful!" Underlying their lament is the notion that people are basically good and that if we are nice and kind, everyone else will be too. "I thought that Christianity and Jesus taught that if you just love people, everything would work out!"

When we consider the course of Jesus's life, the opposition he experienced, the many conflicts he confronted, not to mention his death on the cross, for us to have gotten the idea that Christianity boils down to being nice or the assumption that if we are nice people, everyone else will be too, is a bit dumfounding. Those who invoke the ironic aphorism "No good deed goes unpunished" are closer to the truth of the gospel. "What part of the cross don't you understand?" a friend queries rhetorically.

When in the nativity story from the Gospel of Luke, the writer tells us there was "no place for them in the inn," he offers more than a nice narrative touch or sentimental detail (2:7). He is foreshadowing the resistance of a sinful world to God's love and presence. When the Gospel-writer John, in his prologue, soberly states, "He came to what was his own, and his own people did not accept him" (John 1:11), the Fourth Gospel is saying much the same thing, namely, that something about us human beings prefers, in John's recurring metaphor, the darkness to the light. Christianity is not naïve about the reality of sin and evil. Nor are people helped when churches communicate that Christian faith boils down to being nice.

From the General to the Specific

A more sober understanding of human nature can help a congregation and its members identify and properly name sin and evil, starting with and including their own. I seem to recall that

Calvin asserted confession begins with the house and people of God. Teaching and preaching that take into account the reality of sin equip individuals and congregations to deal with these experiences in ways that are more realistic and therefore more effective than "I thought Christianity taught that if we just love people everything will work out." Teaching about sin is important, as the first section of this chapter has endeavored to do, but bringing these general concepts and convictions to the actual lives of congregations is also important.

To this second task, I now turn. Here I want to pay particular attention to three particular ways sin disfigures congregational life today: leadership failure, abuse of power and bullying, and the adoption of a victim mentality. These three are not intended as an exhaustive catalogue of sin's expression in congregational life. They are proposed more as illustrations. Moreover, each of these three areas is itself a complex matter, and they overlap. Each of them also, in my experience and observation, bedevils congregational life today, resulting in various forms of ill health. By taking sin more seriously, naming it accurately, and speaking of it truthfully, we enhance congregational health.

Leadership Failure

Several years ago I taught a summer school course on pastoral leadership at a seminary of the United Church of Canada. As we began our course, I invited the 40 participants to complete an exercise that was designed to get at our motivations. What excites and motivates us? What helps us to get out of bed in the morning and gets our engines going? This particular diagnostic tool asked people to answer a list of questions that locates participants in one of three motivational groups. Group one were those whose motivations were "affiliative." The affiliators focused on relationships and caring interactions, on seeing that everyone was included and noticing how people were participating or not. Group two were the achievers. They wanted results, outcomes, and products. They wished to make a visible difference. Group three were those whose motivations fell under the rubric of "power and influence." They wanted to change hearts and minds, to influence people and organizations. All three are important. If one were to imagine a dinner party, the affiliators might be welcoming people to the party and helping them to feel comfortable, while the achievers might have spent time planning the menu and making sure dinner was wonderful. The power and influence group might have scrutinized the invitation list and sought to shape a vibrant conversation and help guests make meaningful connections with one another to advance a particular cause or project.

When we were all done, we discovered that we had 23 affiliators, 15 achievers, but only two power-and-influence types among the 40 pastoral leaders in the room—a rather striking imbalance. I reported this to the class without comment and asked what they made of it, curious to see how they would respond. Their initial reactions were self-congratulatory. They noted the strong bias toward concern for people and individuals and the apparent lack of concern for power or influence. After a while a younger woman pastor blurted out a very different interpretation of the results. "Our denomination," she said, "has been telling us that power is bad for so long now, that I'm surprised that even two people would own up to wishing to have the power or capacity to influence others." This was followed by a short, stunned silence. Then another younger woman pastor said, "Yes, and the fact that we have described power as inherently 'bad' doesn't mean that power realities and issues simply go away. They go underground and come out in all sorts of weird ways."

I noted to the class that two vocations commonly chosen by those whose motivation falls under "power and influence" are teachers and political leaders, two of our more troubled vocations in today's world. I said that I would worry about a denomination where only five percent of the clergy, more or less, were motivated to change hearts and minds. The survey exercise and, perhaps even more, the discussion were revealing. We have, at least in some quarters, become ambivalent, at best, about power and influence and, at worst, completely negative regarding such qualities and values. In an earlier period, we were often aware of distorted and sinful abuses of power exhibited in the domination of others and in being high-handed or arrogant. I wonder if today more of the sins related to leadership are of a different nature. Instead of overbearing leadership, we often witness a failure to lead and to exercise the responsibility, as well as to take the risks, leadership entails. Have too many clergy, called to leadership in the church, fallen short not by being dominating or high-handed but by being passive and resigned? To put this claim another way, if the prevailing form of sin among leaders was, at one time, a tendency to grab power, perhaps today the prevailing form of sin is the slide of designated leaders into powerlessness. Leaders, by definition, lead. And yet many congregations today founder because their called and designated leaders fail to lead and to lead effectively.

Let me hasten to add the fault is not always that of leaders alone. While recognizing that I am speaking in generalizations here and that certainly many exceptions exist, congregations seem often unwilling to support and foster good leadership. People in many congregations have such a wide array of expectations that leaders are pulled in too many directions. Many are the congregations today that get the leadership they deserve, namely, poor and inadequate leadership. Congregations, in their sinfulness, want leaders to tell them what they want to hear rather than what they need to hear. Yet if leaders are doing their job, they inevitably challenge those whom they lead to a higher level of realization of goals and values and to a higher level of aspiration. Not a few congregations today have adopted a definition of pastoral leadership that prizes member satisfaction and meeting the diverse array of member expectations over congregational faithfulness.

What are the results of this failure of leadership? Often, what seems to happen is that the most pressing challenges and problems before a congregation are not addressed and acted upon. Over time, two things then happen. Inertia sets in and the problems, whatever they may be (for example, poor stewardship, loss of members, sloppy worship) build in a way that undermines the church's life and mission. In advanced stages, leadership failure tends to create a vacuum into which others step. Of course, some others may provide the needed leadership. But often those who step into such vacuums may have their own agendas and needs.

This emphasis on pastoral leadership ought not be taken to mean that lay people and members of congregations do not have a leadership role to play and a responsibility to be leaders themselves. They most certainly do. Good pastoral leadership tends to enable other leaders; it supports and strengthens a leadership team as well as a positive ethos within an entire congregation. Good pastoral leadership does not mean being the only leader or the pastor doing everything. That is another kind of leadership failure!

The point here is that leadership is relational and involves two parties, the leader or leaders and the led. Both have a crucial part to play. "It takes two to tango," as the saying goes. Nevertheless, my primary point is that sin disfigures the face of leadership and contributes to illness in congregations when leaders fail to lead. Sin here is expressed less in presumption than in servility and resignation. The result is sometimes captured in the lament of people in such congregations who say, "We just seem to be wandering in the wilderness."

Power Grabs and Bullying

If designated leaders are ineffective and refuse to fulfill their important role, we can be sure of one thing: others will, as noted above, rush to fill the vacuum. By the inelegant term *power grab*, I have in mind the attempt of those in congregations who have not been designated or authorized for leadership, or for whom there are no structures of accountability or evaluation, to claim and exercise power in a congregation. Leaders in congregations, by and large though not always, ought to be designated by a clear and open process for filling those roles and authorized by the church to fulfill them. Part of what such designation and authorization of leadership means is that structures are in place to which leaders are accountable and by which their leadership is evaluated. Too often today those who are neither authorized nor accountable are inserting themselves into leadership roles. To use my framework of sin as the distortion of either our freedom or our finitude, power grabs distort our freedom by self-assertions that disregard others and the church as a whole. People put their own needs first, even though they may have been called to something quite different. While many designated leaders are lapsing into the sin of timidity or resignation and failing to lead, others distort human freedom by efforts to dominate and by presumption.

As an example, consider Dan, who volunteered to be a part of the music team for the new contemporary service at his church. All well and good—so far. Dan joined Mike and Sally on the music team and worked with their pastor, David, to plan the new service and get it going. As such new ventures often do, the new contemporary service began on a high note, with great interest and enthusiasm. The first year was a hit. But in the second year the initial enthusiasm waned, and by the third year many in the congregation began to suspect that the contemporary service was an experiment that had failed. Its participants had winnowed to a relatively small group.

The pastor told the worship board that much had been learned from this experiment and that he was grateful for the help Dan, Mike, and Sally, along with others, had provided. He and the board, after further evaluation, which included consulting those who most frequently attended the contemporary service, concluded that the best course was to integrate elements from the contemporary service into the congregation's other two services. Everyone agreed; everyone, that is, except Dan, who it seems had found his place and his group in the contemporary service. Working behind the scenes after the worship board meeting, Dan rallied various individuals against the board and against the pastor. Whispered accusations began to be heard by various members that the pastor was on a power trip and that David had it in for particular individuals, especially Dan, who wasn't being allowed to exercise and share his gifts. The decision to end the contemporary service and to integrate its elements into the other services was made, it was alleged, because David felt threatened by Dan. Dan called people in the congregation with these allegations against the pastor and the board. Suddenly, the congregation was in an uproar.

This is not an unusual story. It might have happened in a mission or outreach program or in the youth ministry. Someone, in this case Dan, was making a grab for power and for turf to meet his personal needs. Though the contemporary service had never been conceived as "Dan's service" or as a vehicle for Dan to share his gifts or garner a group of followers, it had morphed into that. What began as a useful experiment, and had been described as such, became a clique within the congregation. Moreover, no one seemed to know what to do about it. Some were astonished that Dan was willing to manipulate others through distorted information and false accusations against the pastor and lay leaders. Others were astonished that the pastor could be so small-minded or that this was such a big deal to David. "Why not let Dan do his thing?" they asked.

One congregation with which I worked had a variety of worship services, differentiated by musical style and idiom. It would not have been an exaggeration to say that each service was a different person or group doing their thing. In the sanctuary, Ralph did his thing on the organ. In the chapel, Sue did her thing on an electric keyboard. In another setting, Charley did his thing as he presided over the discussion-based service. Meanwhile, Corrie was playing guitar for a family service. From the outside, it looked like a wonderful expression of diversity. From the inside, it looked like a church that had become a loose federation of factions. The congregation was a variety of groups and individuals who had successfully grabbed power and their piece of turf.

Congregations are particularly vulnerable to such power grabbing when they have little realistic understanding of human sin and instead prefer to be "nice" and to avoid conflict or confrontation. In a similar way, congregations are vulnerable to what boils down to bullying behaviors. Bullying isn't much different from the old playground gambit, "If you won't play my game or play by my rules, I'm taking my ball and going home." The issue may be, "If the church doesn't have the rummage sale, or if the time of my service is changed, or the annual mission fair is dropped, I'm dropping or canceling my pledge." The problem is essentially this: I get my way or I leave. Or, what is often worse, I stick around and make life miserable for everyone else.

What are congregations to do in the face of power grabs and bullying? How are congregations to cope with human sinfulness? Of the various means and strategies, all of them have something to do with recognizing such willfulness for what it is: sin. Good congregational practices of decision making, evaluation, term limits, and accountability are the best defense against power grabs and bullying. Such practices put boundaries around those who behaviors are willful. So do clear personnel policies and practices that are uniformly applied. In extreme cases of bullying behaviors, congregations and their leaders may need to plan coherent and consistent strategies to limit and contain the damage some will cause or try to cause. Attempts to be nice and let people do their thing often prove to be no more than forms of enabling or supporting power grabbers and bullies.

The Victim Mentality

I am not quite sure how it has come to pass, but people describing themselves and their experience through a lens or framework that might be called "the victim's tale" is common today. This is not to say that people are not sometimes victimized by others. Certainly they are. Nor is this intended to blame the victim. Most of us are, at some times and in some ways, victims. We may be victims of robbery or of a hit-and-run accident. We may be victims of racial bigotry or of prejudice based on age, gender, or appearance. We may be victims when a company decides to move its plant overseas. The tragedy of childhood sexual abuse and domestic violence are very real and deeply wounding.

That said, being a victim is different from adopting what might be described as a victim mentality. A victim mentality has both an outward and an inward aspect. Outwardly, it may mean that one's story of victimization or suffering is the primary way through which a person is known and describes himself or herself to others. Inwardly, the adoption of a victim mentality means granting control of one's life to the victimizer or to oppressive powers. Their actions determine one's fate and future. Even if the victimization is not ongoing, such a mentality means that a person can never be anything but a victim. Getting over the experience of victimization or moving on is not possible.

Victimization is real, and we do not choose it. A victim mentality, however, is chosen. Jim may have lost a job because he didn't get along with his boss. He was treated unfairly. This is a case of being a victim. We can certainly understand if Jim goes into his next job a little cautious, watching his boss carefully. But Jim adopts a victim mentality when he refuses to give his new boss a chance, when he speaks repeatedly about how his former employer shafted him, and when he undermines his success on the job by having a chip on his shoulder that everyone sees but him. The initial experience was real, but Jim clings to the disappointing experience rather than processing it, learning from it, and coming to put it in perspective.

Moreover, in terms of the understanding of sin I have developed here, a victim mentality is a form of sin—a rejection of freedom and our capacity to exercise it. Jim had rejected his wife's suggestion of counseling. He had declined his pastor's invitation to a men's group where others who had experience loss of jobs might have been a help to Jim. Jim refused to get over his bad experience. He slid into resignation and into powerlessness. To a significant extent, our society seems today to encourage a victim mentality by granting the moral high ground to anyone who is able to narrate a story of being a victim. Too often such an account seems to be enough to legitimate a person or to gain some kind of acceptance or even status. This, of course, encourages people to frame life through such narratives, as well as to describe themselves as victims.

Noteworthy is that Jesus, while addressing himself to victims and speaking honestly of that experience, does not encourage a victim mentality. For example, in the Sermon on the Mount, Jesus counsels those who would follow him, "If anyone strikes you on the right cheek, turn the other also; and if anyone wants to sue you and take your coat, give your cloak as well; and if anyone forces you to go one mile, go also the second mile" (Matt. 5:39-41). He speaks to those who are subject to oppressive Roman powers in first-century Palestine. Many have decried these words for their impracticality or as an invitation to further abuse. This is to misunderstand the paradoxical nature of Jesus' teaching. He is acknowledging that victimization happens. Someone may strike us, sue us, or force us to march. How then does a victim avoid surrendering control to an oppressor? By seizing control and taking the initiative: "Turn the other cheek," "Give them your cloak as well," or "Walk a second mile." All are encouragements to victims not to adopt a victim mentality.

In more recent times, both Gandhi and Martin Luther King Jr. understood the ways those with less power, those who are victims, might take power by submitting to violence, yet maintaining freedom and initiative. Less well known persons have done something similar when they have worked through a particular trauma but have gone on to share their experience with others who struggle with similar problems. For example, many substance abuser counselors have themselves been substance abusers. Victims of domestic violence work with others to deal with the problem. Especially in situations faced by a King or Gandhi, systems of broad social injustice and victimization, not to internalize a victim status or mentality is a huge challenge, yet their examples show that it can be done. Moreover, we find counsel and direction in the Gospels where Jesus does not encourage or sanction a victim mentality, even though he does speak to and sympathize with victims.

For another example of Jesus's capacity to make and hold this distinction, we can turn to the Passion narrative, especially in the Gospel of John. If any moment in the life of Jesus exists when he may be perceived and cast as a victim, surely the crucifixion is one. Particularly in the Gospel of John, Jesus makes clear that his life is not taken from him. Rather, he gives his life (10:17-18). This point is echoed in Jesus' final words in John, when Jesus says, "It is finished" (19:30). He has accomplished what he set out to do. He has completed his mission. He is not a victim. For the followers of Jesus who experienced increasing persecution, this was an important model.

How might this distinction and the contemporary recourse to a victim mentality play out in healthy and unhealthy ways in congregations? One congregation I served went through a two-year process of discernment as it decided whether to become what our denomination refers to as an "Open and Affirming Church." This meant that the congregation would explicitly state its welcome to gay and lesbian people and to their families. It meant the congregation would work to understand the experience of such people and to include them in its life and leadership. During the course of the two years, many different forms of discernment were engaged in, including listening to the testimonies of gay and lesbian people and to the testimonies of their parents. Often these were stories of victimization, being rejected by family and churches or experiencing discrimination in schools, in the workplace, or in the housing market. Often such accounts were met with astonishment—"I never knew"— as well as sympathy and compassion. Both the telling of such stories and the responses were appropriate.

After the congregation had reached a decision to become an Open and Affirming Church, there was a next step. The congregation needed to decide how this designation and its meaning would be communicated on an ongoing basis to those who came to the church and in the wider community. Initially a statement was placed in the congregation's order of worship and newsletter and in other materials. The statement simply said that people whose sexual orientation is to those of their own gender are welcome here and are affirmed in that identity and orientation. Recognizing what gay and lesbian people had suffered, welcome and compassion were extended in Christ's name.

As time passed, this affirmation seemed to the congregation's leaders to be incomplete. A new statement was developed that welcomed all people regardless of race, economic status, age, or sexual orientation. "This congregation welcomes all people," said the statement, "and calls all people to the cost and joy of Christian discipleship." The revised statement attempted, successfully I believe, to do more than simply acknowledge victims of exclusion. It went beyond that to call all people to full discipleship and thus to avoid a victim mentality. Something, the statement asserted, is asked of us, all of us. We have the capacity to make choices, to accept responsibility. Victims can become disciples of Jesus Christ. In this way the congregation recognized the experience of victims of prejudice but did not consider that recognition the end point of its life and ministry. That purpose was Christian faith and discipleship.

Healthy congregations speak to people's experiences of suffering, loss, and victimization. But they do not leave people there.

We come just as we are, to paraphrase the words of the hymn. But, through the grace of God and the power of a community of healing and transformation, we rediscover and reclaim our powers of freedom and as agents who are capable of choice and change. We answer the call to discipleship.

A Concluding Word

You will undoubtedly think of forms of sin in addition to those considered in this chapter. This is, as I indicated earlier, not an attempt to catalogue all such forms but to illustrate several of the ways that sin and the failure to name and acknowledge sin can result in congregations that are unhealthy. It is an attempt to encourage congregations to observe practices and to create structures that put boundaries around human willfulness and that encourage those who lapsed into powerlessness to claim the power God has given to them. By the same token, the Christian conviction is that by naming our sinfulness, turning to God, and with God's help repenting of it, we are on the way to greater health and vitality.

Questions for Reflection and Discussion

1. Alone or in a group, do a free association with the word *sin*. Without thinking too much or censoring first thoughts, what comes to mind?
2. Consider and discuss the following statement from *Dakota: A Spiritual Geography* by Kathleen Norris:

Comprehensible, sensible sin is one of the unexpected gifts I've found in the monastic tradition. The 4th century monks began to answer a question for me that the human potential movement of the late twentieth century never seemed to address: if I'm O.K., and our friends are O.K., why is the world definitely not O.K.? Blaming others wouldn't do. Only when I began to see the world's ills mirrored in myself did I begin to find an answer. Only as I began to address that uncomfortable word, sin, did I see that I was not being handed a load of needless guilt so much as a useful tool for confronting the negative side of human behavior.[3]

This chapter explores the idea that we human beings are both free and finite. Moreover, sin arises when one or the other is overemphasized. How do you react to this understanding of human nature and of sin? Do you find it helpful? Why or why not?

3. Of the three forms of sin in congregational life the author describes, which one concerns you most and why? How do you think congregations can best cope with such forms of sin?

4. Name and discuss another form or expression of sin that you believe common today and detrimental to the life of congregations. Try to describe how this form of sin distorts either human freedom or human finitude.

Chapter 7

The Difference Jesus Makes

The Person and Work of Jesus Christ

W hile the church has expressed its experience and faith regarding Jesus Christ in many different ways, theologians and teachers seeking to give an ordered account of these convictions have generally identified two broad topics: the person of Jesus Christ and the work of Jesus Christ. These two themes of theology can be expressed in two questions: who is Jesus, and how does he help us? As with most such distinctions, this one is useful but not absolute. Who Jesus is and how he helps us are, in the end, bound together.

The body of theological thought devoted to the first question is called "Christology." Who was and who is Jesus? Who was and is this person who is the second person of the triune God? The church's answer is a challenging one. Jesus is fully human and fully God. The answer is also puzzling. How can any one person or thing be fully this and also fully that? In the first part of this chapter, I focus on this great puzzle, or paradox, and some implications it has for the vitality of congregations.

The attempts of the church and its teachers to address the second question, how does Jesus help us? are called "soteriology." This comes from the Latin root word for salvation, *soter*. How does Jesus help us? What has he done and what does he do? Here the church does not give one answer but several. The second part of the chapter explores some of the main ways this question has been answered and their implications for the health and life of congregations.

Who Is Jesus?

All four of the Gospels agree that the public ministry of Jesus began at one defining moment, his baptism. While Matthew, Mark, Luke, and John all tell the story of the baptism of Jesus in somewhat different ways, they are in agreement on this: the preaching, teaching, and healing ministry of Jesus got underway with his baptism by John. While all the Gospel writers agree on this point, in some ways they couldn't have picked a more difficult event to focus on. The baptism of Jesus troubled the early church and continues to fret some people today. After all, if John offered a baptism of repentance for sins, what was Jesus doing in that line at the Jordan River? If this baptism is for sinners, why is the sinless Son of God taking part?

The discomfort of the church with the whole thing is evident in the ways the various Gospel writers handle it. While Mark, as is his style, relates the baptism straightforwardly, Matthew has John the Baptist trying to talk Jesus out of it. "I need to be baptized by you, and do you come to me?" (Matt. 3:14). Luke takes the matter a step further. The actual baptism of Jesus is not even reported, only noted as having happened (Luke 3:21). John shifts the focus further from the actual baptism to the witness of John the Baptist to Jesus (John 1:19-28).

The wonderful, contemporary preacher Barbara Brown Taylor sees this struggle for what it is in a sermon on the baptism of Jesus: "If Jesus had listened to his public relations people, he would . . . have been a friend to sinners, a kind and loving helper, but never mistaken for one of them. He could have stood on shore and offered words of encouragement to those going into the water, yes. He could have held out his hand to those who struggled out of the river in their heavy wet clothes, yes, but he could not under any circumstances have gone into the water himself, unless it was to tap John on the shoulder and say, 'Hey, you go rest. I'll take over now.'" Moreover, Taylor herself points toward the implications of all this for the life and health of congregations: "You see the problem. We spend a lot of time in the Christian church talking about God's love for sinners, but we sure do go to a lot of trouble not to be mistaken for one of them. Guilt by association and all that."[1]

But Jesus, and God in Jesus, does not seem worried about getting into the river, into the mud of life and the muck of sin, with us. From the very first, Jesus does not stand apart, cheering from the shore; he stands with us and for us as one of us. "Sharing our common lot," is the way the Statement of Faith of the United Church of Christ puts it. He risks full entry into our life and humanity. This is the meaning of the word and doctrine *incarnation*. "The Word," as John puts it in the opening words of the Fourth Gospel, "became flesh and lived among us, . . . full of grace and truth" (John 1:14). Jesus embraces our humanity by sharing it, completely.

Just as the account of the baptism of Jesus has troubled some, so the conviction that Jesus was and is fully human has also proven difficult for many Christians from the earliest times. One early instance of this hesitancy to affirm the full humanity of Jesus was known as Docetism. The Docetists claimed that Jesus was not truly human. Rather, he only appeared to be human. Like someone at a masquerade party, he put on a human mask and costume for the occasion, but underneath he was God. The church declared Docetism to be a heresy and said that Jesus was fully and truly human in its earliest statement of faith, the Apostles' Creed. He didn't stand on the shore shouting encouragement or offering a helping hand. He got into the river of life with us, embracing our full humanity with his own. In doing so, God in Christ says to us what Psalm 139 had said earlier, as the psalmist sang in awestruck wonder: "If I ascend to heaven, you are there; if I make my bed in Sheol [the shadowy underworld], you are there. If I take the wings of the morning and settle at the farthest limits of the sea, even there your hand shall lead me, and your right hand hold me fast. If I say, 'Surely the darkness shall cover me, and the light around me become night,' even the darkness is not dark to you; the night is as bright as the day, for darkness is as light to you" (Ps. 139:8-12).

The Christ Who Is Fully Human and the Health of Congregations

Not quite ten years ago a particular event changed my life and that of my family. It happened while I was on a youth mission trip in Nicaragua. I was one of the adults with a group of young people from our church, a group that included my two sons, who were then aged 18 and 22. Within days of our arrival, our eldest son, who had graduated from college the spring before, began to evidence strange and worrisome behaviors. Before long he experienced a psychotic break. When he and I were able to return home to the States, he was diagnosed with the brain disease known as bipolar illness. To exaggerate how devastating and challenging this was for us all in our family would be difficult.

Partly because a number of people from the congregation had been with us on the trip and were aware of the situation, and partly because I simply trusted the care and understanding of the congregation, my wife and I did speak of our son's illness and its terrifying and devastating effects on our whole family. At the same time, we tried to respect that this story was, in the end, his and to honor his privacy.

As this difficult experience unfolded over several of the most challenging years in the life of our marriage and family (and most of all in our son's life), I noticed something happening in the congregation. Others who had a family member who had or was then experiencing the terrors and trials of mental illness began to speak, first with me or another pastor, of that experience. Gradually, this candor went beyond the pastor's study as the congregation embraced mental illness and those who suffer with it. Moreover, in time not only those who had a family member who suffered mental illness who spoke of the struggles, but also people who had experienced a bout of mental illness in their own lives. In this large congregation, that proved to be a significant number of people, as many as fifty to one hundred people all told.

But very few, really almost none, of their stories or struggles came out until we shared our own. Moreover, it became clear that, for some at least, reticence about the experience of mental illness in their own family or personal lives was not only a matter of privacy, which can and should be respected, but something more: secrecy and shame. For many it had not been acceptable to acknowledge even to themselves, much less within the community of Christ, that they or their family had known the harrowing depths of mental illness. They seemingly understood it as a personal failure and a shameful thing.

I understood this. Nearly twenty years earlier, I had experienced a time of severe depression. I had shared it with no one except my wife and doctors. I did not tell friends, colleagues, or congregation. I found it too embarrassing and shameful. But over the years that changed. In sermons and other presentations I would speak, albeit cautiously, of my own earlier experience of depression. I did understand the shame and sense of personal failure attached to mental illness.

Christians would not object were Jesus to stand on the figurative shore and offer words of encouragement to those who suffer, but we do not imagine Jesus getting into the muck and risking being confused with sinners. And we ourselves do not wish to be identified or confused with the broken, with the suffering, with the sin-sick. If we do not face up to our own brokenness, however, we cannot appropriate the real blessings of God's embrace of our full humanity in Jesus. Or to put it in a more positive way, by his full embrace of our finite and limited humanity, Jesus makes of our humanity a blessing and not a curse. We need not flee the inherent vulnerability of being human in order to follow Jesus. Or to put it a slightly different way, the world is not divided between the sinful and the virtuous. It divides between those who are aware of their sin and their need for grace and those who are without awareness of their true condition.

When the awareness that we all stand in need of grace is absent, it fundamentally skews the ministry and health of the church. We become blind to our own need for forgiveness and healing. We pretend that we have it together. We are happy (or not) to help others, but we need no real help ourselves, thanks very much! In this view, Christians are better sorts of people, not sinners in need of God and God's grace.

Author, theologian, and teacher Roberta Bondi says that all too often the church permits and encourages us to be our "noble selves," "our cleaned up and socially presentable selves."[2] That is not without value. We do need to be reminded of our better natures. But there is a problem with an unrelieved emphasis on our noble selves. It does not so readily invite and include our real selves. And, observes Bondi, the real us is who God wants and who God loves. In Christ, God has embraced our real and full humanity, warts and all.

What became evident in the course of our family's experience with mental illness is a pattern of cover-up in the church. We pretend to be okay. We cover up our own brokenness and sin. Our family realized we too had lived, in some measure at least, with the myth of the perfect family. Such pretense was no longer an option. We clung to grace. We drew near to the crucified and risen Christ in new ways.

When our family shared our experience in what I hope were judicious and appropriate ways, and others came forward to speak about their similar experiences, unexpected things began to happen. Honesty and intimacy in the congregation moved to a deeper level. The congregation's caring shifted somehow from what might be called "we strong people will care for you needy people," to "we are one another's companions in the midst of life's challenges." Moreover, this more authentic type of community and bringing our fuller selves to God and to one another eventually led to an amazing new congregational ministry.

Today, fewer than ten years after our family's experience, that ministry includes classes and support groups for people and families experiencing mental illness, a ministry on the streets of downtown Seattle to the chronically mentally ill, and three houses of healing. The houses are residential, spiritual communities where low-income people experiencing mental illness and those recently discharged from a hospital psychiatric unit find a safe home and community, which members of the congregation support and provide. Both the residents and those who support the residence have been changed by this ministry. Truly, from loss and devastation, God brought forth new life and hope.

My point is not to commend ourselves, to use a phrase of the apostle Paul, but rather to indicate how, from our personal experience of suffering and weakness, God's strength and grace became both more real and more abundant. Paul speaks of this too, in 2 Corinthians, reporting that he came to understand, strange and paradoxical as it may seem, God's "power is made perfect in weakness" (12:9). The Christian conviction that Jesus is fully human and that God embraces our full humanity permits and invites us to be more authentic with God and with each other. We are not made acceptable to God because we have arrived at perfection or gotten it (whatever "it" is) right. We are made acceptable to God by God's grace, which comes to us in the one who, yet fully God, became fully human for our sake.

Fully God?

The account of Jesus's baptism provides an entry point into the church's claim that Jesus is fully human and that nothing we can experience is beyond God's knowledge and grace. Another well-known text from the Gospels may serve as a springboard to discussing the church's conviction that Jesus is not only fully human but also fully God. This text is the story of the transfiguration, found in all three of the Synoptic Gospels, Matthew, Mark, and Luke, with small variances reflecting the emphasis of that Gospel and its author. The essential story is, however, much the same, and in each gospel the account of the event comes at a turning point, as Jesus turns toward Jerusalem and the cross.

Taking three of the disciples, Peter, James, and John, Jesus ascended a high mountain where he was filled with light and suffused with the glory of God. Moses and Elijah, two figures emblematic of the law and prophets, joined him, but in the end they faded and Jesus stood alone, which suggests both Jesus' continuity with the past as well as his fulfilling of it. As the three figures stood in glory before the disciples, Peter sought to take charge, blurting out: "Lord, it is good for us to be here; . . . I will make three dwellings [or booths] here, one for you, one for Moses, and one for Elijah" (Matt. 17:4). Peter was not only silenced but also driven to the ground in fear and trembling when a voice spoke out of a bright cloud that hovered above and said, "This is my Son, the Beloved; with him I am well pleased; listen to him!" (v. 5).

In Jesus's transfiguration, the glory of God, evident in Jesus's ministry of preaching, teaching, and healing, is fully revealed in him. In him God is fully present and revealed in a way that has at least two implications. One is that in Jesus's life, teachings, death, and resurrection, we see the nature and way of God. As Martin Copenhaver puts it:

> By observing the way Jesus responded to those who were cast off by life, we can understand God's special care for the out-cast. By hearing about the ways Jesus healed the sick, we can discover that our God is the kind of God who can put to-gether the broken pieces of our lives. By observing the ways Jesus forgave the very ones who rejected and betrayed him, we can realize how far God will go to embrace us with forgive-ness. By studying the ways of Jesus, we need not wonder what God would have us do because we can endeavor simply to do what Jesus did.[3]

Jesus reveals God, but in doing so another thing becomes evident. Jesus who is fully God is also other than we are. Jesus is not simply a model of human beings at their best, but he is the awesome fullness of God, which we can neither wholly compre-hend nor control. Thus, when Peter seeks to put a box around the glory of God manifest in Jesus, he is driven to his knees and told, "Listen to him." Or one might paraphrase, "Don't just do something, stand there!" Because Jesus is fully God, he cannot be captured in a creed or a church, in our best ideas or our best plans, in our temples or our institutions. There is an otherness, a transcendence, and a mystery about this one who is fully God. Perhaps the Gospel of John has no story of the transfiguration because, in many ways, the whole Gospel witnesses to this truth: Jesus, especially in John, reveals the awesome mystery of God. Fourth-century desert "abba" Gregory of Nyssa pointed to this truth when he wrote, "Concepts create idols; only wonder comprehends anything."[4] Peter's booth-building project and our concepts have this in common: they attempt to capture and control the one who cannot be either captured or controlled.

Fully God and Transformative Worship

Some interesting conversations occur on airplanes, especially when people ask what you do and you answer, "Well, I am a pastor." Something a seatmate said in the course of one such conversation made a lasting impression upon me. He told me of his struggle with alcoholism and his recovery by turning to a higher power with the help of Alcoholics Anonymous. He said that he kept a note prominently displayed on his refrigerator with these words: "There is a God, John, and it's not you." While the attempt to usurp the role of God has a history as long as humanity, it took on a new and powerful form in what historians term "modernity," that period beginning with the Enlightenment in the eighteenth century and continuing into our own time.

Both the Enlightenment and modernity have given us great gifts but also some great illusions. Modernity has prized reason, optimism, objectivity, and progress. These gifts have promised humanity greater control over life's changes and chances. But we have sometimes drunk so deeply at the wells of modernity and its promises of control that we have grown blind to our limits and have presumed ourselves to be in charge, sufficient unto ourselves. In many ways, we moderns have, with my seatmate John, forgotten that there is a God and that it is not us. Even the religious exhibit what some have called the "functional atheism" of modernity. We live as if there were no power but our own, no resources other than our own, and no purpose forming and informing life save our own.

This functional atheism has many implications, but here I want to focus on one that has to do with the church, and particularly worship in the church. Worship has many dimensions, but certainly a most basic one is that in worship we seek to be in the presence of God. In some older traditions, going to worship was spoken of as "going to meeting," which did not primarily mean meeting with other people but going to meet and be met by God. Vital congregations, where worship has transformational power, are congregations that help people to be in God's presence. As the teacher of preaching and preacher Fred Craddock has observed, that is "where everyone wants to be, and where everyone doesn't want to be."[5] To be in the presence of God is to be face to face with unconditional truth and burning love. To be in God's presence is to risk being changed and to realize our own finitude. At Jesus's transfiguration, Peter, James, and John were invited to be in the presence of God; they preferred, or at least Peter did, to be busy with activities that might protect them from God. Congregations fall into this trap too. We get so busy "doing God's work" that we forget to be in God's presence.

All too often worship becomes limp and anemic for one reason: we substitute our own agendas and activities for the risk of being in the transformative presence of God. We evaluate worship on the basis of whether it made us feel good or touched us, rather than asking ourselves, "Did we open ourselves to God in praise and adoration?" Or to recall the transfiguration story, did we "listen to him"? Is the focus of our worship ourselves and what pleased us, or is it turning to God? Have we the grace and courage to let God be God for us? Have we had the grace and courage to let the fully human, fully divine Jesus be for us the power of God to heal, redeem, reconcile, and raise all that is dead in us?

Just as some people are troubled by the affirmation that Jesus is fully human, others dismiss the notion that Jesus is fully God. Just as the church faced the heresy of Docetism and its claim the Jesus only appeared to be human, so the church encountered other heresies, such as Arianism, Ebionism, and Adoptionism. These theologies contended that Jesus was not fully God but a lesser deity or a special (but only) human. Today, we can hear this sentiment in those who say, "Jesus was a great teacher, a truly spiritual person, a wondrous human being (but no more)." Of course, people are entitled to their opinion, but as a pastor I sometimes wonder if doubts that Jesus is fully God, as well as fully human, are a form of self-protection. Are our doubts a booth we build around the one who might change us? But when the church and its worship no longer are a place where we meet and are met by the holy, mysterious, majestic, and merciful God revealed in Jesus Christ, well, something crucial is missing.

The Paradox

The church's conviction that Jesus is fully human and fully God is, among other things, a paradox. By definition, a paradox is something that cannot logically be true and yet is true. Christianity is full of paradoxes. Do you want to be great, important, and significant? Then, said Jesus to his disciples, you must become little, like a child, and least, like a servant. Or here is another paradox: do you long to find yourself, to really know who you are? Here's what you do, said Jesus: you lose yourself, forget yourself, and give yourself away in loving, praising, and living for God. Losing yourself is how you find yourself. And a third paradox of Christian faith is that we will have enough (money, power, love) only by giving these things away.

All of these are paradoxes. That is, they are statements that don't make logical sense but are nevertheless true. The Christian claim that Jesus is fully human and fully God is one of the biggest and most mind-boggling of these paradoxes. We will not figure it out or solve it by digging a blood sample out of the wood of the cross—supposing that wood were found—and studying the DNA. Nor will we get it by saying something like, "He was human on the outside but God on the inside." The rational mind bumps into a dead end here.

Perhaps because of the limits of reason, the way we humans often deal with paradoxes is by breaking the tension. We resolve the paradox in favor of one pole or the other. Either Jesus is fully human or fully God, but he is not both. Holding the two poles—fully human and fully God—together is difficult. But paradoxes are like batteries. Without both poles, the batteries have no charge, no electricity. The nineteenth-century Danish theologian, Søren Kierkegaard, once observed that faith is holding the tension of polarity, resisting the temptation to collapse one pole into another. My colleague Martin Copenhaver makes a similar point when he observes: "There may be times when we are embarrassed by Jesus, embarrassed to think that the source of all wisdom and power, the very meaning of our lives, the very image of God, can be found in the one whom the world rejects as an obstacle and sheer folly. But that is OK. When we are closest to the embarrassment of it, we may just be closest to the truth of it. To make faith claims about Jesus any easier to understand or accept is to diminish their power."[6]

The Work of Jesus Christ

For purposes of discussion and study, distinguishing the person and the work of Jesus Christ can be quite useful, but in the end they are not wholly separable. By his full entry into our human experience and by his transcendent glory, Jesus helps us. And the work of Christ is what it is because in him the fullness of humanity and the fullness of God coexist. The two—person and work—go together. Nevertheless, this distinction has value, for person and work expose different aspects of the whole event and experience of Jesus Christ. Thus we now move to the work of Jesus Christ. What does Jesus do, and how does he help us?

While I turned to two key stories from the New Testament as points of entry into the person of Jesus Christ, I take a different approach to examine the work of Jesus Christ. Here I draw upon the work of one theologian and author, Gabriel Fackre. Fackre taught for many years at Andover-Newton Theological School and has been a leader in developing a broadly ecumenical and centrist approach to Christian faith. In Fackre's helpful narrative theology, *The Christian Story*, he describes and evaluates four different and major understandings of Jesus' work, each of which is very much alive in congregations today. As with most such frameworks, we may not feel that any particular congregation is an exact fit with one model or another. Many pastors and congregations draw from several, which the church year and the witness of the Scriptures themselves encourage us to do. Nevertheless, congregations tend to lean toward one or another. Moreover, this framework serves to make clear that more than one legitimate understanding of the work of Jesus Christ exists, and that whatever our own may be, we can be deepened by being aware of the limits and strengths of our perspectives.

The four models of the work of Jesus Christ that I briefly discuss, following Fackre, are: Jesus as example and teacher, Jesus as substitute and savior, Jesus as conqueror and lord, and Jesus as presence. In each case, Fackre develops the model by (1) discussing the issue or problem it addresses; (2) its locus or the segment of Christ's life to which it gives particular attention; (3) its focus, that is, the target of Jesus' work; (4) the action involved in that work; and (5) its outcome or what difference it makes.

Jesus as Example and Teacher

When Jesus is understood as teacher and example, the issue or need is that we human beings lack knowledge of God's truth and lack commitment to what little we do know. We do not understand the ways and will of God. How can we be saved from our blindness and our complacency? The location of Jesus as example and teacher is the Galilean ministry of Jesus as teacher, preacher, and healer. Here we are taught that life's purpose is to love God and neighbor. The focus of this powerful teacher and inspiring example is to change our hearts and minds. We need one who teaches us the pattern of the life God intends, and we need an inspiring example of selfless love. Particularly in Galilee, Jesus confronts human ignorance, heals the sick, and proclaims God's way and presence. This model gives prominence and content to Jesus' proclamation of the kingdom of God. By word and by deed, Jesus discloses that love of God and neighbor is what God asks of us and intends for us. The outcome of this model, Jesus as teacher and example, is illumination of our darkened minds and inspiration of our apathetic spirits.

Jesus as teacher and example has been particularly popular in the nineteenth and twentieth centuries and among liberal Protestants. Perhaps not surprisingly, it has had strong appeal among the more highly educated as well as those who place a high value on reason and a rational understanding of religion. This suggests some of the limits of this model. It may not as fully address the human experience that is other than rational. Even more seriously, this model underestimates the power and depth of human sin. One critic diagnosed this weakness when he said, "We need more than good advice; we need Good News."[7] Still, Jesus as teacher is hardly limited to modernity and liberal Protestantism. In the First Gospel, Matthew presents Jesus as, more than anything else, the teacher. In Matthew, Jesus is the authoritative teacher in the mode of Moses, the one who conveys the new covenant and who is to be obeyed.

Jesus as Substitute and Savior

Ignorance and apathy are the issues addressed by the first model. But for those who understand the work of Jesus as substitute and savior different urgent issues are addressed by the work of Christ. These are the issues of human sin and the consequent burden of guilt. A vast gulf has opened up between us, the loving God, who intends fellowship with his creatures, and those very creatures. By our sinful choices, we are separated from God. Not only that, by our sin we have incurred the righteous judgment and wrath of God, who demands satisfaction. But at Calvary, which is the locus of this model, our sin is overcome by the costly sacrifice of Jesus who substitutes for us and suffers our sin. Forgiveness does not come without a cost, and the cost is the suffering of sinless and innocent Jesus. In this model of the work of Christ, the locus shifts from Galilee to Calvary and the cross. Jesus takes our place, enduring the consequences of our sin. The change effected is not first in us but in God. God's judgment is satisfied, God's righteous wrath appeased. The outcome is that our sin is cancelled and we are forgiven. We are saved from eternal death for life with God. This model has been particularly strong in the various forms of American Evangelicalism.

While a strength of the substitute and savior depiction of the work of Christ is the seriousness with which it takes human sin, a weakness is the way it reduces the whole gospel and its picture of Jesus to one moment—the cross—and one action—sacrifice. As a consequence of this reduction, the substitute and savior model overlooks the meaning of the incarnation that Jesus Christ is the eternal Word of God. In this model, such neglect of the incarnation plays out in pitting God and Jesus against one another. An angry God requires a sacrifice. This seems to drive a wedge between God and Jesus, as an angry God is pitted against a forgiving Jesus. The New Testament does not support such a dividing of God. Rather, as Paul says, God was in Christ "reconciling the world to himself" (2 Cor. 5:19). To believe in the incarnation, the Word made flesh, is to believe that the work of Jesus is the work of God. In addition to this problem, the substitute and savior model tends, again because of its reductionism, to fall short when it comes to describing and emphasizing the ethical life of Christians.

Jesus as Conqueror and Lord

Like the model of Jesus as substitute and savior, Jesus as conqueror and lord takes sin seriously. In fact, this model understands sin and evil much more broadly than the previous picture of the work of Jesus Christ. Sin and evil are not limited to personal life. They are powers at work in the world. This is the great issue: the powers of sin, death, and evil and the many ways they distort and diminish life and God's intention. Jesus as teacher and example gives particular emphasis to the Jesus of Galilee, and Jesus as substitute and Savior takes us to Calvary and the cross, while this third model of the work of Jesus Christ takes us to the Easter event and the resurrection as its locus. The resurrection is the action of Jesus as conqueror and lord and marks the defeat of powers of death, sin, and evil. With the triumph of the resurrection, every alien power that would hold us in bondage or that would destroy our lives is met, dethroned, and stripped of its power and pretension.

This model is sometimes also referred as *Christus Victor*, or Christ victorious, which came to prominence as a theme for resistance and hope during the Nazi period in Europe. It has also contributed to later liberation theologies and their understanding of poverty and oppression as alien powers and foes of God. All the rival powers and principalities of which Scripture speaks, including death, have been conquered. The outcome of this defeat of evil and death is a bold life of faith, freed from paralyzing fear and acting with hope in the final consummation of God's reign.

A particular strength of the Christus Victor model of the work of Christ is its emphasis on sin and evil at work in the structures of history and society, but it may miss the more personal dimension of sin and estrangement. The political and societal may, in other words, eclipse the personal. Likewise, in this model the deity of Jesus, his great power and vitality, may be so evident that his humanity drops away.

Jesus as Presence

Like the first model of the work of Jesus, that of teacher and example, this model tilts less toward the cross and resurrection and more toward the life of Jesus, particularly to Bethlehem and the incarnation. Here, and as it is expressed in the Fourth Gospel, the Word of God is made flesh, dwelling among us in grace and truth. For the Jesus as presence model, the issues are not so much sin, ignorance, or evil, as they are the temporality of life, that is, life's transience and our mortality. How can mortal life be vested with immortality, the profane with the sacred, and the ordinary with the holy? By God's full entry into this realm in Jesus, beginning at Bethlehem. That is the locus for this model of the work of Jesus Christ, the place where the eternal intersects the temporal, where the sacred enters and transforms the profane. In some measure, this understanding of the work of Christ may be more characteristic of the Eastern church and Eastern Orthodoxy, while the emphasis on cross and resurrection are more the precinct of Western Christianity.

With this model's concern for the transience and temporality of life, human sin and its gravity tends to be underplayed. Moreover, the ministry of Jesus in Galilee as teacher and healer, prophet and preacher, tends to be reduced, sometimes to nothing. The concern of this model to address personal finitude tends to overlook the ethical mandates of love of neighbor and service.

Though none of these models is fully adequate, each of them does have significant strengths. In this way, they help us understand how different eras and traditions have understood and appropriated the work of Christ. Of course, other depictions of the work of Christ exist, and these models do not exhaust the possibilities. Nevertheless, these four models continue to be prominent in our time and are clearly grounded in both Scripture and tradition.

The Work of Christ and Vital Congregations

What implications for congregational health does the work of Jesus Christ have? I want to suggest two particular implications, one having to do with life together in the body of Christ and a second that bears more on congregational understanding of mission and ministry.

One contribution of Fackre's four models of the work of Christ, or any similar typology, is that it suggests to congregations that more than one understanding of the work or significance of Jesus Christ is legitimate. The human tendency is to pit the varied understandings of the work of Christ against one another and to argue, "Ours is right, yours is wrong." It can be enormously helpful simply to understand that different ways of looking at this exist, all informed by Scripture and having a place in the broad tradition of the church. Such a depiction of the varied models of the work of Christ helps people in congregations and denominations to understand where others in those bodies are coming from. Just as the body of Christ is made up of many parts, so the understanding of the work of Christ across time and cultures cannot be reduced to one authorized and final version.

Such an enriched understanding of the work of Christ may help us to understand and appreciate our brothers and sisters within our own congregations, as many of today's congregations are made up of people from varied traditions and backgrounds. It can also help us to understand and appreciate other congregations and denominations. Finally, this typology invites us to be aware of the strengths and the weaknesses of our understandings of how Christ helps us.

One way to illuminate the power of these various models is to pay attention to the hymns and songs different congregations tend to sing and to sing most often. Hymns like Charles Wesley's "Love divine, all loves excelling" and Harry E. Fosdick's "God of grace and God of glory" may fit well in congregations where Jesus as example and teacher are prominent. "Rock of Ages" or "Blessed assurance" suggest Christ as substitute and savior, while "A mighty fortress is our God" or "Jesus Christ is risen today" may be a fit for Jesus as conqueror and lord. Finally, hymns like "Let all mortal flesh keep silence" or the haunting "O come, O come, Emmanuel" convey the themes of Jesus as presence.

A second implication of these various understanding for congregational health is to explore how each plays out in a congregation's understanding of its mission and ministry. When a congregation is influenced and shaped by a particular model of the work of Jesus Christ, whether it be Jesus as example and teacher or Jesus as substitute and savior, or one of the others, what are the consequences and weaknesses of its mission? To these questions I now turn.

Mission and the Work of Christ

I remember the evening we first sat down with members from our new sister congregation, a large African-American Baptist Church in Seattle. They were aware of the significant low-income housing ministry conducted by our congregation, which at that time operated ten buildings in downtown Seattle, with nearly one thousand units of housing for people who had come out of shelters for the homeless. They were eager to hear about this ministry. In particular they wanted to know how we did evangelistic outreach in and through this housing ministry. I could almost feel the members of our United Church of Christ congregation cringe when that question was asked. "Well," said one, "we don't really try to convert people in our housing. In fact, there is no real 'religious' program. We simply try to offer homeless people a roof over their heads and some security." Our conversation partners from the Baptist church were as clearly taken aback by this response as members of our congregation had been by their question. One way to interpret this disconnect was that for our congregation, Jesus was primarily example and teacher of selfless service, while for our Baptist counterparts, Jesus was substitute and savior who promises a fundamental transformation of people's lives through the forgiveness of sin, and not only a roof over their heads.

Each had something to learn from the other. The Baptists were eager to learn the particulars of mounting such a successful ministry of housing. Our United Church of Christ congregation also had something to learn, though I'm not sure we grasped the possibility as readily as our counterparts. That lesson may not be that our housing should come with revival services. But it may be that many of our most intractable human problems in twenty-first-century America have a spiritual component that ought not be overlooked. In other words and in this specific instance, housing the homeless is clearly an act of Christian mercy and care for our neighbors in need. But it may not go far enough. While manipulating conversion and taking advantage of people in need are dangers to be avoided, addressing people's need for spiritual transformation with sensitivity and respect is also possible.

In some respects, this discussion points out strengths and weakness of both Jesus as example and teacher and Jesus as substitute and Savior. Congregations like my own, in which the former is prominent, may be helped in their mission and ministry by finding ways to address the deepest spiritual issues, the sense of hopelessness and worthlessness that afflict many in our society. Sin and guilt are real. Likewise, our Baptist counterparts may be helped by the clear ethical impulse that shaped such a ministry of service and brought it to impressive realization.

Or to put this example in somewhat different terms, a weakness and limitation of the mission of congregations shaped by Jesus as example and teacher is underestimating the power and tenacity of human sin and the need for fresh turning and new birth. Especially where addictions have taken hold of people's lives, the work of Christ may be more than providing human services to the neighbor in need. It may be spiritual renewal and redirection through dramatic change and reorientation of life.

But this encounter also points to the limits of congregations whose understanding of the work of Christ is primarily as substitute and savior. This model tends to shape a reductionist understanding and embodiment of mission. Mission is reduced to "saving souls" by rescuing people from eternal damnation, but not necessarily by addressing concrete issues of ongoing life, human need, and injustice. Moreover, the societal roots of injustice and evil tend to be overlooked in preference for a focus on individual salvation. In some sense, the mission of congregations shaped by Jesus as substitute and savior gives such priority to salvation that ethics are eclipsed, while the opposite may be true for congregations shaped by Jesus as example and teacher. There ethics eclipse salvation.

What about congregations where the work of Jesus is seen through the prism of conqueror and Lord? In some expressions, say, communities shaped by various liberation theologies, mission can become so highly politicized that individual needs and people are overlooked. We are engaged in a cosmic battle so large that individuals (and families) are sacrificed to the cause. Christian mission in such congregations may rally people to social activism, but neglect the roots of personal faith and personal health as people shoulder the problems of the world, going forth to battle what the Scriptures refer to as "the cosmic powers . . . and spiritual forces of evil" (Eph. 6:12). Whereas congregations influenced by Jesus as conqueror and lord run the risk of such thorough-going engagement in the world as to be blind to personal lives and personal ethics, congregations where Jesus as presence is the operative model may run opposite risks.

Such so-called spiritual congregations may invite people into another world or dimension that does not connect Sunday with Monday, the spiritual life with the real world. Spirituality under the influence of Jesus as the presence of the eternal within the transient and temporal need not necessarily have this outcome, but it certainly can. It risks a kind of Gnostic (*gnosis* means "special and secret knowledge") variety of Christian faith. Christian faith is for the select and truly spiritual, and thus an elite and otherworldly understanding of mission and ministry. "Come and chant very ethereal and mystical strains, and get away from it all." Christianity risks becoming a spiritual vacation for the Jesus as presence congregation, while Jesus as conqueror and lord calls us forth to battle in ways that may lead to spiritual burnout.

Just as each of the various models of the work of Christ has strengths and weaknesses and each is helped to be aware of other models as correctives, so congregations can be strengthened in their understandings and practice of mission by other models of the work of Christ. When one model becomes predominant, at the expense of all others, a congregation's mission and ministry tend to be reduced and narrowed. In different understandings of the work of Christ, our mission may find greater breadth and balance with healthier congregations being the outcome.

The core convictions of the church about the person and work of Jesus Christ are crucial to congregational vitality, for they both fundamentally ground and enrich the life of congregations. Congregations ought not avoid the basic and central questions, "Who is Jesus?" and "How does Jesus help us?" While much more could certainly be said regarding the person and work of Christ, this exploration begins to suggest some of the current implications of these core convictions for healthy congregations today.

Questions for Reflection and Discussion

1. The author speaks of Christian conviction about the person of Jesus ("fully God and fully human") as a paradox too often resolved by choosing one side or one pole at the expense of the other. Which side of the paradox (fully human or fully God) seems most prominent in your congregation?

2. Take a look at the hymns about Jesus that your congregation sings most often. What kind of understanding of the work of Christ do they convey?

3. Which of the four models of the work of Christ speaks most to you personally? Why?

4. Is there another model of the work of Christ that makes sense to you or speaks powerfully to you?

5. The author says the church's faith is that in Jesus we come to see that nothing we can experience is beyond God's grace or knowledge. It's one thing to affirm this in concept, another in experience. Can you think of a personal experience in which you did not think to find, or be found by, God, but where you were surprised by God's presence and power?

Chapter 8

The Power of Reform, Renewal, and Growth

The Holy Spirit and the Christian Life

I n some congregations the emphasis on the Holy Spirit is
constant, but in most the Holy Spirit can seem almost an
afterthought. "Growing up," quipped a friend whose church
formation was also in mainline Protestantism, "it seemed it was
the Father, the Son, and the Other One."

Pentecostal forms of Christianity, which emphasize the presence and power of the Holy Spirit, are today sweeping through
much of the Southern Hemisphere, particularly in Latin America
and Africa. The twenty-first century may be a time when the
Holy Spirit is no longer an afterthought or an enigma. Moreover, a recovery of a more fulsome experience and appreciation
of the Holy Spirit is also overdue in North America and congregations there. This chapter explores two related dimensions of
the Holy Spirit's role and work that are particularly germane to
the vitality of North American congregations: the Spirit as the
power of God to reform and renew congregations that have grown
dull or rigid, and the Spirit as the power that transforms individual Christians from spectators to participants in the Christian
life. But first, a brief overview of the Holy Spirit.

The Holy Spirit: A Brief Introduction

Sometimes theologians distinguish among the roles of the various persons of the Trinity through prepositions. Thus, one writes,
"The third article of the creed affirms that God is not only *over*
us and *for* us but also at work *in* us."[1] Such formulations always
have their limits as well as their strengths, and this one does too.
To speak of the Holy Spirit as God in us does rightly emphasize
the Holy Spirit as God's presence in our lives. This emphasis may
also, however, lead to taking the role of the Holy Spirit in a too
individualized way. To be sure, the Spirit does work in the lives of
individuals, but not only there. The book of Genesis describes
the Spirit at work in the drama of creation as the wind moves
upon the waters. The Old Testament books of Judges and the
religious prophets recount the Spirit at work animating various
figures and empowering the prophets in their work to renew
and reform God's people. In the New Testament, the Spirit is at
work in the conception of John the Baptist, then in the conception of Jesus. The Spirit is upon Jesus at his baptism and as his
ministry begins. In Acts the Spirit not only falls upon the first
disciples but also comes to Samaritans, Ethiopian eunuchs, and
Gentiles. The Spirit is God's presence *in* us, but it is also God's
presence at work in the world and God's power to create and
renew communities and social structures.

Another Christian teacher, David H. C. Read, offers a different concise description of the triune God and of the Holy Spirit.
According to Read, the Trinity speaks to us of "God who is
everywhere and *always* (God the Father), God who is *then* and *there*
(the Son), and God who is *here* and *now* (the Holy Spirit)."[2] This
formulation also has its limits, suggesting that Jesus is only in the
past, but it does help us see that when the church speaks of the
Holy Spirit, it affirms that God continues to act and to do so
both in society as a whole and in the lives of individuals. Theologian Daniel Migliore describes the problems when the Holy
Spirit is not given sufficient emphasis in Christian life and
teaching: "When the work of the Holy Spirit is forgotten or
suppressed, the power of God is apt to be understood as distant,
hierarchical, and coercive; Christocentric faith deteriorates into

Christomonism; the authority of Scripture becomes heteronomous; the church is seen as a rigid power structure in which some members rule over others; and the sacraments degenerate into almost magical rites under the control of a clerical elite."[3]

The Holy Spirit is present throughout the entire sweep of the biblical story from Genesis to Revelation. But the three most prominent and sustained portrayals of the Holy Spirit in the New Testament are found in three parts of the canon: in the two-volume work of Luke-Acts, in the Fourth Gospel, and in the letters of Paul.

From the beginning in Luke-Acts, the Holy Spirit is a major player. In the Gospel of Luke itself, the Holy Spirit is repeatedly active in the nativity story. This new birth, God's new initiative, is a work of the Holy Spirit (Luke 1 and 2). Moreover, when Jesus is baptized and begins his ministry, he receives and is led by the Spirit (Luke 3 and 4). Likewise, in Luke's second volume, Acts, the Holy Spirit gives birth to the new community in Jerusalem at Pentecost (Acts 2). Subsequently, the Spirit leads the ministries of the church and drives new turns in the church's story (Acts 3, 8, and 15).

Luke-Acts discloses two crucial themes in its portrayal of the Spirit. First, the Spirit is reformist or transformist. That is, when the existing structures of religion and society have grown rigid and unresponsive, the Spirit takes matters into its own hands and works both within and outside those structures. In Luke's nativity story, the aged, country priest Zechariah and his hitherto childless and now older wife Elizabeth will conceive and bear a son, John, who will be the prophet of the Messiah. An unlikely peasant girl Mary conceives by the Holy Spirit. The Spirit does not work through the Roman emperor or the governor of Judea or the high priest or at the center of Jewish life in Jerusalem, but rather works through an ancient rural priest, through a barren woman, through a peasant girl, and in the Judean wilderness. While this may have several implications, one is that the structures of religion and society have grown rigid. God must act in new and unexpected ways, through surprising people, in out-of-the-way places, and through the Holy Spirit to bring renewal and transformation.

But here's a second and complementary theme: while the Spirit moves in unexpected ways and people to bring reform and renewal when existing structures and institutions have grown rigid and self-serving, nevertheless, the work is characterized by continuity with God's work in the past. Over and over again in the nativity story, at Jesus's baptism, and in his ministry, the Scriptures of the Old Testament are prominently displayed to ground and explain what is happening and provide continuity with the past. In Acts also, Scripture and Spirit are held in close relationship, as at Pentecost when Peter draws upon the prophet Joel to explain this outburst of wind and fire (Acts 2:17-21). In other words, the Holy Spirit is God's living power for renewal and transformation, but it is not a rejection of all that has gone before. The Spirit's work does not mean "God's doing a new thing, forget all that old garbage," which sometimes seems to be communicated when some claim the Spirit's mandate or blessing. As evidenced in Luke-Acts, the Holy Spirit is God's living power for renewal and transformation, but the Holy Spirit does not annul or disregard the past promises of God. Rather, it fulfills them, if in ways that are unexpected and disruptive of established orders.

When we turn to the Fourth Gospel, John, we find a different yet similar set of affirmations regarding the Holy Spirit. John's most sustained teaching about the Holy Spirit is found in that portion of the Fourth Gospel known as the "Farewell Discourse," John 13–17. Here, on the eve of his crucifixion and resurrection, Jesus prepares his disciples for life after he is no longer present with them in human form. Jesus says he must go so that the Spirit may come. When he goes to the Father via the cross, he will send the Spirit to the disciples. John speaks of the Spirit in several ways—as comforter, advocate, and teacher. In all these ways and others, John presents the Spirit as the continuing presence of Jesus to guide, strengthen, comfort, and vivify his followers in the time to come.

John communicates four particular points about the Holy Spirit in this teaching. First, the Spirit is given, not gotten. Jesus will send the Spirit. The Spirit is not something human beings grasp or achieve, manipulate or control. It is God's gift. Second, the Spirit does not teach on its own but always in the name—the spirit—of Jesus. Similarly, the role of the Spirit, according to John 14:26, is to "remind you of all that I have said to you." The Spirit's function is to "re-present" Jesus. Both the second and now third points keep the Spirit tied to the life, teachings, death, and resurrection of Jesus. While the Spirit in Luke-Acts is closely connected to Scripture, here the Spirit is closely bound to Jesus. The Spirit is in the name of Jesus and represents his teaching for a new time. No Pentecostal or Spirit-led enthusiasm will supplant or set aside the teachings and life of Jesus and his way. Fourth and finally, the Spirit, according to John, "will teach you everything" (14:26). Jesus cannot possibly teach all that his followers need to know, for they will confront new situations and challenges in the future. In that future the Holy Spirit will guide and teach in Jesus's name and in continuity with his life and ministry.

As in Luke, in John we see the Holy Spirit is not discontinuous with all that has gone before. The Spirit maintains the tradition but keeps the tradition alive and living. In this regard, the distinction of theologian and art historian Jaroslav Pelikan is germane. Pelikan notes the difference between tradition and traditionalism. Tradition is the living faith of the dead; traditionalism is the dead faith of the living. The Holy Spirit serves the former, keeping the tradition alive and ever new. The Holy Spirit has more than once challenged traditionalism, the dead faith of the living.

With this witness of the Scriptures regarding the role and nature of the Spirit, and reserving Paul's teachings on the Holy Spirit for the section "The Christian Life" below, we turn next to the role of the Holy Spirit in the life of vital congregations.

The Holy Spirit and Healthy Congregations: Structure and Spirit

John Gardner, the founder of the citizen's lobby Common Cause and former secretary of health, education, and welfare, writes:

> Organizations are created by their founders to serve vibrant, living purposes. But all too often the founding purposes fade

and what finally gets served are the purposes of institutional self-enhancement. It happens in hospitals to the detriment of patients, in schools to the detriment of students, in business to the detriment of shareholders and customers, and in government to the detriment of taxpayers. It is rarely the result of evil intent: It happens because means triumph over ends, form triumphs over spirit, and the turf syndrome conquers all.[4]

To his list of examples, Gardner might have added another: it happens in churches to the detriment of a congregation's members and the community in which the congregation exists. Churches too forget or lose touch with their founding vision and living purposes. Congregations as well as denominations begin to serve and maintain themselves. What appears to institutional insiders to be important may seem irrelevant to many whose identities are not so tied up with the institution and who see other challenges. As Gardner points out, this seldom results from evil intent. More often it results from unquestioned, long-standing loyalties, from a position that prevents or conditions perception, as well as from what institutions and organizations reward and what they do not. Sometimes they reward behaviors that are actually counterproductive, for they only assure that a failing system continues unchallenged.

Gardner describes the experience of decline: "Motivation tends to run down. Values decay. The problems of today go unsolved while people mumble the slogans of yesterday. Group loyalties block self-examination. One sees organizations whose structure and processes were designed to solve problems that no longer exist. If regenerative forces are not at work, the end is predictable."[5] The good news is that regenerative forces are usually present both in the church and in other settings. Christians call that regenerative force the Holy Spirit. The bad news is that the work of the Holy Spirit is often disruptive, challenging, and disturbing. But without the Holy Spirit, as Gardner says, "the end is predictable." The end is declining congregations. The end is spiritless churches and Christians. The end is congregations moved more by fear than by faith.

A Case in Point

The adult-forum education program of a downtown congregation had begun in the 1960s. At its height, the forum drew audiences of three hundred people or more who would come to hear the mayor, senators, university presidents, authors, pundits, and activists. The forum's focus was contemporary social and political issues. Its purpose was not to tell people what to think, but to help them reach their own decisions. Still, few of the speakers could be described as conservative; most fit the label "liberal." While the forum included debate and differing perspectives, the range of opinion was not great. Most speakers appealed to the liberal and activist views of most congregation members. The forum became widely known in the community. It was a point of pride for the congregation.

Thirty years after its founding, the forum audience had diminished to fewer than one hundred people most Sundays. The speakers generally were still liberal in outlook and many of high quality. But not only had their numbers diminished, the forum audience was discernibly graying, as was the church itself. Meanwhile, downstairs in the church's lounge a growing number of younger church members seemed to congregate simply to visit. Sometimes they ended up there because, in the rush to get the whole family out the door, they arrived late for the forum. Others said this was their time to see friends, to visit, and to simply be. Still others said that for some reason, the forum no longer met their needs. "I'm already on information overload," said one young woman.

Meanwhile, the forum occupied a crucial time in the congregation's schedule and quality space in the church building. It met between the two services, and, by an unwritten rule, nothing except Sunday school was to be planned that would conflict with the forum. Integral to the congregation's identity in the wider community, the forum was viewed as the key to the church's success in attracting new members. Whenever the possibility of changing the Sunday morning schedule or doing different programs emerged, the cry went up, "We can't change the

forum. That's what brought me to this church." While it may
have been true for a time that the forum brought many to church,
a quick analysis of new members over the past five years suggested this was no longer the case. Still, the myth of the forum
was strong. "This is the most important thing this church does.
Besides, this is how we attract new people." The congregation's
adult education board was the de facto forum board, devoting 90
percent of its time and energy to identifying topics and recruit-
ing speakers. No other ongoing adult education programs were
offered. The mantra was "the forum cannot be changed." It had
become a sacred cow.

But the forum was, as noted above, changing. Moreover, the
church and the community in which it was set were changing.
Conversations with the younger adults downstairs indicated they
were longing for something in their church experience that focused more on spirituality than on social analysis. They wanted
smaller, interactive groups. They had a felt need to grow in faith's
basics: Bible study and prayer. The issue was not that they were
disinterested in social issues, but that they wanted these ap-
proached, as some put it, from a spiritual perspective.

In many ways, this congregation's story of the forum is a
classic congregational case of what Gardner describes and what
has happened over and over again in both large and small congregations. Group loyalties blocked self-examination. The problems of today were going unsolved as people repeated the slogans
of yesterday. The structure and program of Sunday mornings
seemed increasingly to be designed to solve problems and serve
needs that had ceased to be as urgent. The issue was not that the
forum was bad or wrong, nor certainly that its loyalists were
either. Rather, the issue was that changes in the environment had
created new challenges and needs.

To put this particular example in a somewhat larger framework, the forum was a fine example of civic faith that worked
well in a time when congregations depended on the larger society and on strong, stable families to provide spiritual basics and
Christian formation. In other words, the assumption then was
that new people coming to the church already understood core
Christian convictions, knew something of the Bible and its sto-

ries, and were participating in meaningful social networks. They were already Christians. Therefore, the church could busy itself with social and political issues or what might be called "applied discipleship."

While this assumption was probably never very sound, it worked reasonably well with the generations born before and up to World War II, in an American Christendom where the Protestant mainline congregations were the religious establishment of American society. But by the 1980s and '90s, this was no longer the world in which we lived. Nor was it the world in which the church ministered. Increasingly, the world had become a place of religious pluralism, secularism, and social and family networks jeopardized by divorce, drugs, and disarray in other institutions, such as public education. Increasing numbers of those who came to such a congregation had little or no previous church background. Instead of coming to the church via Sunday school or a church-related college, more and more newcomers' prior experience of spirituality had been in some sort of 12-step group or other recovery program. This world was characterized by a surprising new interest in spirituality. And yet this congregation's only consistent program of adult religious education, the forum, was in fact not religious or spiritual in any readily recognizable way.

Was the Holy Spirit at work here? Was the Holy Spirit stirring in the downstairs lounge where people gathered who felt needs that they could not quite articulate? Was the Holy Spirit at work in the larger culture and the shifts and changes there? Would the Holy Spirit challenge something as dear to long-time church members and as self-evidently valuable and important as the forum? Would the Holy Spirit lead a new pastor to ask questions about the forum and its place in the church when it was a program created by one of his most revered predecessors?

The eventual outcome, after several years of experiment, was the creation of a new small group ministry and a new Wednesday evening menu of classes and groups focused on faith basics. The forum continued, but now there were other options that responded to different needs and recovered an older focus on Christian formation, albeit in a new way. The new programs and ministries were not without precedent in the Christian community's life. Destroying or demonizing the forum was not necessary. But for three years the congregation and its leaders struggled to respond to the prompting and the challenge of the Spirit's movement. If the congregation had proven unable to respond and to allow regenerative forces to work, the end would have been predictable.

A Second Case

Every year the congregation held its annual meeting, as stipulated by its bylaws, on the fourth Wednesday of January. Every year a portion of the congregation gathered for a meeting that was sometimes exciting, as there might be a heated, even acrimonious, debate prior to a vote, but was often boring, as endless reports were given and nominations voted. Usually the annual meeting was some combination of the two, hum-drum and conflict. Occasionally someone would say, "You know, this feels a lot like the annual meeting of a business; I expected church to be different." "How," someone might answer, "did you expect it to be different?" "Well, I'm not sure," said the first person. "I just thought it would be somehow, you know, more spiritual. I didn't know Robert's Rules was a Christian thing." And, of course, Robert's Rules is not a Christian thing. It is a set of rules of debate for adversarial situations, originally created to adjudicate a border dispute between the United States and Canada. But as Robert's Rules has become the norm for meetings in a variety of civic settings, Robert's Rules has also become the norm for many congregations. Is there another way? Is church supposed to be different? Was the Holy Spirit at work in such a question?

My denominational forebears, the Congregationalists, were known as the people of "the meeting." The Congregationalists met early and often. But their meetings were different from most of today's meetings. Their meetings were animated by the belief that God's will was best discerned in the presence of the gathered community of believers whose minds were formed by Scripture and whose hearts had been shaped by prayer. When these early Congregationalists met, it was not, they said, to discern the will of the majority. Rather, pointing to the early church and the book of Acts as their inspiration, they met to discern the leading of the Spirit and the mind of Christ.

As time passed in New England and among Congregationalists, the meeting, in which matters of civic and faith life were considered and the guidance of the Holy Spirit sought, became two meetings. There was the town meeting for civic matters and the church meeting for matters of faith. The church meeting continued, for a time, to be one that sought to discern the Spirit's leading, while the town meeting became a laboratory of a newly emerging democracy. In the latter, the will of majority ruled. Gradually over time, even the church meeting began to resemble the town meeting. Participants debated as different factions tried to sway others. Votes were counted. Parliamentary procedure was followed. As often happens, the church had been shaped by the culture, rather than the other way around, as some hoped. The point is not that democratic town meetings are wrong. Much is right with them. Rather, the church is called to something different, and that difference involves the Holy Spirit.

Moving toward an experience of congregational meetings that was different and had room for the Holy Spirit meant reaching back into some of the denominational history just cited, as well as into Scripture. In Acts, we can see the Christian community involved in debate, conflict, and decision making. Particularly instructive examples are found in Acts 1, 6, and 15. In these chapters, we see congregations engaged not in parliamentary procedure but in the ancient spiritual practice of discernment. Denominational history, Scripture, and spiritual practices were brought to bear as one congregation attempted a shift in the style of its congregational meetings.

Today, more members of the congregation understand that when the congregation gathers, it seeks not simply the will of the majority but the guidance of the Holy Spirit. Today, such meetings are punctuated by silence, during which those gathered are invited to listen for and seek the Spirit's guidance. Today, during discussion of particularly difficult issues, the congregation listens to someone speak and then prays together "May the Holy Spirit speak through us," to remind itself that the Holy Spirit is the voice for which it listens. Today, the floor at such meetings is perhaps a little more open to all speakers, not because everyone has a right to speak, but because they never know through whom the Holy Spirit will speak. Today, congregational meetings are different from the meetings of another civic group or business's annual meeting. This congregation has recovered its older tradition of the meeting and of the role of the Holy Spirit in its life.

The Holy Spirit and the Christian Life

The focus of the first section of this chapter has been on introducing the Holy Spirit and exploring its role in the renewal of congregations that have lost vitality, clarity of purpose, or their distinctive nature as the church. The Holy Spirit is God's presence for transformation in congregations, in denominations, and in the world. The Spirit moves to enliven structures that have grown rigid and, at least sometimes, self-serving. But this is not the only area of activity for the Holy Spirit, especially as it bears on vital and healthy congregations. The Spirit also has an important role in the lives of individual believers who make up vital congregations. To this we now turn.

The Christian Life

The brief formulation of the Trinity with which this chapter began suggests the Holy Spirit's role in the lives and maturation of Christians. The Holy Spirit is God *in* us. God is not only *over* us and *for* us, but *in* us to guide, empower, and bring us to maturity as Christians. Theologians have described the work of God the Father, Jesus Christ, and the Spirit in us by using three terms to describe aspects of the Christian life and process of maturation: *justification, sanctification,* and *vocation.*

Before moving to a closer examination of each term and the experiences they describe, I want to make clear that these are not completely discreet movements of the Spirit in the lives of Christians; they overlap. Moreover, they are not to be thought as rigidly sequential. While to a degree one aspect follows another logically as faith matures, a person never outgrows the need for any of the three aspects of the Christian life, and people may experience these different movements in a different sequence altogether. Finally, God through the Spirit is active in each of the three elements of the Christian life. We cannot say, for example, "Justification is God's work; sanctification is our work." With these caveats in mind, let us turn to a closer examination of this classical depiction of the Christian life.

Justification. As the pastor and popular author Eugene Peterson observes, "We preachers are often much better at preaching grace than receiving it and living by it ourselves." I get that, because it pretty well describes my experience. I got grace as a concept, but in my early ministry I behaved as if everything depended on me, on my hard work, and not on God's grace. My labors would make, establish, or justify me to God, myself, and others. My work would make the church successful, though I'm not sure I had any real idea of what success for a church meant, other than institutional growth. Like many who have traveled this road, I ran into a significant obstacle: an experience of a disabling and terrifying depression. It pretty well stopped me dead in my tracks.

Amid that several-year-long dark night of the soul, God was at work, even if I was only half-functioning. The concept of grace became real for me. In new ways, I came to rely on God's justification of me. Both words—*grace* and *justification* migrated from my head to my heart. I came to see I was "put right" (justified) by God and grace, not by my hard work or success. In a remark to a newspaper reporter, the South African bishop Desmond Tutu captured well the meaning of justification, at least for me. "We tend to turn the Christian religion into a religion of virtues," Tutu says, "but it is a religion of grace—you become a good person because you are loved. You are not loved because you are good."[6] This justification, or being put right and made acceptable, is grace—that is, God's work. We cannot earn it or deserve it. We cannot justify ourselves, though that does not keep us from useless self-justifying speech and behaviors. Just as life itself is a gift, so new life or justification or forgiveness is too.

Sanctification. The word *sanctification* means "to make holy," which may or may not be an aid to understanding. It does not mean "to make holier than thou." It is not about false piety, religious pretense, or self-righteousness. Sanctification is about

maturing in a life of grace. Many people today may mean something like sanctification when they say of another, "She is a truly
spiritual person," meaning the person is centered in a presence
and power not her own. Moreover, compared to many people,
she is free of self-preoccupation and therefore truly available for
others. She lives a life of relationship with God and others that,
while not fleeing from suffering—not at all—is characterized by
a basic sense of gratitude and even joy.

Sanctification is the work of the Spirit as we mature in the
life of faith. By staying close to the means of grace, that is, the
Word and Sacraments, by living into the practices of faith (for
example, sabbath keeping, prayer, discernment), and by serving
God and our neighbors in the world, we open ourselves to the
Spirit, who is able to make us whole and holy.

Vocation. *Vocation* is not another word for a job. Vocation is
what God has called us to be and to do in order to be participants in God's work of mending a broken world. Vocation is
about being partners with God. We can do this through the work
that we are paid to do. We can do it when we get home from
work, turn on the computer, and start writing, or when we walk
out the door to go and start chopping vegetables for tonight's
dinner at the homeless shelter in town. We can do it by building
relationships or by building houses. The word *vocation* comes from
the Latin word *vocare*. The English word *calling* also has its roots in
this Latin word. That means having a vocation involves listening
for the calling and direction of the Spirit in our lives and amid
our experiences. Our vocation is what we can't *not* do.

Vocation was an especially prominent theme for the Protestant reformers as they sought to overcome the tendency of the
medieval church to divide people into first-class Christians (priests
and monks) and second class (laity). Both Martin Luther and
John Calvin taught that we have multiple vocations in different
arenas of our life. For Luther, the arenas were family and work
(generally the same, given the structure of work in his day), community, and church. Luther said vocation is all about service, and
we discern our vocation by noticing what our neighbor, broadly
understood, needs. Calvin expanded on this and said another
clue to our vocations is our gifts. For both Luther and Calvin, all

Christians are called to multiple vocations, which take many more forms than that of the ordained priesthood.

As I said, justification, sanctification, and vocation are not fixed, as in sequential stages, but they are distinguishable aspects of the Christian life that flow from and to one another. At least in the experience of many through history, they are how God through the Holy Spirit works *in* us. Moreover, they involve a kind of Christian two-step. We are mended in order that we may become menders. We are freed up in order to exercise our freedom in a life of service to God and God's world. We are loved so that we may love. Receiving and giving, gift and task—both are elements to the Christian life.

The Christian Life and Healthy Congregations

In her little book *Speaking of Sin*, preacher and author Barbara Brown Taylor includes this recollection: "I remember a classmate of mine, a Lebanese Presbyterian, who threw a theological temper tantrum during his first semester in seminary. 'All you Americans care about is justification!' he howled. 'You love sinning and being forgiven, sinning and being forgiven, but no one seems to want off that hamster wheel. Have you ever heard about sanctification? Is anyone interested in learning to sin a little less?'"[7]

In the way that outsiders have of sometimes seeing the obvious truth that insiders miss, this Lebanese Presbyterian hits a theological nerve. Perhaps because frontier evangelism, revivals, and "walking the sawdust trail" have played such a large and unique role in Christianity in America, many congregations and Christians in this country apparently seem quite content to do justification over and over again and never experience other dimensions of the Christian life. In some congregations, the every-Sunday message is "Christ died for your sins." In others the message of justification is a more tepid version of grace, simply "God loves you unconditionally," or as theologian Paul Tillich put it, "You are accepted."[8] But as Taylor observes, "Forgiveness is a starting place, not a stopping place." She then adds, "Most of us prefer remorse to repentance. We would rather feel badly about the damage we have done than get estimates on the cost of repair.

We would rather learn to live with guilt than face the hard work of new life."[9]

The author of the New Testament's First Gospel, Matthew, never tires of making the same point: grace requires a response. Grace is not an ending, but a beginning. Thus Matthew gives us a parable that I have found disturbs many people in contemporary congregations, the parable of the wedding feast (Matt. 22:1-14). All goes well through part one of this parable, as all sorts of people are invited to the wedding feast. Part two (vv. 11-14) is dicey. Here the host of the feast, the king, enters the hall and lays his eyes on a guest who hasn't dressed for the occasion. He has the poor fellow tossed out, way out "into the outer darkness." In my pastoral experience, most congregations find this troubling, if not offensive. We are all for grace (the free invitation to the feast), but we draw a line when it comes to having to do something—to change, to respond to grace with something that looks like a new and different life (putting on appropriate attire for the feast).

A truncated Christian life—all justification, no sanctification or vocation—takes shape in various ways in congregations. One is a constant reiteration of God's love with no articulation of God's expectations. This one-sided emphasis is then repeated in human relationships. So, for example, someone volunteers, with a great flourish of enthusiasm and all sorts of new ideas, to chair a church retreat. He talks about how this will be "the best ever" and about the new ideas he and others bring to the table. Two months later the pastor receives a phone call from the enthusiastic new retreat chair. Only he isn't. "I've gotten really busy at work, I'm going to have to resign right now." "But," thinks the pastor, "you've got to be kidding. The retreat is just a month away, and besides, what about all that enthusiasm, not to mention the commitment, you made?"

But the pastor says none of this. Perhaps fearful of causing offense or losing a member, the pastor says, "Sure, no problem, I understand. Listen, hope things settle down for you at work. Is there any way I can help? See you Sunday, I hope?" Clearly, at times in our lives we cannot fulfill every commitment, and we must apologize and ask for people's gracious understanding. Clearly, congregations must be able to offer the same when true emergencies arise. But sometimes that's not what happens. For whatever combination of reasons, someone loses interest or is a chronic over-promiser or discovers the pay-off will not be what was hoped and bags it. And too often pastors and congregations say nothing. All grace, no expectation. Justification without sanctification and vocation. When this becomes the norm, it is what Dietrich Bonhoeffer called "cheap grace"[10] and what can also be aptly described as sentimentality, or love without cost, sacrifice, or commitment.

Ten minutes after the meeting is supposed to start, a board member rushes in. "Sorry, I'm late." "Again," thinks the chair. "Oh, that's all right," chirps another member. Another ten minutes pass and two more people walk in and go through the same set of words and gestures of extravagant remorse. "I'm so sorry. Traffic." "Again," muses the chairperson to herself, who after four months of this behavior is doing a slow burn.

In congregations where this becomes the pattern and where "we don't say anything—it just wouldn't be nice," meetings tend to be frustrating and not very productive. In another, healthier congregation, a nominating committee member calls the board chairperson before asking current board members to serve a second term on the board. The chairperson is asked about attendance patterns, tardiness, participation, and follow-through. The chronically late person is not asked to serve again. Or if she is, the nominating committee member or the chair talks with her about how the coming-late thing affects the group's life and functioning and gets a commitment to a change of behavior. As Taylor notes, we too often prefer remorse, "I'm so sorry," to repentance—that is, a change in our behaviors. This is a simple, some might say trivial, example, but multiplied and built into a pattern in church life, it becomes a regular and energy-sapping infection.

While justification without sanctification and vocation can put Christians and congregations on a hamster wheel of sin and forgiveness without change of behavior patterns, another and larger dimension to this unhealthy distortion of the Christian life needs to be addressed. That is, congregations may provide no real structures or practices that help their members grow in discipleship and in Christian maturity. They may talk about

discipleship or about the "priesthood of all believers," but somehow there is no flesh on the bones. Members of a congregation
may be left wondering, "How would I really do that—I mean,
'grow in discipleship' or discover what sanctification and vocation actually mean in my life?"

Today, vital congregations seem to emphasize two old but
new themes that help people move beyond justification to maturity in a Christian life. These are Christian practices and a focus on discernment of gifts. Both enable ordinary Christians and
church members to take greater responsibility for their own faith,
to move from being receivers to also being givers. As I argued in
a previous chapter, there is a time for learning to receive. There is
also a time for giving. Receiving and giving are not an either-or
but a both-and. Through Christian practices and discernment of
gifts, healthy congregations help make real the baptismal ordination to ministry and call to discipleship of their members.

Christian Practices. Over the past two decades we have
seen a resurgence of interest in faith practices or spiritual disciplines.[11] Such practices, whether keeping sabbath, discernment,
testimony, or hospitality, provide focused ways through which
the Spirit can work to further Christianity maturity. These practices support sanctification as they weave faith and life together
into an increasingly organic whole. They infuse faith into our
way of life and being. They give specific expression to the idea
that faith, and justification by faith, require and enable a new way
of life.

Some congregations have focused their congregational life
around one or more practices that become both marks of their
identity and the focus of their ministry.[12] Others have developed
resources and studies on a variety of practices that individual
congregational members or small groups within the congregation emphasize for a year or season. Most practices have ancient
roots as well as contemporary expressions. The life of many congregations already demonstrates a variety of practices, but these
ongoing practices may not have been identified as spiritual practices or explored in depth. My point is this: congregations that
speak of, teach, and embody spiritual practices provide specific
and identifiable ways for people to grow in the Christian life,

ways that allow the Spirit to build on the experience of justification something that more nearly resembles sanctification as faith becomes a way of life.

Discernment of Gifts for Ministry. Another specific way congregations can put flesh on the bones of sanctification and vocation is through ministries aimed at helping people discern and claim their gifts for ministry, that is, service to God and to others. In too many congregations, the only consistent options for service are participation in the management of the church itself. While this has a place and can be a form of ministry, church management is not for everyone. Congregations need to acknowledge and honor those who understand their daily work as Christian vocation. But beyond that important emphasis, congregations can also assist their members in Christian maturation by offering programs for discernment of gifts for service to God and to God's world.

In 1 Corinthians in particular, and in his general treatment of the work of the Holy Spirit, the apostle Paul links the Spirit to gifts for ministry that are given to every believer. "To each," writes Paul, "is given the manifestation of the Spirit for the common good" (1 Cor. 12:7). While many congregations affirm this principle in theory, not many have done much to help their members identify and practice their gifts for ministry in a consistent way. Increasingly, however, one finds congregations that include gifts discernment seminars and retreats among their core ministries. Through such ministries a congregation may help people move from a theoretical or conceptual affirmation of vocation to claiming and practicing one's Christian vocations.

In the congregation I most recently served, we offered several gifts discernment events throughout every year. The long form for discernment was completed in a retreat setting and a short form could be completed in a three-hour evening session. We encouraged all new members to participate in at least the short form, saying that part of our ministry as a church is to help members identify and practice their vocations. Those who completed such seminars might join existing ministry teams that offered a place for their gifts, or they might join with others to start a new ministry team. While not everyone was expected to be a member of a ministry team, everyone was encouraged to see their vocation, God's calling to them, as a part of the Christian life that our congregation wanted to support.

A fuller appreciation of the person and work of the Holy Spirit is overdue in many of our congregations and denominations. All too often the Holy Spirit has been relegated to the sidelines or margins of the church and associated primarily with congregations that practiced such gifts as speaking in tongues or ecstatic worship experience. But this view, as the Scriptures make clear, is a far too limited understanding of the Holy Spirit's role. In a time when the transformation of congregations and people seems increasingly urgent, the Holy Spirit is God at work in such change in and renewal of congregations, communities, individuals, and families. The Holy Spirit is at work to renew congregations that grow rigid and lifeless. The Holy Spirit is at work to enable Christians to grow in maturity in faith and in the Christian life. What could be more important?

Questions for Reflection and Discussion

1. The author describes the Holy Spirit as reformist and transformist, saying that when existing structures of religion and society have grown rigid and unresponsive, the Spirit can often be found working within or outside those structures to effect renewal. Name one such event or experience that fits this criteria and description for you. Describe the role of the Holy Spirit.

2. The author tells the story of one congregation's adult education program, the forum, and how the Spirit was at work for renewal. Can you think of some similar experience in your congregation? What happened? What role do you think the Spirit played?

3. One prayer of invocation goes, "Come, Holy Spirit, break us open and make us new." How do you respond to this prayer? What in it speaks to you? What in it disturbs you?

4. Of the three movements or aspects of the Christian life—justification, sanctification, and vocation—which one is the most familiar and congenial to you? Which is the least familiar or congenial to you? Why is that, do you think?

5. Share an experience that helped you identify a gift for ministry that is yours. Or share an experience that helped you discern your vocation or calling as a Christian.
6. How would you evaluate the balance of grace and expectation in your congregation? Do you find your church encourages remorse (feeling sorry) or repentance (the hard work of new life)?

Chapter 9

This Thing Called Church, Part 1

Ecclesiology

Perhaps the most neglected branch of theology is the theology of church, or ecclesiology. Battles over the Bible and authority have brought the theology of revelation and Scripture to the fore, and concern over the mystery of evil has kept the nature of human beings and sin before us. Conflicting beliefs about Jesus Christ have put the person and work of Jesus in the spotlight, and new growth of Pentacostalism has prompted attention to the Holy Spirit. But Christian conviction about the church has often, it seems, gone missing.

Theologian Ellen Charry, who teaches at Princeton Theological Seminary, puts the matter directly: "I am increasingly realizing that a number of our ministerial students have no ecclesiology to speak of. For them the church is a voluntary not-for-profit organization run like a local franchise."[1] This mix of not-for-profit and business (local franchise) models for the church is perhaps understandable given the pervasiveness of the consumer economy, including churches that compete in the free-market of spirituality in North America. Moreover, many new forms of church have emerged in our time. Noteworthy is that many omit "Church" from their names. Where I live, one can go to "Quest," "Mars Hills," "Anchor Pointe," "Spirit of the Sound," or any number of "Christian Faith Centers" or "Christian Fellowships."

Still, without an ecclesiology formed and informed by Scripture and tradition, clergy and congregations can find themselves seriously misled and confused about their identity and purpose. If our efforts to be and build congregations do not rest on a core of Christian conviction about what the church is, we tend to go to default options from the culture. The church becomes an entertainment experience with audience ratings, a purveyor of spiritual goods and services, a religious club for people who share the same worldview and experiences, a coalition united around a set of causes or sociopolitical agendas, or simply a gathering place where people have their individual spiritual experiences. Without an ecclesiological foundation, the focus of faith often tends to fall entirely on individuals and their spiritual life or salvation. The biblical sense of the church as a people or body is lost.

Consider, for example, the "congregation" (in this case, I use the word advisedly) that gathers around the compelling personal presence of one preacher and leader. A number of such charismatic leader and followers operate in North America. Some are televised. Many are not. Some do wonderful things. Some use and abuse their members or participants. All are centered on the dynamic leader. When something happens to that person, say a mental breakdown or accusations of sexual harassment or financial malfeasance, the church usually goes from boom to bust in short order. Or when the charismatic founder dies, "the ministry," as it is often referred to, simply dies also. The church is the ministry of that one person. Usually, in such instances, there has been no real church. There has been a charismatic leader and his or her followers. This is but one of the common distortions of church today. Lacking core Christian conviction about this thing called church, distortions and pseudochurches flourish, although only for a time. Established and more traditional congregations that lack a sufficient ecclesiology often lose their sense of identity and purpose.

Ecclesiology: A Brief Introduction

The name of this branch of theology comes from the Greek word *ekklesia*, which means "a people called" and "the visible assembly." Church is not the building nor is it the leader. It is people gathered into community in response to God's call in Jesus Christ. Church happens, as Jesus said, where "two or three are gathered *in my name*" (Matt. 18:20; italics, author's emphasis).

Churches, like other organizations, develop their structures, systems, and rituals for governance and continuity. These can be quite important, for they sustain common life and work, but such structures are in the end provisional. In the apostle Paul's words, they are "clay jars," and not to be confused with the "extraordinary power [that] belongs to God" (2 Cor. 4:7).

The Scriptures contain a host of images for the church, ranging from salt of the earth to bride of Christ, from royal priesthood to God's field. The church is God's planting and the temple of the Holy Spirit, the new Israel and God's elect from every nation. These various images stress one thing that distinguishes church from either a not-for-profit organization or local business franchise: the church belongs to and owes its existence to God and not to us. God has created and claimed the church for God's purposes.

The church, then, is not simply whatever we want it to be or what we choose to make of it. The church exists prior to its members or participants. Charry puts it this way: "Theologically speaking, 'the church' is an institution given a peculiarly honorable identity and high calling by virtue of her owner who sets the corporate culture into which members are acculturated."[2] The owner is God. "We are his people, and the sheep of his pasture," says the psalmist (Ps. 100:3). Thus, the church is not simply a consumer-driven entity that exists to meet the religious needs of those who come to it. Churches may meet people's needs, but they must do more than that. At least potentially, they transform people by drawing them into a larger purpose and identity. "Once you were not a people," writes Peter, "but now you are God's people" (1 Pet. 2:10).

Several of the most prominent metaphors for the church in Scripture have long been at the forefront of ecclesiological thinking: people of God, body of Christ, and temple of the Spirit. Noteworthy is that each of the three correlates, in some measure, with one of the three persons of the triune God. Like God who is communal, the three in one, Christian life is communal. It is not lived in isolation. God's clear intention, to judge from the biblical story, is to create a people to serve God. All three of these metaphors for church depict Christian life as being part of a people and community. Before considering some of the ways a sound ecclesiology can strengthen and correct today's congregations, I want to comment on these three scriptural depictions of the church and its life and purpose.

The Church as the People of God

This understanding of the church draws on and connects the church to its Jewish legacy and to the Old Testament Scriptures. As the exodus event transformed the Hebrew people into a people called and set apart by God, so the new exodus, the crucifixion and resurrection of Jesus Christ, calls and sets apart a people of God, the church. This people owes its being to God. The people of God are called to be faithful to this creating, redeeming, and sustaining God. And, as Israel itself was blessed to be a blessing to all the peoples of the earth, so the people of God, the church, also are called by God to be a blessing to others. God calls the church not to receive special favors or protection but to carry out a unique vocation: service to God and to the world God loves.

The Church as the Body of Christ

The apostle Paul in his various letters articulates this powerful image for the church: "Now you are the body of Christ and individually members of it" (1 Cor. 12:27). For Paul, this way of understanding the church connected the living Christ and his followers. We are his body in tangible form, continuing his life and his ministry. Not only does this image connect Christ and his followers, it also allowed Paul to deal with the perennially challenging matters of unity and diversity, the parts and the whole. "If the whole body were an eye, where would the hearing be? If the whole body were hearing, where would the sense of smell be?" (1 Cor. 12:17). Just as the parts of the body need one another, so the individuals who make up the church need one another. None are sufficient unto or by themselves. Moreover, the whole is more than the sum of its parts. Together the church, its members and individuals, has an identity greater than any one person or group of people. Together it is the body of Christ.

The Church as the Temple of the Spirit

While the church as the people of God has a particularly Old Testament resonance and the church as the body of Christ can be traced to Paul's thought and letters, the church as creation or temple of the Spirit is especially evident in the story of the early church found in the Acts of the Apostles. In Acts, Luke's second volume, we read that, following the crucifixion and resurrection at the end of the Gospel of Luke, the disciples are told by Jesus to return to Jerusalem and to wait there for the power of the Spirit (Acts 1:4-5). On the Day of Pentecost, the Spirit comes—powerfully—to create the church. The disciples no longer cower and hide. They burst forth into Jerusalem to declare the acts of God in all the languages of the known world. Throughout the book of Acts, the Spirit leads and empowers the church for its mission, whether in Judea, Samaria, or throughout ever-widening circles of the Mediterranean world. Moreover, Acts makes clear that the Spirit is not the possession of a chosen few individuals or groups. The Spirit is poured out on all, as Peter says in Acts 2:17, quoting the prophet Joel, and is shared by all believers.

Each of these three biblically shaped understandings of the church—people of God, body of Christ, and temple of the Spirit—offers important and different, though complementary, emphases. *People of God* reminds us that the church is a community. *Body of Christ* connects the church to Christ's ministry of preaching, teaching, and healing. *Temple of the Spirit* emphasizes the role of the Spirit, which "blows where it chooses," as Jesus said in John 3:8, to refresh and empower the church. All three have this truth in common: the church is God's gift and creation. The church is not simply what we make of it nor is it whatever we want it to be. The church is what God makes, and is making, of us. Or to draw on the words of the great preacher and theologian of the early twentieth century, P. T. Forsyth, "The church rests on the grace of God, the judging, atoning, regenerating grace of God which is his holy love in the form it must take within human sin. Wherever that is heartily confessed and goes on to rule we have the true church."[3]

Ecclesiology and Healthy Congregations

Lutheran pastor Michael Foss argues that the central challenge facing many congregations today is to shift their dominant paradigm from being cultures of membership to cultures of discipleship. When Foss describes what he means by a culture of membership, he turns to the model of the now-ubiquitous health club. Writes Foss:

> I don't want to push the analogy too far, but for the sake of illustration, let's think of the membership model of church as similar to the membership model of the modern health club. One becomes a member of a health club by paying dues (in a church, the monthly or weekly offering). Having paid their dues, the members expect the services of the club to be at their disposal. Exercise equipment, weight room, aerobics classes, an indoor track, swimming pool—all there for them, with a trained staff to see that they benefit by them. Members may bring a guest on occasion, but only those who pay their dues have a right to the use of the facilities and the attention of the staff. There is no need to belabor the point. Many who sit in the pews on Sundays have come to think of church membership in ways analogous to how the fitness crowd views membership in a health club.[4]

Foss argues that this understanding has misplaced the true purpose of the church and distorted its nature. The point is not membership. The church does not have clients, members, or consumers of goods and services. The point is discipleship. The church exists to form and sustain individuals and a people who are followers of Jesus Christ, who are his disciples. Rather than buying into a consumer model of the church, where the customer is king and the church simply meets customers' needs, the church does more; the church redefines our true needs. The church transforms people according to the life and pattern revealed by God in Jesus Christ. It unites them with others who are committed to this way of life.

Nevertheless, perhaps because we have grown so accustomed to thinking of ourselves as consumers of various goods and services, the membership ethos is hard to break. I have noticed, for example, that in many congregations, when a new group gathers for the first time, the default option for introductions tends to take the form, "My name is _____, and I have been a member of First Church for 30 years (or 15 years or 1 year)." As a way of introducing ourselves, length of tenure at that particular church, to be sure, provides some useful information. And there is much to be said for loyalty and commitment. But something else often seems to be going on during such a ritual. A pecking order is established based on length of membership. An insider-outsider dynamic is suggested. Indeed, as Foss notes, "The membership model identifies who is in and who is out. No wonder those outside the church consistently say that church people are more judgmental than others."[5]

I recall a struggling congregation with which I worked. One Sunday when I was free from my pastoral responsibilities, I went to visit this small church. I parked on a nearby side street and walked to the front door, which was closed. I pulled on the door and found it would not open. It was locked. The Sunday service was to begin in just minutes. I knocked on the door. After a while, an older member of the congregation pushed the door open and invited me in saying, "We usually don't open this door; everyone knows to come in through the back door." Well, this arrangement was very cozy and friendly if you were part of the "everyone" who made up the aging and shrinking cohort of the congregation. If not, you hardly felt welcomed. In fact, had it not been that I had some prior relationship to the congregation, I am sure that finding the door locked I simply would have left. The message was clear: members only. However, and here's the crucial point, the congregation's members were oblivious to the message of the locked front door as well as to the implications of their confidence that "everyone knows to come in through the back door." In truth, they might just as well have had a sign over the door, like a kids' clubhouse, "Members Only."

Congregations and clergy seemingly have often misconstrued or misunderstood the closing scene in the Gospel of Matthew where Jesus meets the disciples on a mountain and charges them with the Great Commission: "Go therefore and make *disciples* of all nations, baptizing them in the name of the Father and of the Son and of the Holy Spirit, and teaching them to obey everything that I have commanded you" (Matt. 28:19-20; italics, author's emphasis). Somehow it seems we have heard Jesus say, "Go therefore, and make *members* . . ." That is not quite the same thing. Frankly, making disciples seems to me both more interesting and more valuable.

The shift to a culture of discipleship that Foss advocates implies an ecclesiology different from the culture of membership. A culture of membership, partly shaped by the ethos of consumerism, turns the church into a provider of goods and services dubbed religious or spiritual. Moreover, it is "our church" or "my church," not "God's church." A person, couple, or family may go to such a church to have a wedding or funeral, to participate in a small group for personal growth, or to receive inspiration for their work week. Nothing is wrong with any of this, except that it stops short of a full realization of the nature of the church as the people of God or the body of Christ or the creation of the Spirit or all three. The church in such a model remains something we go to in order to take or receive from. It may meet our needs and thrive or disappoint them and lose our interest or engagement. But the church in this model has missed what may be our most fundamental human need, and that is to lose and to forget ourselves in commitment and relationship to that which is greater than self and self-interest.

Congregations that honor the Reformation teaching that the church is "the priesthood of all believers" too often today have become something that looks much more like the congregation of all consumers. The clergy, or "staff," and a core of lay leaders produce some product called "ministry," which is consumed by the congregation. An adequate ecclesiology would stress that all baptized Christians are called to ministry and the church's various activities and programs exist to, as Paul put it, "equip the saints for . . . ministry" (Eph. 4:12). When ministry is a commodity created by the few to be consumed by the many, it misses the point. Moreover, an unhealthy dynamic is created between those who provide and those who consume.

At times in the past and in some churches and denominations in particular, clergy or other church leaders may have had so much power and authority that they have perhaps been indifferent to the needs, desires, and opinions of church members. I am not at all advocating, however, this stance as the antidote to religious consumerism in which the customer is king and religious experience a product. Yet perhaps in response to the excesses of authority located in clergy or church structures in some congregations or denominations, we have swung in the other direction. Yes, congregational leaders, whether clergy or lay, must take seriously the experience of congregational members. And yet, the church is not driven simply by people's needs and wants (which happen to be pretty much endless). The church is driven by God's dream and purposes for creation.

The Church: A Typology

I want to push a little deeper on these themes by turning to a typology of congregations developed by sociologist of religion C. Kirk Hadaway in his helpful book, *Behold I Do a New Thing*.[6] Hadaway's typology might be thought of as a practical ecclesiology. That is, he describes actual rather than ideal congregations. The typology is informed by the Scriptures and theology, but for the most part it depends on language derived not from either the Bible or theology but from observation of actual congregations.

That said, Hadaway makes clear that no one congregation perfectly fits any of the four types reviewed in his typology. This typology, like any such device, offers useful distinctions, but the types are concepts and constructs developed for discussion. Real congregations are more complex than any typology. Most congregations are a mix of elements from different types. Still, it is usually possibly to discern the dominant type for a particular congregation, and in doing so to see what their working ecclesiology is as well as what their strengths and weaknesses are.

Church as Club or Clan

When classifying and comparing congregations by size, churches with two hundred members or fewer are by far the most numerous in North America. Many congregations have fewer than one hundred members. Often such congregations resemble a club or a clan or an extended family. In fact, they may be an extended family, made up of the friends and relatives or two or three dominant families. Like a club or clan, such a congregation has a thick or dense and generally unwritten culture. Newcomers, including pastors, often find out the dos and the don'ts by observation, or, in the case of the don'ts, by doing something that "isn't done here." Often the only way into such a congregation is by birth or marriage. Membership is by blood, but not the blood of Jesus Christ!

Members often describe this type of congregation as particularly warm, friendly, and family-like. "Everybody knows everybody," people say. But it's not quite true. Everybody knows everybody who is part of the club or clan. Visitors, newcomers, even those who have become official members but who don't quite belong, often describe such a congregation as "cold and unfriendly." Ironically, both those who say, "This is really a warm church," and those who say, "It's cold" are correct in their observations and experience. It all depends on where you stand or sit or where you are located. Are you on the inside or at the margins or an outsider?

In such congregations, the pastor is not ordinarily the leader. Leadership and power often reside with two or three key lay people or one or two families of particularly long standing and great influence. Ministers tend to act more as chaplains to the group; they are religious functionaries rather than leaders. The pastor can become the leader, but it ordinarily takes a long time and considerable patience or cunning on the part of the pastor.

Such congregations do emphasize community and belonging, which are important attributes of the church. We ought to want our churches to be places of belonging and community where people are known. The problem here, according to Hadaway, is that the purpose of the church has been lost, or in sociological language, "displaced." Hadaway argues that the purpose of churches is, very broadly speaking, "to change lives."[7] But in the church as club or clan, this purpose has been forgotten. The purpose has become the satisfaction and comfort of the members. Thus, Hadaway's image for this type of church is the easy chair or recliner! Often such churches seem like little more than another social gathering or group, except that they are adorned with a certain amount of religious language and symbolism.

According to Hadaway, the key to health lies in recovering the church's purpose, that is, changing lives by making disciples, which according to Hadaway is not an impossible undertaking. Still, those who advocate such a shift of focus ought to be prepared for some resistance, which at times can be pretty stiff. The key is to ask consistently, steadily, and relentlessly the purpose question, "Why are we here? What is the purpose of the church?" and then to build on that question with scriptural teaching that returns or leads the church to its true nature and purpose as the people of God, body of Christ, and creation of the Spirit.

One of the things I value most about Hadaway's typology is that it sees a positive potential and future for smaller congregations. The tendency in some quarters today is to write off the smaller membership church. This is a mistake, if only because so many of them exist. Such congregations can and do change lives, make disciples, and grow Christians. Pastors and lay leaders in such congregations are well advised, indeed, to find the places in the congregation where these things are happening and fan those warm embers into flame. Find the experiences and settings in that congregation where lives are being changed and people are growing in faith and discipleship, and highlight those. Build on them. Encourage them. Strengthen them. And be prepared for the fact that change is slow and, especially in smaller congregations, requires great persistence. By repeatedly reminding the congregation in different ways of its basic purpose, renewal can happen. Such renewal is contingent on having a healthy theology of the church, one that discerns a purpose for the church beyond the comfort and satisfaction of its members.

The Church as Charismatic Leader and Followers

Some struggling congregations, whether small or large, believe the answer to their problems lies not in recovering their sense of purpose as church but in finding the right, attractive pastor or leader. "If we just had somebody like _____," and here the name of some former much admired pastor or televised preacher is inserted, "then we'd be going like a house afire."

Just as the church or club or clan is partially onto something with its emphasis on belonging and community, those who express a longing for a charismatic leader are also onto something. Churches do need leadership. But these wishful thinkers are also overlooking something. True leaders do not use an organization or congregation to satisfy their needs for power or control, status or achievement. True leaders help a congregation more fully realize its purposes and deal with its genuine challenges. Genuine leaders are not primarily focused on their own needs but on those of the congregation as the church of Jesus Christ.

The churches of charismatic leaders and obedient followers are not especially common numerically, but they do tend to be highly visible. Some have television, radio, or Web ministries. Some employ cable channels or extensive advertising. Others get their charismatic leader out in public as well as on television or radio. Their operations tend to be large and growing. Hadaway's image for this type of church is a guided missile, but he notes the missile is often misdirected!

As I noted earlier in this chapter, these operations are given to cycles of boom and bust, depending on the fate, fortunes, and longevity of the charismatic leader. Moreover, when that person does pass from the scene, whether by death or some other development, such churches often fade rapidly and go on, if they do, as shadows of their former selves.

As is often the case, the strengths and weaknesses of the church as charismatic leader and faithful followers are closely related. The church has a sense of direction. Leadership is clear. Power vacuums do not exist. But once again purpose has been displaced. In the church as club or clan, the de facto purpose is the satisfaction of the members. In churches built around a charismatic leader, the purpose has become the satisfaction of the leader. In some sense, lives may be changed by such a church, but often they are not changed in healthy or faithful ways. Responsibility is given over to the leader who has the answers and who protects followers. People surrender the capacity to think for themselves or to question. There is little broad participation in decision making. Such a situation may offer a great deal of security but provides little room for growth or change. Again, biblical understandings of the nature of the church and its purpose, such as people of God, body of Christ and creation of the Spirit, have been diminished or lost altogether.

The Church as Company or Corporation

Many of the larger Protestant and Catholic congregations fit this type. Here church is defined by its programs. "Community Church? Isn't that the one with the great youth program?" "First Church, that's the one that has that amazing housing ministry." "Second Baptist has the largest Sunday school in the state." "Holy Rosary boasts a parochial school of nine hundred students." To be sure, many if not most of these programs and congregations do great things. The churches are known for Meals-on-Wheels programs, legal clinics, boys and girls clubs, credit unions, low-income housing and more. They do change lives. In this sense, their purpose, according to Hadaway, is not displaced but in place.

And yet dangers and distortions are present. Such congregations often fall victim to the peculiarly American myth of measurement. They count the numbers to measure their ministry.

That's okay, so far as it goes, but it doesn't go far enough. Much about the church and the life of faith cannot be measured or quantified or achieved by "working the program." The church is not a company or corporation, though you might not know that by hanging out in the office complex of this type of church. Indeed, Hadaway's image for this type of church is a factory.

I have observed two particular foibles of such, often great, churches. One is that members of such congregations are permitted and encouraged to be doers, actors, givers, and leaders. But they are not similarly encouraged or permitted to be receivers. Members are the "haves" and the recipients of their programs are the "have-nots." But, as I suggested in an earlier chapter, such a view distorts who we are and eventually leaves our ministries spiritually underfunded. Those who are "haves" in some ways are "have-nots" in others. And, however much such congregations may talk about grace, they have a tendency to get caught up in a religion of good works and achievement. "This is a great church because of this or that outstanding ministry or program." "We are special because we belong to the church that does so many good things in the community." The church should do such ministries, but in response to grace, not to earn it.

The other thing that tends to happen in such congregations is the programs or ministries take on a life of their own. The tail begins to wag the dog. Whether it is the rummage sale or the neighborhood meetings program or the annual event for this or that group, the means take precedence over the ends. For example, in a congregation I once served, we had an annual afternoon service and tea for what were called "shut-ins," members of the congregation who lived, by and large, in nursing homes and similar facilities. A tremendous amount of planning, money, and human resources were put into that annual event. Planning began months in advance. Transportation had to be worked out, as well as questions of access and dietary restrictions attended to. Invitations needed to be made, flowers arranged, name tags created and filled out. For half the year, the event was the primary focus of a board of 12 people and demanded additional attention from several part-time staff. When the day came, the event was a lovely affair.

But over the years something happened. An event that had been attended by nearly one hundred people became gradually smaller: from 70 to 50 to 25 to 20. What had changed? A once numerous and aging cohort had died. The church, once made up of many elderly, had grown younger. The average age was once 66 and one third of the congregation's members were over 80. But the average age was now 42. Still, the Special Service and Tea marched on as if it were still 20 years earlier! The program had a life of its own that no longer fit new realities.

When effectiveness or pay-off for a particular program declines in the program-driven church, what often happens is that folks simply work the program harder rather than asking, "What's changed?" So congregations that see declining numbers at a worship service that seemed successful in the 1960s and 1970s may, instead of asking what's changed and how might we respond, simply keep doing what they have always done, only with greater effort and anxiety and without apparent results.

The point is this: the purpose of changing lives after the image and pattern of Jesus abides; programs do not. They are but means to achieve the chief purpose of the church. Programs can be, and must be, renewed, revised, and replaced as circumstances change.

The Church as Incarnational Community

Here, Hadaway shifts to more theological language to describe what he understands to be a type of church most congruent with its purpose. The church as incarnational community lives (incarnates) its purpose, that is, changing lives. This definition of the church's purpose—changing lives—should not be taken in a too restrictive way. Hadaway does not envision quick-and-easy, overnight change. Nor does change stop with individuals. A community where lives are being changed will be a changed community with a wider impact on the society around it. About this purpose, Hadaway writes:

> We must be transformed into people whose eyes are open to the signs of God's kingdom. Transformation is a magical

process, but it does not happen all at once through the wave of a wand, a trip down an aisle, or the praying of a prayer. We move from insight to understanding to a new incarnation, as a new way of seeing becomes a new way of being. The process is continuous. . . . The problem, of course, is that people don't want to be transformed or don't see the necessity. Whether the old system is working for us or not, it is our world, and from the inside we cannot see it for what it is. We must be jolted out of the old and into the new.[8]

Transformation often begins with provocation, disorientation, loss of control, and emptying.

Like the church as club or clan, community and a sense of belonging are evident in the church as incarnational community, but the overall purpose is that of changing lives—spiritual formation and transformation. Like the church as charismatic leader and followers, leadership is strong in the church as incarnational community, but the purpose is not to meet the leader's needs. Like the church as company or corporation, effective ministries and programs exist in the church as incarnational community, but they are not ends in themselves. Changing lives and growth in faith is not wholly subject to quantification or measurement.

In the church as incarnational community, lives are changed, but not by the church. The agent of change is God. The church provides the vessel or, to use a different image, the baking pans in which the yeast of God's realm activates the lives of individuals. The church does ministries of service and is curious about those served, building authentic relationships. But it also asks those who perform service to reflect on their experience, what they received as well as what they gave, and where and how they experienced God. Preaching and worship and liturgy are not a performance by the preacher or choir but an opportunity for the innately disturbing and provocative Scriptures and the gospel to get at us, to speak to us, and to be heard. The sense of community is not an end in itself. The community experienced in groups and classes is in service of growing people of faith.

The community of the church grows because its members and participants are growing in faith. Hence, Hadaway's image for the church as incarnational community is the grove of aspen trees. Individuals are linked in community, but community growth depends on the growth of individuals. Individual members are asked to be open and responsive to the work of the Holy Spirit in their lives. God is not so much a concept to be discussed as an experience to be attentive to and possibly to be shared. Instead of asking people to further programs with predetermined goals, we create places for surprise, for the unexpected things that God may do as we take risks and step outside our comfort zone. Rather than developing an array of sometimes-competing programs and jurisdictions (for example, social action versus music and the arts), we nurture the church as incarnational community, one that is a social system of three interdependent parts: inviting, growing, and sending.

Like any typology, this one has its limits. No living congregation perfectly fits any type. Perhaps some congregations do not look like any of these types. Nevertheless, Hadaway's work and church typology helps us get at some crucial questions, ones that can be shaped by ecclesiology. What is the purpose of the church? What is the role of ordained ministers and designated leaders? What does belonging mean? By what criteria is success or faithfulness measured or evaluated? What role do a congregation's programs and ministries play in the overall life of a church?

In a time when vision and leaders who cast the vision are greatly emphasized, Hadaway pushes us to an important prior question, that of purpose. Ordained and lay leaders often serve a congregation best by simply helping a congregation be reasonably clear about its purpose and doing those things that further that purpose. If, as Hadaway proposes, the church exists to change lives, to make disciples, and to grow people of faith, leaders will keep that large purpose before a congregation. This purpose is shaped by a theology of the church that understands the church's God-given nature and calling. Forgetting or neglecting this, congregations easily devolve into clubs or personality cults or service agencies with their associated liabilities and distortions of the gospel message.

This is not all that can be derived from theological conviction about the church. Also important for healthy and vital congregations is clear theological thinking about the sacraments of the church and the nature of ministry, both lay and ordained. In the next chapter, "This Thing Called Church, Part 2" we turn to these topics and what they have to do with healthy congregations. But the crucial and concluding point echoes the beginning of this chapter. The church has a theological nature, role, and purpose given by God and disclosed in Scripture and tradition. The church is not to be defined by individual needs and desires alone, though congregations and their leaders ought always be cognizant of such needs. The church is not to be created in the image of other entities in our society, whether not-for-profit agencies, franchised businesses, or consumer services, though it can learn from them all. Healthy congregations are informed and grounded by a sense of identity and purpose that challenges lesser identities and purposes. Healthy congregations have a high sense of the church's calling and mission in the world, borne of a deeply formed and constantly renewed ecclesiology.

Questions for Reflection and Discussion

1. Of the three scriptural and theological metaphors for church (people of God, body of Christ, and creation of the Spirit), which one speaks most powerfully to you? Which least? Why?
2. Consider the proposed shift from a culture of membership to a culture of discipleship. What excites you about this? What concerns you? What questions do you have?
3. After reading the typology of four types of congregations, does one best fit your congregation? How does this typology help you to evaluate your church's strengths and needs?
4. In your congregation, what are some examples of lives being changed? How are people having their "eyes opened to the signs of the kingdom," as Hadaway describes it? How might those be reinforced or strengthened?

Chapter 10

This Thing Called Church, Part 2

Sacraments and Ministry

This chapter continues our focus on ecclesiology, the theology of the church. But now we turn from more general concern with the church's nature and purpose to more specific aspects of church life. In particular, this chapter focuses on the church's sacraments, baptism and communion, and on ministry. What implications do the sacraments have for church health and vitality? And what is ministry and "the ministry"? What is the meaning of ordination? What are ordained ministers to do? What is the ministry that belongs to the laity?

The Sacraments: Some Preliminary Thoughts

Different congregations and denominations have different traditions for how frequently and in what manner the sacraments are celebrated. Some celebrate the Eucharist or Lord's Supper (Eucharist, Lord's Supper, and Communion or Holy Communion are ways different denominations speak of the same sacramental meal instituted by Jesus). Some churches offer this sacrament in each Sunday worship service, as well as at other times during the week. Others celebrate this sacrament somewhat, or even much, less frequently. In some traditions, Communion is celebrated quarterly, in others monthly. The form and understanding of baptism also vary considerably. Some congregations and denominations baptize infants, others do not. Some practice baptism by immersion. Other congregations make a much more moderate, essentially symbolic use of water in baptism.

As a child and pastor of the Congregational/United Church of Christ, my experience has been with the less frequent celebration of the Lord's Supper. To some extent, this practice is characteristic of those denominations that drank most deeply at the font of modernity and its high emphasis on reason. At least to some moderns, the sacraments seemed too material and were thought primitive. Today, in such traditions, a rebalancing is often evident in a new appreciation and more frequent celebration of the sacraments.

Whether the sacraments are celebrated more frequently or less so, whether they involve a generous use of water, bread, and wine, or a more limited and symbolic use of the elements, the implications for the life and health of congregations remain much the same. Those implications are, I believe, significant, and often much more significant than we realize.

What Is a Sacrament?

Not only do different church traditions do the sacraments in different ways, they vary in what is considered a sacrament. For the Roman Catholic Church there are seven sacraments; for most Protestant denominations only two, baptism and communion. Catholics add to this list confirmation, penance, extreme unction, ordination, and matrimony. Protestants have limited the designation "sacrament" to those acts in which Jesus himself participated, that is, baptism; or that he instituted, that is, communion. But besides this functional definition, what is a sacrament?

Author Frederick Buechner offers a helpful and mercifully nontechnical definition of sacrament. He contrasts rituals and sacraments. "A sacrament is the breaking through of the sacred into the profane; a ritual is the ceremonial acting out of the profane in order to show forth its sacredness. A sacrament is God offering his holiness to men; a ritual is men raising up the holiness of their humanity to God."[1] One might abridge this even further: a sacrament is something God does; a ritual something we do. In baptism and communion, God is present and active; indeed, God is the primary actor. God is present and active throughout all creation, but God has specifically promised to be present to us in the sacraments.

The Sermon Preached by a Sanctuary

Ten years ago, the congregation I served decided to do a renovation of its sanctuary. Some of the work was simply maintenance and updating of electrical systems. Some of the work had broader, theological implications. The end result was a sanctuary that itself preaches a sermon. After the renovation, we would take baptismal preparation classes into the sanctuary to point out what this sacred space says about the Christian life and how it forms the congregation.

Our tour began in the low-ceilinged, winding entryway. This opened into a huge, oval-shaped sanctuary with a soaring ceiling and accented by simple stained glass in the windows that allows the space to fill with light. I suggested that in some ways, walking through that entryway into the sanctuary is like returning to the womb. Thus, it allows worshipers to experience a legitimate dependence. Worship is that. It is a return to the Source and Author of our existence, a drawing near to that which is larger than self and, in so doing, regaining our sense of perspective.

Coming out of the low entryway and just before stepping into the area of the nave, we came to the baptismal font, positioned in the center before one enters the area of congregational seating. A very large and beautiful glass bowl rests, illuminated, upon a wooden frame. Both the glass of the font and the water resting in it catch the light. Prior to the renovation, another much smaller font had been located at the far side of the rail that separated the nave and chancel. It sat, largely unnoticed, off to the side. It held no water, refracted no light. On Sundays when there were baptisms, the font was moved from the side front to the center and filled with water. Now the new baptismal font and its location proclaim the message: We all enter into the community of faith and the Christian life through the waters, and new birth, of baptism. Moreover, our entry into this life and community is through an act of God and an experience of God's grace. Our admission does not depend on our dress, station in life, looks, race, or anything else about us. It is God's doing and a gift.

Next, we came to the area of congregational seating. Once the seating had been straight rows of long pews facing forward. In the renovation, the pews, arranged in three sections, still face forward but are angled in a herringbone fashion to emphasize the experience of a gathered community. People can more nearly see one another, the gathered body of Christ. In front of the congregational seating and in the center of the slightly raised chancel area (now open as the rail had been removed) stands a plain-yet-elegant table where Communion is celebrated. While baptism is the sacrament, the act of God, by which we enter into the community of faith, communion is the sacrament that sustains and feeds us on the journey of faith. To the right of the table stands the pulpit, because our other primary means of sustenance on the journey of faith is the proclamation and hearing of the Word.

Above both table and pulpit hangs a large wooden cross. It dominates the sanctuary, hanging both before and above the entire congregation. Without a word, the cross says that we make our faith journey, from baptism through life, under the sign of the cross. It speaks of discipleship, its cost and its joy. But the cross also stands as our destination, full fellowship with the triune God.

Thus the sanctuary itself preaches a sermon and shapes faith. Worshipers return weekly to our Source and Author, having entered into the Christian life and community of faith through the waters of baptism, to be nurtured by the breaking of the bread and by the breaking open of the Word in the midst of the gathered community and under the sign of the cross. At the conclusion of the service, worshipers are reborn out of the birth canal and with the benediction sent again into the world. The worship experience in this space permits a legitimate dependence, but worshipers are not allowed to remain dependent, either physically or psychologically. We are sent again into the world, but sent having learned once more who and whose we are. "You are a child of God, a disciple of Christ, and a member of the Church. Go, now and be who, by God's grace, you are."[2] Thus does one sanctuary preach its own sermon and form a congregation's life.

Baptism and the Healthy Congregation

"He's not sure he completely understands baptism, and we're having a difficult time explaining it to him," said the father of two boys, one soon to be confirmed and, prior to his confirmation, baptized. "He is concerned that he may not understand enough or really be, well, good enough." I was not surprised. The boy, age 14, was very bright, able, and extremely conscientious. He was worried that he might not have sufficient grasp of Christian beliefs or that his life didn't measure up to the stature of Christ.

"Remember," I said, "that none of us deserves baptism. None of us understands enough, or is 'Christian enough' to qualify. It is, after all, grace, gift. While we should make every effort to prepare, our role really comes on the other side of baptism, in our response. Sometimes," I suggested, "we can become too focused on ourselves, whether we have a sufficient grasp of Christian faith or whether we are really morally or spiritually 'good enough' for baptism. But baptism is not, first of all, about us. It is about God. This conviction is particularly evident in infant baptism. God's love and grace precede our understanding, even our comprehension."

This conversation, and the father and the son's concerns, are not unusual. We human beings are often focused on ourselves. Sometimes we think too highly of ourselves, and sometimes we are overly critical. Such self-examination is not, of course, all bad nor all wrong. But, in some measure, baptism and the Christian life direct our focus elsewhere. They direct our concern away from ourselves to the holy, merciful, mysterious, and majestic God who births creation and each of us. Just as Jesus was not the main actor at his baptism but was a passive recipient, we are not the main actors at our baptism. Something happens to us and for us. Something, someone intrudes, breaks in, tears open the heavens, as it says in Mark's Gospel. This is God's doing. It's grace.

In my church tradition, we tend to be doers, activists, and highly responsible people. This is good and commendable. But it can become a heavy burden. We take the weight of the world—of life itself—upon our shoulders. It may prove a crushing weight. Baptism brings into focus one of the great, liberating truths of the Christian life: it's not about you. It's about God, what God has done, what God is doing, and what God will do. And, as Paul wrote to the Philippians, "The one who began a good work among you will bring it to completion at the day of Jesus Christ" (1:6).

I recall the story of the great prophet Elijah (1 Kings 18–19). Elijah took on the prophets of Baal, the house-prophets of the corrupt Queen Jezebel and King Ahab in Israel's Northern Kingdom. Despite the overwhelming odds of five hundred prophets of Baal to his one, Elijah was victorious. He routed the prophets who took their orders from the manipulative royalty. The triumph was great. But then, in a perplexing turn of events, Elijah fled, seemingly overwhelmed and unable to cope. Arriving on Mount Horeb and huddling in a cave, Elijah heard the voice of the Lord ask, "What are you doing here, Elijah?" Perhaps stung by the Lord's seeming lack of support and understanding, Elijah answered, "I have been very zealous for the LORD, the God of hosts; for the Israelites have forsaken your covenant, thrown down your altars, and killed your prophets with the sword. I alone am left, and they are seeking my life, to take it away." Perhaps the key words are "I alone am left." Elijah believed he was the last faithful Israelite. Not so, says the Lord, who announces that there remain in Israel seven thousand who have not bent the knee to Baal and insists that Elijah is to go and anoint a new king and his own prophetic successor (1 Kings 19:13–14, 18). Elijah believed it was all up to him, and that he *alone* was left to defend and serve the cause of right. God indicates otherwise. Many faithful followers remained, said the Lord, even those who would succeed the prophet Elijah and carry on the struggle.

Baptism offers a similar word of judgment upon our grandiosity as well as a word of grace in times of discouragement. It is reported that Martin Luther, when despondent, used to touch his forehead and say, "I have been baptized," by which he meant, I belong, by God's grace, to Jesus Christ, and nothing can undo this truth. Though I may feel down in the dumps, alone, and overwhelmed, an objective truth and reality exist, to which I may cling and in which I may find hope and renewal: *I have been baptized*. God's act, by which I have been named, claimed, loved, and called is the foundation. No matter how discouraged I may feel, no matter how worthless or ineffective I may think I am on any given day, I can take heart, for I have been baptized.

Healthy and vital congregations help their members, as well as the congregation as a body, hold in fruitful and faithful tension the *gift* and the *task* aspects of faith and of life. Through the corrective lenses of Christian faith, we see life is both gift and task. Baptism and life have both a passive and an active aspect. Baptism has both an objective (what God has done) and subjective (what we are to do) side. When we forget that life is gift, that we have been claimed by God, and that baptism has an objective nature, the task of life can overwhelm us and crush us, as it had Elijah (and many since). But when we forget that the gift entails the task and that grace invites and requires response, then grace becomes cheap. The gift of the healing, washing, forgiving, and renewing waters of baptism implies the task. You have been claimed, named, and called by God; go now and be who you are. Grace may be free, but it is not cheap.

Indeed, more pastors and congregations probably find themselves confronted with situations where the task element has been forgotten and grace is presumed. Although most pastors have met someone like the 14-year-old who was so conscientious that he was not sure he deserved baptism, pastors more often face the other side of the coin. A mother calls the pastor and says, "You don't know us, but my grandparents are members of your church. We're going to be visiting in town next weekend, and we'd like to have our baby baptized." "What congregation are you active with at home?" asks the pastor. "Well, none, really," says the mother. "Actually, church is not our thing. But this will mean a lot to my grandmother."

In such a situation, the pastor has the hard task of explaining that baptism is not a social convention or a magical rite. It entails a commitment, a task. Parents promise to be faithful disciples and to ensure their children are raised within the church in order that they may come to know their identity as proclaimed in their baptism: child of God, disciple of Christ, member of the church. Moreover, the congregation itself enters into a covenant before God with those parents and their child. They will support both parents and child as the newly baptized one grows in Christ. When these covenants mean nothing, the gift of grace becomes cheap, for the task has been forgotten.

Giving the gift aspect of baptism too much emphasis leads to a failure to responsibly exercise the freedom God grants to us human beings, which encompasses our capacity for independence and creativity. By the same token, emphasizing only the task can lead to an exaggeration of freedom and responsibility as we forget or deny that we are finite and limited beings who remain, in some sense, forever dependent. We are both, finite and free. Life, and life in Christ, is both gift and task. When these two aspects, which come to focus in the sacrament of baptism, are not held in right relation or balance, our lives as congregations or individuals become unbalanced. Either we feel frequently overwhelmed by demand and responsibility, or we discern no call to use our gifts and no capacity to act responsibly.

Baptism signifies many things: forgiveness, calling, washing, new birth, dying and rising with Christ, incorporation into the body of Christ, and beginning among them. But in the midst of these many meanings, baptism crystallizes the nature of Christian life in a healthy balance of gift and task, grace and responsibility.

Because the congregations I have served tend to emphasize our freedom and responsibility and pay less heed to grace and free gift, we began to annually observe a "renewal of baptism" (not rebaptism) on the Sunday when the story of the baptism of Jesus is the Gospel text. Here Jesus is acted upon. He is a receiver of God's confirmation and of the Holy Spirit. But this action is immediately followed by the beginning of Jesus's ministry, his response. Other congregations offer a similar renewal service during the Easter Vigil or on Sundays when baptisms are celebrated. Because baptism is understood as a sacrament and, by definition, something God has done, it cannot be done again. Nevertheless, baptism can be remembered and its covenant commitments renewed. When we offered this opportunity, people came forward to have one of the pastors touch water to their foreheads, speak their name, and say, "Remember your baptism and be thankful." Worshipers' tears testified to the power of this moment and to our need for the reminder of God's grace and God's calling.

The Sacrament of Communion and Healthy Congregations

Like baptism, which has many meanings, communion does also. Forgiveness, Christ's presence, penance, community, hunger, feeding, Christ's body and blood, memorial, and sustenance are among the many dimensions of the meal Christians share. Here I want to focus on one among these many meanings and its potential for contributing to congregational health and vitality.

Paul's first letter to the church at Corinth is preoccupied with the problems of congregational factionalism and divisiveness. He notes that some in the congregation regard themselves as spiritually "in the know" and look upon others as the unenlightened. Those in the know possess the spirit and the gifts, while the unenlightened, in the view of the enlightened, lack both significant gifts and spirit. But Paul questions just how enlightened and in the know these, whom he refers to as the strong, really are (1 Cor. 8:9). He detects a lack of the highest gift, the one that orders all other spiritual gifts: the gift of love.

Thus, Paul's famous hymn to love in 1 Corinthians 13 is not a text created for weddings but a text for divided, squabbling congregations: "If I speak in the tongues of mortals and of angels, but do not have love, I am a noisy gong or a clanging cymbal. And if I have prophetic powers, and understand all mysteries and all knowledge, and if I have faith, so as to remove mountains, but do not have love, I am nothing. If I give away all my possessions, and if I hand over my body so that I may boast, but do not have love, I gain nothing" (1 Cor. 13:1-3).

When Paul turns to the topic of the Lord's Supper, this same concern and critique is evident. Paul tells the Corinthians that they are missing the whole point. "When you come together, it is not really to eat the Lord's Supper. For when the time comes to eat, each of you goes ahead with your own supper, and one goes hungry and another becomes drunk" (1 Cor. 11:20-21). Paul charges the Corinthians with failing to discern the body (v. 29) and warns that this will bring the judgment of God.

What does Paul mean by discerning the body? He is not referring to later church controversies over transubstantiation, that is, the doctrine of the Roman Catholic Church that the bread and wine were transformed into Jesus's actual body and blood. That controversy lay hundreds of years down the road. What Paul meant by "discerning the body" is simpler. He meant, "Do you notice others in the congregation? Are you aware of your sisters and brothers in Christ, or are you only tuned in to your own needs, your own pressing hungers? Do you who claim to be enlightened even notice your weaker brothers and sisters, or are you in such a hurry to get your share of the power food that you neglect and embarrass them? Do you see (discern) the body of Christ, the church and gathered community and the needs of your brothers and sisters?"

One of the ironies of contemporary church life is the extent to which Communion has been individualized and this concern for the community, the body, pretty much lost. We receive our individual wafers or cubes, drink from our tiny individual cups, and sit alone in our pews deep in private prayer or simply passing the time as the meal is served. We do not discern the implications of the sacrament for life together in the body of Christ. We may not, like some of the members in Corinth, eat the meal all up before others even get there, but do we see that one meaning of *communion* is community? Do we see that how we celebrate the sacrament often reflects the limits of our own communities, their fractures and failures, as well as their strengths and health? In my experience, we don't do all that well at making the connection between how we celebrate Communion and how we function as a community. Communion is a religious thing. Congregational divisiveness or factions or broken relationships, well, that's between individuals or something for the pastor and deacons to deal with.

I recall the story of the Palestinian Christian priest Elias Chacour who finally tired of presiding at the sacrament in his congregation, knowing that many in the pews hated each other, had not talked with one another in years, even decades, and bore grudges dating to the previous generation. One Sunday Father Chacour locked and barred the doors to the church. Then he told the congregation that he had no intention of presiding at the service and sacrament or of unlocking the doors until those at odds with one another confessed their sins, offered forgiveness, and made peace. What followed, after a stunned silence, was nothing sort of remarkable. A policeman got to his feet, confessed his misdeeds, and asked forgiveness. Others followed. When the Lord's Supper was finally celebrated, it was no longer a mockery. It was a sacrament in which members of the congregation recognized one another as the body of Christ.

While the situation in our congregations may not be as intense as in the war-torn land of Palestine, theologically informed understandings of communion help us make the connection between our life together as a people and community and the sacrament we celebrate. In some traditions, for example among Moravians, this aspect is made prominent by preceding Communion with a time of confession of sin in which members of the church speak with others, making peace and washing one another's feet.

Many congregations today celebrate the kiss or greeting of peace as part of their liturgy. Often, however, it too lacks theological funding and understanding. The greeting of peace becomes a time to chat, to offer a breezy good morning, to comment on last night's football game. But such practices mistake this moment. It is our moment to offer peace to one another in the same way God has offered peace to us. Moreover, it properly belongs with the sacramental rite, not first thing in the service after the announcements. Furthermore, it can be informed by the teaching of Jesus in the Sermon on the Mount, where he urges people not to offer their gift at the altar without first making peace with others.

The point is that the sacrament of communion, as Paul makes clear, is not just about my individual spiritual life or experience. It is not my private time with the Lord. It is not simply about my personal standing with God. The sacrament of communion has everything to do with community and the health of our life together as the body of Christ.

I recall the congregation with which I once worked where members said, "We need to strengthen our sense of community. We don't know each other. We don't get along all that well."

"What do you want to do about that?" I asked. "Tell me, when do you experience your greatest sense of community?"

"When we eat together, when we have a potluck," they answered without hesitation. "That's interesting. Community has something to do with eating together? I'm just curious, what is Communion like around here?"

"Gloomy," one person immediately said. "We don't have it very often, just four times a year," said another. "People say that having it more often would lose its specialness. But Communion doesn't seem to have much to do with our sense of community, anyway. It's all about how we've betrayed or failed Jesus, isn't it? It's pretty somber. Mostly individual. A time for silence and meditation."

"Well," I asked, "I wonder if you'd be willing to take a look at that? I wonder if you might be willing to reconsider Communion and its relationship to the strong sense of community that you say you lack but wish you had."

"We might be able to do that," they said. Subsequently, the congregation spent time looking at both the texts that speak directly of the Lord's Supper and at the many texts and stories of Jesus eating with others. They paid attention to what eating together meant in their own lives. They then prepared for a festival Sunday focused on Communion during which the sacrament would be celebrated with both reverence and joy. "This was a wonderful Sunday for us," they reported afterwards. "We're considering more frequent Communion and looking at ways to share Communion that put us in touch with God and each other."

Of late, many sociologists and family counselors have reported the single best indicator of family health is one practice. Families that eat at least one meal a day together have a much higher chance of being happy and healthy, as well as surviving, than families that don't. The table and gathering around it regularly and predictably is, it turns out, important to family health. Maybe it's not that different in the church?

The Ministry: Ordained and Lay

Another crucial element of our understanding of church is what ordained ministry means. I recall my first interview with a congregational search committee. It seemed to be going pretty well. Several of its members, speaking almost at once, were talking about all the things they imagined and hoped their minister would do in the community. Serve on this town council, get involved at the senior center, work with bored and aimless youth in town, and more. As the possibilities for community involvement became more numerous, I became more depressed. Their expectations seemed endless.

Having come to the conclusion earlier that they would never actually call me to be their pastor, for they were more conservative than I, I decided, "What the heck, you may as well say what you're thinking. Nothing to lose.""Listen," I said, "I hear all these things you expect your pastor to do in the town. I just want you to know that I am not interested in being a Christian *for* you. I am, however, very much interested in being a Christian *with* you." "What a stupid thing to say," I thought later. "They were actually interested in you. But you finished that!" Imagine my surprise when a week later the chair of the committee called to say they would like me to be their candidate for presentation to the congregation! I suspect it had something to do with my candor at that moment.

Sometimes we pastors try to be Christians for our congregations, running all over the community, serving on every imaginable board, showing up at every rally, speaking to every issue, responding to each crisis. Whether because our congregations have fostered such expectations or because it makes us feel important and needed, we have become confused about what ministry is, who ministers are, and what they do. What is the role of those who have been ordained to the ministry of Word and Sacrament? And what is the ministry to which all Christians are called?

By virtue of our baptism, all Christians are ordained for ministry, that is, service to God and to our neighbors. All of us are called to love God with all our heart, soul, and mind, and to love our neighbors as ourselves (Matt.22:37-39). Within this baptismal calling are two broad categories and assignments. Ordained clergy are called, in Paul's words, to equip the saints for ministry. Ordained clergy are not called to do the ministry of the laity for them or instead of them. Ordained clergy have been given special training and education for preaching and teaching, administering the sacraments, and providing pastoral leadership in the body of Christ. The ministry of the ordained is to care for and build up the body of Christ through these pastoral duties. The ministry of the laity is to represent Christ in and to the world. This ought not be understood to mean that the ministry of the ordained is primary and the ministry of the laity secondary. The word *laity* comes from the Greek word *laos*, which means "people." Clergy are among the laos. And clergy are ordained to guide congregations in equipping members to carry out the ministries to which they have been called.

But there seems to be a lot of confusion about this. We sometimes have too many people managing the church and not nearly enough people out in the world practicing their vocations as Christians in the arenas of family, occupation, and community. By the same token, it sometimes appears that some clergy really want to be lawyers, politicians, social workers, or therapists instead of pastors and teachers of the church. Nothing is wrong with being any of those—except that the church needs pastors to do the job to which they have been called.

At one church and ministry committee meeting, a candidate for ordination was asked, "What is the meaning of ordination?" A look of confusion and alarm flitted over the candidate's face. "Ordination . . . It's for full-time Christians, for those who will serve the Lord, you know, on a full-time basis as pastors or teach-

ers or missionaries." "Oh," said the lay member of the committee, "so I'm a part-time Christian?" "Well, I didn't mean that
exactly," said the flustered candidate.

Still, that message often is conveyed. We have two classes of
Christians, full- and part-time, really committed and sort of involved. But this betrays a serious misunderstanding of the ministries of both the ordained and the lay. Ordained clergy are not
more special or more spiritual than other Christians, nor are they
full-time. Rather, they have specific functions, different tasks, from
others in the community of faith. They have the task of leading
worship, preparing sermons, seeing that the sacraments are properly celebrated, and giving pastoral leadership to the church. The
laity of the church have the primary task of representing Christ
in the world, in their workplaces, and in the work they do, in
their relationships with people, and in their citizenship. While
laity have an important role in congregational governance and
leadership, that role must not eclipse their role in representing
Christ to the world. These general guidelines are not, of course,
rigid categories, but they do suggest directions and distinctions
that may guide the church and give new vigor to the ministry of
the whole people of God, the laos.

Sometimes the confusion comes, as I indicated earlier, when
clergy themselves take on almost the whole task of representing
Christ to the world. But other times the confusion comes when
lay people try to take over the roles and responsibilities to which
the ordained have been called. For example, a layperson may
wish to preach or celebrate the sacraments on a regular basis.
Certainly, there are times and places for laity performing these
tasks, but not all the time. Nor is it appropriate, as sometimes
happens, for a layperson to become a kind of chaplain to a group
of their closest friends, performing the sacraments for them. They
lack the training, but not only that; the congregation has not
called them for that task. Nor does the congregation often have
the means to evaluate and hold them accountable for their performance. In recent years, the ministry of the laity too often has
been understood to mean only that laity do what the ordained
do. When this happens, the laity's role in representing Christ to
the world may be eclipsed. Certainly, there are appropriate times

for a sermon by a layperson. I have served in congregations where trained laity have done a wonderful job as readers of Scripture. And the church has identified many appropriate roles for lay leaders as teachers, group leaders, and mentors. My point is not to say that lay members ought not be involved in worship leadership, but that this role ought not be allowed to obscure the primary calling of laity, to represent Christ to the world.

Too often congregations tie up many of their lay members doing tasks in the church. Far too little focus is given to the ministry of the laity in and to the world through their jobs. Congregations are increasingly redressing this imbalance by such activities as creating gifts discernment ministries; organizing groups where professionals in a particular field (law, health care, criminal justice) study, pray, and reflect together; or planning trips where groups go to do ministry in another part of the world.

When ordained clergy don't do their job, the church suffers a loss of clarity and direction. When laity don't do their job, the world suffers neglect and absence of faithful witness. The whole and healthy church needs both parties to own their ministries, to be authorized and equipped, to be supported and held accountable, and to be thanked and acknowledged. Ours is a shared ministry but it is not the same ministry. "Now there are varieties of gifts," writes Paul, "but the same Spirit; and there are varieties of services, but the same Lord" (1 Cor. 12:4-5). Healthy congregations are clear about the different responsibilities of their ministers, both lay and ordained.

Questions for Reflection and Discussion

1. How would you say the meaning of baptism is understood by and interpreted to people in your congregation? What meanings of baptism are given greatest emphasis? Which are given the least?
2. Baptism, according to the author, suggests both the gift and the task aspects of Christian life and faith. Do you think these are held in balance in your congregation or are they out of balance? If so, in which direction?

3. How is Communion celebrated in your congregation?
   Does it help you to "discern the body" or does it hinder
   that?
4. The author writes that the task of the ordained is to equip
   the church for its ministry through preaching, teaching,
   administering the sacraments, and giving pastoral care and
   leadership; the laity's role is to represent Christ in and to
   the world. What excites you about this statement? What
   questions do you have about it? What concerns do you
   have?

Chapter 11

What Time Is It?

Eschatology

When the apostle Paul writes to the congregation at Rome regarding relationships with others in the community, he counsels, "Owe no one anything, except to love one another," which seems like a rather large "except." Three verses later Paul adds, "Besides this, you know what time it is, how it is now the moment for you to wake from sleep. For salvation is nearer to us now than when we became believers; the night is far gone, the day is near." Knowing what time it is helps Christians to know what is important and what is not. Thus *eschatology*, that is, teachings about "the last things," and ethics interact. "Let us then," continues Paul, "lay aside the works of darkness and put on the armor of light; let us live honorably as in the day, not in reveling and drunkenness, not in debauchery and licentiousness, not in quarreling and jealousy" (Rom. 13:8, 11-13).

Do We Know What Time It Is?

Where are things heading? What does the future hold? Will history, as we know it, have an end or consummation? And what happens to us when our own endings come? Is there a final judgment? Will Christ come again? All of these are eschatological questions. From the Greek term *ta eschata*, "the last things," is derived the theological term *eschatology*. The doctrine of eschatology summarizes Christian convictions regarding the fulfillment, destination, and end of life.

You may have detected a certain ambiguity in these words. The last things, the fulfillment, destination, and end, cover a lot of ground and include many different questions. Does "last things" refer to a chronological end to the world? Or do these terms denote something slightly different: the *ultimate* end, as in the goal and purpose of history? Here's another ambiguity in these terms and questions: Is this eschatology thing about the future of all life? Or is it mainly about individual lives, my life, the lives of those I love, and what happens to us after we die? But here is something not at all ambiguous: whether Jesus comes or we go, we do not have forever. Biblical thought is linear, not cyclical. Time does not move in an ever-repeating circle. It moves from beginning to end, from creation to consummation. "So teach us to count our days," writes the psalmist, "that we may gain a wise heart" (Ps. 90:12).

Such is the eschatological perspective of Christian faith. Or as a favorite benediction of mine has it, "Life is short and we do not have much time to gladden the hearts of those with whom we walk the way. So be swift to love, make haste to be kind, in the name of our companion on the way, Jesus the Christ." The eschatological nature of Christian faith poses an urgent question that contemporary culture, and all too often the church, would rather avoid: do we know what time it is?

When it comes to framing that question as well as providing hope for the future, the language of Scripture is the language of metaphor and symbol. This language attempts to express what cannot be fully expressed in words. For example, John of Patmos, suffering under Roman persecution, writes in the book of Revelation: "Then I saw a new heaven and a new earth; for the first heaven and the first earth had passed away, and the sea was no more. And I saw the holy city, the new Jerusalem, coming down out of heaven from God, prepared as a bride adorned for her husband" (Rev. 21:1–2). Rome shall not endure forever, affirms

John, but God shall be God. Or, Paul says, "So it is with the resurrection of the dead. What is sown is perishable, what is raised is imperishable. It is sown in dishonor, it is raised in glory. It is sown in weakness, it is raised in power. It is sown a physical body, it is raised a spiritual body" (1 Cor. 15:42-44). In the end, affirms Paul, God triumphs even over death. This language is more poetic than scientific. We invite misunderstanding when we try to turn such metaphor into literal description.

Perhaps for this reason such themes and texts are often best conveyed through hymns and music. For example, one version of the familiar harvest and thanksgiving hymn, "Come, ye thankful people, come" moves from the annual harvest to the eschatological one.

> For the Lord our God shall come, and shall take his harvest
>   home;
> From his field shall in that day all offenses purge away,
> Give his angels charge at last in the fire the tares to cast;
> But the faithful ears to store in his garner evermore.
>
> Even so, Lord, quickly come, to thy final harvest home;
> Gather thou thy people in, free from sorrow, free from sin,
> There, forever purified, in the presence to abide;
> Come, with all thine angels come, raise the glorious harvest
>   home.[1]
>   —Henry Alford, 1844

In spirituals of the African-American tradition, eschatological themes are also prominent.

> I want to be ready,
> I want to be ready,
> I want to be ready
> To walk in Jerusalem just like John.[2]

Or,

> Keep your lamps trimmed and burning,
> Keep your lamps trimmed and burning,

Keep your lamps trimmed and burning
For this work's almost done.[3]

And Julia Ward Howe's great hymn of the Civil War era is reso-
nant with eschatological themes and images.

My eyes have seen the glory of the coming of the Lord;
who is trampling out the vintage where the grapes of wrath
    are stored;
And has loosed the fateful lightning of a terrible swift sword;
God's truth is marching on.[4]

The language of these hymns is not, as some popular
eschatology is, the language of prediction; it is the language of
hope, that is, faith applied to the future. The God we trust in
present life is the God we also trust in the future. Whether the
concern is with the end and consummation of all life or the final
completion and destiny of our personal lives, Christian faith affirms that history moves toward conclusion and that the end is
God.

Eschatology: A Brief Review

Throughout this study I have been aided by the work of theologian Daniel Migliore, and on this topic of eschatology I again
turn to his insights. Migliore helps to order the array of scriptural
texts as well as theological themes by his observation, "Eschatology
has traditionally focused on four clusters of symbols of the end
of history and the completion of human life."[5] These four symbols are the *parousia* (second coming of Christ), the resurrection
of the dead, the last judgment, and eternal life (heaven) and eternal death (hell). Migliore is careful to use the word *symbols* when
speaking of these clusters of Christian eschatological themes. They
do not describe literal realities captured in our human words but
realities too great for words.

As I noted in an earlier chapter, we do not understand these
matters in the modern sense of the word, that is, understanding
as fully explaining them and with complete certainty. No, we

understand in that older sense of "standing under" great mysteries of which we glimpse only a part. We see a part, but we cannot see the thing whole.[6] The apostle Paul makes a point similar to this one about understanding when he writes, "For now we see in a mirror, dimly, but then we will see face to face. Now I know only in part; then I will know fully, even as I have been fully known" (1 Cor. 13:12). These four clusters of symbols help us express what is not easily described, and we now move to them.

The Parousia of Christ

A Greek word meaning "arrival" or "coming," *parousia* refers to the return or final coming of Christ. The essential point here is that Christian hope is not hope in and for abstract things like joy, peace, freedom, or justice; our hope is hope in *someone,* not something. Moreover, and at odds with some popular eschatology, the Christ who comes again will be the Christ who has already come. He will not take off his cloak of compassion and mercy to reveal a holy avenger or terminator. We hope in one we have known and whose will and way has been revealed in our midst.

The Resurrection of the Body

This cluster of eschatological symbols challenges the preponderance of Greek and Platonic thought in the early centuries of Christianity's development. Greek philosophical thought emphasized the immortality of the soul. To this way of thinking, the body was viewed as not only transitory but evil. The body was the prison house of the soul. At death, the eternal soul was released and continued on. Christians, in contrast, have believed that death is real and complete, but in the final victory of God's grace a new creation occurs, a resurrection of the dead, not as an invisible soul, but as a whole person. Nevertheless, the Scriptures do not describe the nature of the resurrection or the body in the resurrection, they only suggest it. Thus, Paul writes: "But someone will ask, 'How are the dead raised? With what kind of body do they come?' Fool! What you sow does not come to life unless it dies. And as for what you sow, you do not sow the body that is to be, but a bare seed, perhaps of wheat or some other grain. But God gives it a body as he has chosen, and to each kind of seed its own body" (1 Cor. 15:35-38). The concern is less with what or how, which Paul dismisses as foolish. He affirms who, God, and why, the fulfillment of God's love.

Last Judgment

The final two clusters of eschatological symbols, last judgment and eternal life, or heaven, and eternal death, or hell, are ones that we tend to see through the great (and some not so great) art of the Middle Ages and Renaissance. The works of Dante, Michelangelo, the Bosch brothers, and many, many more have said much more than do the Scriptures, which contain only the most limited depictions of judgment, heaven, or hell. In the Scriptures, judgment and a final judgment are a way of affirming one clear conviction: our choices and decisions do matter. There are consequences, eternal consequences, to how we live our lives. We do not, Christians believe, live lives of no consequence. On the contrary, what we do and don't do in this life counts. While we do not earn our way into God's good graces, we are accountable for how we have used the gifts entrusted to us.

Eternal Life and Eternal Death

When our second child was small and my wife and I and his older brother would be speaking about something that had happened before he was born, Nick would sometimes ask, "Where was I then?" His brother would say, "You weren't even born," which while accurate seemed dismissive. When Nick asked, "Where was I then?" we answered, "You were with God." This, obviously, is not a scientific description but a faith statement. In a somewhat similar way, Christians have said to those who asked, "Where will I be after I die?" that "You will be with God." Eternal life is just this, life with God. In the Gospel of John, eternal life is seen as something that begins not on the other side of the grave but on this side. Trusting in the Word made flesh and dwelling among us, Jesus Christ, we participate in a quality of life Jesus called eternal life. We are with God, here and now, and will be with God then and there. To be in hell is to be cut off. It too starts in this life when we choose, again and again, to cut ourselves off from God and from others. Even then, God does not give up, for as the creeds of the Church affirm, "Christ descended into hell." God keeps trying to find us.

Thus ends our brief tour through the eschatological symbols and themes of Scripture and theology. Because they address mysteries and not problems, they are symbols and metaphors and not solutions or precise explanations. Because we moderns have been successful at solving many problems, we tend to think of most everything in a problem and solution framework. But some things are not problems to be solved; they are mysteries with which we must live. Christian thinking about the last things respects that mystery while affirming that the God who has created life and our lives, and the God whose grace we have known in this life, is the final and the ultimate reality. As the creedal statement of the United Church of Canada puts it, "In life, in death, in life beyond death, God is with us. We are not alone. Thanks be to God."

Christian Conviction about the Last Things and Vital Congregations

Next we turn to three particular points of connection between the life of congregations and eschatological conviction. First, how does Christian conviction about one last thing, death, influence the ministries of congregations and how they treat death and the related matters of mortality and aging? Second, I consider how eschatology is often transformed from a matter of mystery and faith into one of prediction and control in what some refer to as the "new apocalypticism." In the process of such transformation, Christian convictions regarding the last things are often severely distorted, resulting in destructive consequences. Third, I weigh the role of eschatological conviction in liberating our often-constricted imaginations and challenging our complacency.

The Denial of Death

Not long ago a large church-related continuing care and retire-
ment facility asked me to contribute my thoughts to their process of formulating a new mission statement. This fine facility
operates like many today with levels of care, known in this field
as "continuing care." Most residents move in when they are still
able to live in their own apartments independently, caring for
themselves, and going about their lives. When the need arises,
the next level of care is assisted living, where residents continue
to occupy a smaller apartment of their own but have nursing and
support services close at hand. Meals are prepared for them, house-
keeping services provided, and daily or more frequent check-ins
from staff members are offered. Beyond assisted living, there's a
third level called the care center, where people receive around-
the-clock care and are often in bed most, or all, the time. The
idea is that as people become more frail or ill, the level of care
increases, but that once entering such a facility you have what
care you need until your death.

The gist of what I suggested to the mission-statement draft-
ing group was that the facility offered, among other things, a
place to die with dignity. As a person became more vulnerable,
he or she would be safe and supported in humane ways until
death. When I conveyed these ideas to the relevant person, I was
thanked, but in a way that indicated my suggestion was not quite
what they had in mind. Sure enough, when the mission statement came out, it did not contain a word about death, dying, or
death with dignity. This was, said the mission statement, a retire-
ment facility for active living. The mission statement spoke of a
rich community life among active people. Nothing is wrong, of
course, with that, except that it belies a good bit of reality. At any
rate, the promotional material suggested a seeming reluctance
to mention death, morality, or dying in such a public way. Even
aging was couched in terms of staying active, enjoying the
amenities of the city, and the facility's many social functions and
programs.

A similar pattern was evident in a friend's report of a recent
visit to a major bookstore. She looked for the section headed

"Aging." There she found two bookcases of many shelves chock full of books. But virtually all of them, she reported, were on one theme and its variations, "how to stay young." The stock was not so much about aging, as it was about not aging, or even anti-aging. She added that she was only able to find books about Alzheimer's disease by locating the neurology section of the store.

Both examples illustrate something that is hardly news: we live in a culture that denies the reality of death. Healthy congregations, congregations that contribute to healthy lives, face death with a certain openness, honesty, Christian confidence, and calm. Healthy congregations do not collude in the denial of death and aging. As I noted above, Christian conviction about the resurrection of the dead does not deny death. Jesus Christ died and was buried. We too will die, and our bodies will be buried or cremated. When our bodies are lowered into the grave, we know that Christ has gone there before us and hallowed every tomb. But we face our personal mortality and that of those we love with the conviction that God and God's grace, and not death, are the ultimate and the lasting reality. Healthy folks and vital congregations do not dwell on death, but they do not pretend it doesn't happen either. Nevertheless, many congregations do not speak of death openly, honestly, or often. To be sure, Easter comes each year with the empty cross, flowers, and songs of life eternal. Death is acknowledged, but more as something that has been conquered or disposed of. Easter can become yet another instance of the denial of death.

Such denial of death goes beyond silence. It is more subtle and multifaceted than that. The friend who reported about her experience in the bookstore happens to be a gerontological psychologist. When I asked about her current research and writing interests, she spoke of a new clinical diagnosis in which she was interested, called Mild Cognitive Impairment, or MCI. "MCI," she said, "is thought by some to be a precursor of Alzheimer's disease, while others do not believe the two always go together." My friend pointed out that there are millions to be made by pharmaceutical companies producing new drugs to treat MCI. She wondered if the diagnosis had been created to fit the drugs or if it was something real. She noted that it fit well into the anti-aging impulse evident not only in the bookstore but also in many products and services marketed today. She asked, finally, "Is something really wrong with becoming a little less mentally sharp as we age? Why are we so intolerant of various forms and levels of ability and cognitive function? Are there not perhaps gifts that those who are differently abled or at different stages on life's journey have to give the rest of us?" With the diagnosis and pharmaceutical treatment of MCI, were we turning natural aging into a problem to be fixed? Maybe. Then again, maybe not. These were questions she hoped to cast light on in her research. But given our proclivities as a society, the possibility exists that we prefer to view natural aging and the aged as a treatable condition rather than as realities to be faced.

The answers to questions about the different aspects of aging, as well as diagnoses such as MCI, are complex. But, speaking broadly, we seem to view our mortal nature, death and dying, our aging as well as the aged as problems to be solved rather than realities to be lived with courage and grace and in the context of community. In some respects, the movement in support of active euthanasia reflects similar impulses: death is not to be lived within faith and community but is to be hastened by eliminating the dying.

Such questions and issues suggest some of the many and complex issues that hover around aging in our times, issues that are likely to become only more complex and more urgent as the baby boomer generation ages and as more new drugs become available. Do congregations and clergy, informed by Christian convictions and faith, address these matters with courage and honesty? Or do congregations and clergy collude in society's denial of death and marginalization of the aged or infirm by a massive silence about them?

Of course, churches don't only keep silence. We also participate in the charade that, as one author put it, old people are just like young people—except older. We tend to support two sorts of ministries for older folks. We either try to keep them busy—with often-pointless activities or mindless volunteer work. Or we take care of them—with Meals on Wheels and Friendly Visitor programs. We do not recognize that elderhood is a distinct age with its own gifts as well as challenges, its own rhythms and purposes—its own vocations.

Shall we deny death too by failing to speak of it? Or, emboldened by faith and the Christian conviction that "whether we live or whether we die, we are the Lord's" (Rom. 14:8), shall we speak honestly and openly of death, neither preoccupied by it nor pretending it does not exist? Healthy congregations are those where life's difficult and challenging realities are not hidden but named and faced. Such congregations do not provide an escape from reality but a deeper entering into reality. In so doing, they affirm the incarnation's truth: that in Christ, God has entered into and embraced our full humanity.

Congregations that are willing to be more forthright about aging and mortality would have many possibilities to explore. Preachers and teachers could address the kinds of questions raised in the preceding discussion as well as those new questions posed by the field of bioethics. The biblical texts and theological doctrines that address these questions would be explored clearly and honestly. In addition, congregations could affirm the gifts of aging through mentorship relationships between the old and the young. Specifically focused gifts discernment programs could explore the work (spiritual and psychological) of the aged and their time in life. Most of all, congregations could in a variety of ways name mortality not as a condition to be fixed but as a reality to be faced and a gift to be received.

When Mystery and Faith Become Prediction and Control

The various clusters of Christian symbols regarding the last things are symbols that stretch language to the breaking point. Words and images such as "new heaven and new earth," "new Jerusalem," "spiritual body," and "the coming of our Lord Jesus Christ" are not literalistic descriptions, nor are they attempts to predict future events or timetables. In fact, Jesus' own words specifically discourage such predictions or speculation about dates and times. We read, "But about that day and hour no one knows, neither the angels of heaven, nor the Son, but only the Father" (Matt. 24:36). "So when they had come together, [the disciples] asked him, 'Lord, is this the time when you will restore the kingdom to Israel?' He replied, 'It is not for you to know the times or periods that the Father has set by his own authority" (Acts 1:6-7).

For the most part, the Scriptures are not only reticent in speaking of the future and last things, they also discourage speculation about the future in favor of faithfulness in the present. They are not concerned, as the saying goes, with the temperature of hell or the furniture of heaven. They specifically discourage the "sky surfing" of those who scan the literal or figurative heavens for Christ's return. The Scriptures are concerned that amid times of chaos and fear "the love of many will grow cold" (Matt. 24:12) and that his followers will be overcome by fear (Luke 21:9). They are very much concerned about encouraging steadfastness and faithfulness in the present, born of the conviction that nothing "in all creation, will . . . separate us from the love of God in Christ Jesus our Lord" (Rom. 8:39).

Nevertheless, these cautions have not stopped many from turning metaphor into timetable. There is, as *Newsweek* magazine said several years ago, a contemporary "boom in doom." The most recent expression of this outlook is the multivolume *Left Behind* series by Tim LaHaye. Prior to this series, probably the most popular book in this genre was Hal Lindsey's *The Late Great Planet Earth*. But many others have been published, from Ray Stedman's *What on Earth's Going to Happen?* to David Wilkerson's *Racing Toward Judgment,* and more. And many more such videos, books, and television shows will undoubtedly appear in the future, if for no other reason than the cryptic one given by essayist and journalist William Dean Howells: "No artist ever starved by underestimating the taste of the American public." Most of these works draw selectively on Scripture and take words out of context to create timetables for apocalyptic end times. These are often combined with scenarios of nuclear war and ecological disaster. Not only that, but they counsel readers to rejoice in terrors, crises, war, and violence as signs of predicated events that move us ever closer to the millennium.

Where has all of this come from? In the nineteenth century, Englishman John Nelson Darby developed a way of interpreting the Bible called "dispensationalism." Dispensationalism gradually took hold among American evangelicals and the just-beginning fundamentalist movement. Darby's ideas were further popularized by C. I. Scofield in his Scofield Reference Bible (1909). Dispensationalism organizes history into periods, or "dispensations," which in itself is a quite defensible technique for giving order to historical material. But Darby's seven dispensations just happen to place us at the end of the sixth dispensation and awaiting the seventh and final one, the millennium, that is, the thousand-year rule of Christ. The Dispensationalists then picked up some references in 1 Thessalonians and the book of Daniel to augment their dispensationalism with new doctrines of the rapture and the tribulation. Prior to the tribulation, which ushers in the millennium, true believers will be raptured into the presence of Jesus Christ, where they will be safe from the terrors of the great tribulation, when the earth will flow with rivers of blood. One other feature of dispensationalism is the interest of twentieth-century Dispensationalists in the modern state of Israel, in which they see the fulfillment of dispensationalist readings of the Old Testament. Thus events in the Middle East are closely watched as signs drawing us ever closer to the rapture, the tribulation, and the millennium.

The story of Darby, Scofield, and dispensationalism is one answer to the question of where the "boom in doom" and the new apocalypticism have come from. Another answer to the question is more psychological. These ideas play upon people's fears, especially their fears of the future and its unknowns. As New Testament scholar Robert Jewett writes in his study of the new apocalypticism, *Jesus against the Rapture*, "The appeal of the New Apocalypticism is as old as mankind itself: to achieve mastery over a threatening future. It reaches back to the first reading of entrails or tea leaves, to the first gazing at the clouds and the positions of the planets to grasp the future."[7] Mystery and faith are replaced by prediction and control, or the illusion of it. The fearful are told they and theirs will be raptured up to safety, while everyone else who is not in their group will meet a terrifying end.

What's wrong with the new apocalypticism, and how does it cause congregations to lose health, not to mention sanity? What is wrong is that such schemes rip the Scriptures out of context to "prove" an already arrived at agenda. It magnifies minor biblical themes and neglects major ones. The Bible is turned into tea leaves to be read for secret messages rather than the plain teachings for God's people. But perhaps even more pernicious is that the life, ministry, death, and resurrection of Jesus largely disappear from such accounts or take a very secondary role in the march of dispensations and signs.

You can save yourself by joining the select group, but not a thing can be done for society, the world, or creation. Such ideas as these let people avoid any responsibility for crisis or disaster, not to mention the common life of their community or nation. The words of the prophet Micah, "What does the LORD require of you but to do justice, and to love kindness, and to walk humbly with your God?" (Mic. 6:8), and Jesus, "You shall love the Lord your God with all your heart, soul, . . . mind, and . . . strength. . . . You shall love your neighbor as yourself," (Mark 12: 29–31), vanish. When this happens, congregations are no longer conveyors of good news. Recalling our discussion of sin, congregations lapse into weariness and timidity in the face of life's challenges. Nothing can be done but watch for signs of the end. When this happens, human beings have lost their capacity for choice and responsibility. Frequently, such congregations become completely dependent on their leaders, who often exploit this dependency.

The teachings of the New Testament about the last things move in just the opposite direction. There we find encouragement of realistic hope and of responsibility, as well as concern for the creation God loves and for all God's children of whatever race, religion, nation, or status. Each of the synoptic gospels— Matthew, Mark, and Luke—has a chapter in which Jesus speaks of the future after his crucifixion and resurrection. Each one speaks of history's troubles and travails: war, famine, flood, and peril. But Jesus tells his disciples (and us) these things not in order to terrify us but just the opposite, in order to encourage us. He doesn't say, "Get out while the getting's good," but rather, "Know that such things will happen, but do not let them throw you off course." He doesn't say, "When you see these things happening, it's time to pull the kids out of public school and turn in your voter registration card for a gun permit." Quite the contrary: these are the signs that it's a good time for God's people to be present and accounted for. These are times when the witness of the faithful matters greatly.

God has told us in advance that we can expect false messiahs and alarmists of all sorts, that there will be wars and rumors of war, earthquakes and diseases that we don't—at least for the time being—know how to explain or cure. We are not told these things so that we can bail out before the crash comes, but so we can hang in there continuing to follow Christ by loving our neighbors, seeking justice, loving kindness, and walking humbly with our God. We are told these things so that we won't be scared to death, because if we are, we will be part of the problem of the timid and resigned and not part of the solution of the faithful and engaged. God has something else in mind besides panic. Call it a certain Christian calm. Call it endurance. Call it hope. In times when fear runs high, Christian courage and calm curb violence and open the door to the renewal of lives and communities.

Our own times are characterized by a new batch of genuinely frightening dangers: ecological collapse, wars, and terrorism. To the credit of the new apocalypticism, it takes these dangers seriously. These are not to be treated with a kind of Pollyanna indifference or by smiling and saying, "Everything will be just fine." But neither are people of faith to withdraw from responsibility in fear and fatalism, as the new apocalypticism seems to urge.

Journalist Molly Ivins tells a wonderful story of two little boys in East Texas, John Henry Falk and Boots Cooper. In their games, they were Texas Rangers riding broomstick horses. One day John Henry's mother sent them down to the chicken coop to rout out a snake that had been doing considerable damage there. They mounted their brooms and galloped down to the chicken house to investigate. They looked all around the nests on the bottom shelf but couldn't find a snake. Then they stood up on tiptoe to see the upper shelf and found themselves face to face with a big ol' chicken snake. They were so scared that they both tried to run out of the hen house at the same time, doing considerable damage both to themselves and to the hen house.

Watching the commotion from the front porch, Mrs. Falk couldn't help but laugh. When the boys made it back to the house, she said, "Boys, what is wrong with you? You know perfectly well a chicken snake cannot hurt you." One of the little boys responded, "Yes ma'am, but there's some things'll scare you so bad, you hurt yourself."[8] I can't think of a better cautionary tale for our times than that!

Jesus said, "In the world you face persecution. But take courage; I have conquered the world!" (John 16:33). Healthy congregations encourage their members to live with realistic hope amid times of danger and challenge. By doing so they serve as the salt to the earth and light to the world that Jesus envisioned. When congregations become places of fear, fatalism, and withdrawal, their life belies the gospel, the good news they claim to preach.

Eschatology and the Liberation of Imagination

One reason Christian fundamentalists like Darby, Scofield, and their latter-day followers developed dispensationalism and the new apocalypticism was because the dominant spirit of the age, and often of churches, was as relentlessly optimistic as their own was pessimistic. Theological liberals embraced modern notions of inevitable progress through education, science, and technology. However, the Darbyites did not see a world getting better and better but worse and worse. Their dispensational scheme confirmed their view of a world going to hell in the proverbial handbasket. But they were, at least then, a distinct minority. The majority view, particularly in North America, was that the world was getting better to the point that not a few preachers predicted the ushering in of the kingdom of God in their lifetimes. Where the Darbyites saw the millennium on the other side of the great tribulation, the prophets of progress saw the kingdom of God just around the bend on the highway of human achievement.

Recall my earlier discussion of sin as either making too little of ourselves, rejecting our God-given freedom and falling into despair, on one hand, or, on the other, failing to take account of our finitude and limits, grasping for a power and control greater than is ours and being distorted by false pride. While dispensationalism seems rooted in a rejection of human freedom and a fall into despair, theological liberalism of the modern era went the other direction. Biblical eschatology was considered outmoded and superstitious and was replaced by liberal theories of progress. "Human history, like all of life," observes Migliore, "was a steadily upward-moving process. Education and modern science virtually guaranteed the progress of the human race."[9] Moreover, the kingdom of God ended up looking remarkably like a modern democracy that experienced widespread material prosperity thanks to science and technology. Of course, both of these things— democracy and prosperity—were great accomplishments, but something was lost when eschatology and Christian conviction about the future were reduced to the liberal theory of progress. A biblical vision of the kingdom of God was reduced in size and domesticated.

The Matter of Advent

As a young and even not-so-young pastor, I struggled with the season of Advent. Advent is that time of the church year that includes the four Sundays prior to Christmas. I expected, as did most of the people in congregations I served, that Advent would entail preparation for Christmas, nativity stories, greens, the scent of hot cider, and Christmas carols. Advent is a preparation of sorts for Christmas, but not this sort. Rather than taking us right to Bethlehem and sweet baby Jesus, Advent begins annually with a reading from one of those apocalyptic chapters of the Gospels I mentioned earlier. Often people came to church expecting childbirth, only to hear texts about the world groaning in labor, about the end of the age, and the second coming of Christ. In other words, Advent is biblical eschatology, not Victorian Christmas.

As I studied the Advent lessons of the Revised Common Lectionary, I wondered, "What in the world am I to do to with this?" Watching congregations as they heard these strange ancient texts about Jesus coming again, teaching that we are to be watchful for the Lord's coming, and warning us about false messiahs, I could see people in the congregation also wondering,

"What in the world are we to do with this?" I could see some asking themselves, "Why aren't we singing Christmas carols?"

Advent begins not with the first coming of Christ but with the second. Advent begins not with a baby in a manger but with Jesus riding in on the clouds. Although Darby and his followers had learned to love these parts of the Bible, more mainstream congregations have not. It is all too strange, too weird, and jarring. We have embraced the ethos of modernity, including progress, optimism, and reason. We prefer something that fits into that world. But, it turns out, the point of biblical eschatology is to shake up our settled worlds. That is the point of these grand, sweeping, strange, poetic, and startling visions of a new age, the coming of Christ, a new creation where the lion will lie down with the lamb, the child play over the hole of the snake. Jesus will appear as a thief in the night when we are dozing, and people who are "marrying and giving in marriage" will suddenly see the hidden glory of God (Matt. 24:38).

Though these parts of Scripture are challenging, eschatological themes and texts contribute to healthy and vital congregations by reminding us of the distance between our version of the good life and God's own, more startling, impossible possibilities. Congregations of the affluent and privileged, which would be most congregations in North America, are tempted to ignore the very different realities of life for many of the rest of God's children. We are tempted to identify our way of life with God's kingdom. Eschatology jars us out of our complacency. It paints a larger and more unexpected hope than we had imagined or thought possible. In doing so, we see reality more clearly. We are less likely to be complacent in the face of injustice. When we sing an Advent hymn like "Wake, awake, for night is flying" with the words, "Midnight's solemn hour is tolling; His chariot wheels are nearer rolling; He comes! O church, lift up thine eyes!" our lives are judged by Christ and his coming.[10] Our complacency is challenged. Congregations shaken out of their complacency tend to be congregations that see new opportunities for reaching the lost, for serving the least, for speaking truth to power, and for seeking forgiveness and reconciliation. We don't have forever. The time is at hand.

In an earlier chapter, I mentioned the experience of one of my children becoming critically and dangerously ill while we were on a church mission trip in Nicaragua. Not only was he ill but his illness was also of a particularly terrifying and heartrending kind, a bipolar illness. I remember one of the Scripture texts for that week was from 1 Corinthians. Paul writes: "I mean, brothers and sisters, the appointed time has grown short; from now on, let even those who have wives be as though they had none, and those who mourn as though they were not mourning, and those who rejoice as though they were not rejoicing, and those who buy as though they had no possessions, and those who deal with the world as though they had no dealings with it. For the present form of this world is passing away" (1 Cor. 7:29-31). This is a text informed by eschatological hope and conviction: "The appointed time has grown short . . . the present form of this world is passing away."

I confess that these words had not meant much to me in the past. But in the midst of our crisis, they came alive, for it truly did seem the present world was passing away and an utterly new time was at hand. I had been too concerned about my personal welfare and comfort. I was too preoccupied with the sermon I was to preach there in Nicaragua. I was too caught up finding a particular gift at the right price to take back. I had worried about the times of flights that were suddenly now totally irrelevant. And I had not cared enough about what was truly significant: being compassionate and being strong in the face of danger. When one of your children is critically ill, only a very few things really matter. You protect them as best you can, get help, and pray a lot.

In the face of the world I had known passing away before my eyes, my scale of values was turned upside down. I thought I had come to help people in Nicaragua and found myself instead completely relying on them. Getting back home in time for the annual meeting of the congregation seemed idiotic, as now I wondered if we would get back home at all. Teenagers in our group ministered to me, holding me as I wept. I was less the pastor and more a human being in need of grace and help. In the midst of such times, we get a good deal more real with one another. The church itself "gets real" too. Healthy congregations know how urgent and important simple acts of kindness and compassion are. They see that these acts have eternal (eschatological) significance. At the same time, many things we normally get upset about and are caught up in are revealed as belonging to the world that is passing away. It didn't matter if I got a Nicaraguan rocking chair! Healthy congregations learn the meaning of "majoring in the majors" and "minoring in the minors." Often unhealthy congregations are revealed by just the opposite, that is, their preoccupation with minor matters and blindness to major ones.

With time, those strange and troubling Advent texts became very precious to me and to congregations I served. I gradually discovered they do prepare us for the joys and trials of Christmas in North America but not in ways we expect. They prepare us by helping us put the seasonal activities, including the buying and selling, the grieving and rejoicing in a much larger, eschatological perspective. Our seasonal buying and selling is not of ultimate importance. What is important, what matters ultimately, is the new creation in Jesus Christ: participating in his love, his reconciliation, his new life. Where are those at work? Do we have eyes to see them? How are we responding? At Advent we need more than to have our cultural Christmas festivities blessed and sanctified. We need God, God whose thoughts are not our thoughts, whose ways are not our ways (Isaiah 55). Christian conviction about life's fulfillment and purpose puts things in a better, an eternal perspective. In doing this, those strange Advent texts and themes can help shape congregations that, rather than reinforcing and sanctifying the culture around us, provide an imaginative alternative where people find water for their parched souls and bread for hungry hearts. This conviction might mean welcoming the Prince of Peace is a time for the serious work of peacemaking and forgiveness in our families and congregations. It might mean this is time when we await with eager hearts the birth of new possibilities for mission and service. It might mean we gather for seasonal activities not only with our friends or loved ones but also with the stranger and alien in our midst.

Sometimes congregations lose vitality because their imaginations have atrophied and their visions have grown too small.

They have no place for talk of "a new heaven and a new earth" or "when Christ shall come again," because they have settled into the world as it is, only asking us to be a little nicer to each other. Our God is after bigger game. Jesus did not come only to help us adjust to this world, but to enter a whole new world. Churches that have a place for the wild hopes and dreams of the Bible's last things tend to be places of possibility, imagination, and hope. Such congregations see fresh possibilities for welcoming the spiritually homeless. Such congregations dream dreams of making a difference in the lives of people in their community. Such congregations are alert and watchful in their worship, prayer, and reading of Scripture for God's new coming in their midst.

This brings to conclusion my review of basic Christian convictions, from revelation to last things, and some of their implications for vital congregations. If churches are to be faithful and alive, it will be in no small part because we believe these convictions and doctrines to be saving truths pertinent to life and to congregations today. The final chapter examines the role of the pastor as theologian and ways the teaching ministry of the church, understood in broad terms, may contribute to refunding the theological foundations of congregational life.

Questions for Reflection and Discussion

1. Of the four clusters of symbols for "the last things"—the second coming of Christ, the resurrection of the dead, the last judgment, and eternal life (heaven) and eternal death (hell)—which speaks most powerfully to you? Why?
2. How would describe the culture of your congregation regarding death, mortality, and aging?
3. What are some of your own fears or concerns about aging? Do Christian convictions about death speak to those? How, and how not?
4. According to the author, eschatological texts and themes can challenge our complacency and expand our imagination. Read either Isaiah 11:1-9 or Revelation 21:1-5 several times in a prayerful and meditative way. What words or

verses speak to you or touch you? Which are most comforting? Most challenging?

5. According to New Testament scholar Robert Jewett, the
   appeal of the new apocalypticism is "as old as mankind
   itself: to achieve mastery over a threatening future."[11] Do
   you agree or disagree with his assessment? Why or why
   not?

Chapter 12

Pastor as Teacher; Congregation as Learning Community

P art of what drew me to the ordained ministry was a particular image of that calling: the minister as a field-based teacher and scholar. It is in many ways a rabbinic model. *Rabbi* means "teacher." Rabbis were teachers who were based not primarily in the school, university, or academy but in the community—in congregations and in the public square. There in the midst of life their task was to teach and to interpret a way of life for the people and community in which they lived. How does the faith of our people and tradition relate to this concern or that question of the day? How do the stories of our faith speak to a challenge in someone's life? How are the pastors and teachers of the church like the scribes of the kingdom of which Jesus spoke when he said, "Therefore every scribe who has been trained for the kingdom of heaven is like the master of a household who brings out of his treasure what is new and what is old" (Matt. 13:52)? Such scribes brought the old wisdom and ancient stories to new times and places. As a young man, I found such an understanding of ministry both compelling and challenging.

Does such an image of the office and calling of the ordained clergy have any meaning or relevance today? Or is it hopelessly romantic and outdated? Can the ordained function as field-based and community-based teachers and theologians, or have other more pressing or culturally appealing or relevant roles rendered this one either passé or simply way down the list of priorities? Ministers, pastors, priests, and rabbis can do so many things. There are so many possible understandings of our role and responsibility. How can one take pride in the calling?

Another way to ask these questions is to frame them in terms of congregations. Can congregations be teaching and learning communities? Or is that asking too much or too little? Are congregations to be something more or something different from this? Again, the possible and appropriate understandings of the purpose of congregations are many. Congregations may be centers of personal healing and spiritual growth, communities for activism and social change, centers of family life and nurture, institutions that offer an array of programs to meet varied human needs, or communities of worship.

While pastors and congregations must make choices among the array of possible priorities before them, my argument is not so much that the pastoral role of teacher and theologian and the congregational one of a teaching and learning community are to be preferred to others. Rather, my argument is that such an understanding gives order and coherence to the many functions and activities of clergy and congregations. We are in the business, or so it seems to me, of teaching and embodying a way of life, a particular way of being human in relationship to God. In all that we do, both as religious leaders and as congregations, we teach. Sometimes the lessons we teach are not consistent with the faith and values we profess, but right or wrong, faithful or derelict, we teach, we model, we form, and we inform.

This book is written with the conviction that the great truths of Christian faith, our core convictions, are saving truths. They make a difference. They make a difference by forming humans who are humane and truthful. They make a difference by pointing the way when we have lost our way and the way. They make a difference by shaping congregations and communities to become more vital. These saving truths create and sustain congregations. Those who seek and find such congregations discover a healthy community in which to grow, struggle, be changed, and be sustained. In the midst of the many forces that regularly distort and diminish life as God has created it to be, these saving truths create God's intended community. Most of all, these truths save by bringing us into relationship with the true and living God.

I envision pastors and congregations teaching these saving truths not only in formal ways through classes and study, but also, and perhaps even more important, in the informal ways that communities always teach: through role models and mentors, by interpreting shared convictions in times of crisis and loss, and by giving shape to those convictions in our daily ways of living. To be sure, this is not an easy endeavor, nor is it even one that will be completed in a person's lifetime. But those caveats make this calling, at least for me, more compelling. To be one among others who conveys and interprets the faith once received in fresh and lively ways and to be a community of learning and teaching (what organizational consultant Peter Senge has called a "learning organization" in his book *The Fifth Discipline*) seem to me to be tasks worthy of a lifetime.

That I draw inspiration for this understanding of both ministry and congregations from the Jewish faith is perhaps revealing. The Jews have long known what it is to struggle to sustain a particular faith and way of life amid societies that were not necessarily friendly to them. This, it seems to me, is increasingly the situation of Christians. We live in a society that is officially secular, is religiously pluralistic, and in values and lifestyles offers more a smorgasbord than a set menu. For the most part, I do not regret these realities. I am not among those who believe a Christian way of life can or ought to be legislated and mandated for all citizens. Faith is not a political ideology or agenda. While it should speak to political and social issues, faith that is captured in a political ideology or agenda has become something other than the faith and way of Jesus Christ, who came not to lord it over others, but to serve (Mark 10:42-43).

But the secularization and pluralism of North American society, as well as the political activism of what is termed the Religious Right, give a new priority to teaching and formation, to
the minister as teacher and practical theologian, and to the congregation as a teaching and learning community. Neither ordained ministers nor congregations can assume, as we once did,
that most people who come of age in North America have learned
the basics of faith simply by growing up here. By basics, I mean
the core convictions, biblical stories, hymns, and practices that
constitute the way of life of believers. While counting on the
culture to form Christians was probably never a very good idea,
there may once have been a time when clergy and congregations
could rely more on the culture at large to do so. That is no longer
true. These changes in our culture and in the place of the church
bring the pastoral role as teacher and theologian and the congregational role as teaching and learning community into higher
relief.

Vital congregations in this new time will look more Jewish
in the sense that they will be more intentional about teaching
and embodying a way of life, about doing Christian formation.
Not long ago, the pollster George Gallup Jr. set out to determine
what those who seek a church today most want from that experience. He noted three things in particular: sermons that are instructive and believable, opportunities to deepen one's own
spiritual life, and a church that helps people to have a better
understanding of the faith. We might think of these things as the
roots of faith. As any farmer or gardener knows, trees whose
roots are not planted in healthy soil and nurtured with water and
occasional fertilizer will not long bear fruit. In some measure,
the problem of mainline congregations has been that we have
gone to the trees decade after decade, asking a great harvest of
fruit (programs of service and activism, ministries of outreach
and care) without tending the roots. The result is predictable.
This is not to say Christian or congregational life is an either-or:
either roots and spiritual growth or fruits and ministries of service and care. Root-bound congregations are in as much a danger as fruitless ones. Roots or fruit is not an either-or; it is a
both-and, as any healthy apple tree testifies.

Minister: Pastor and Teacher

In my denominational family (United Church of Christ), the word *minister* is defined by two other words that are, at least in theory, intrinsically related. They are *pastor* and *teacher*. As I have suggested elsewhere,[1] that theory of relationship is good, but in practice the pastor function often seems to eclipse the teacher function. We clergy become counselors, therapists, helping professionals, crisis managers, and general caregivers, all under the rubric of pastor. There is a reason for this: a lot of lives and families are troubled and at sea. Pastoral care is often an urgent priority. Moreover, specific training in the art of pastoral care has become a central part of the preparation of many ministers through seminary courses and Clinical Pastoral Education, a movement that took hold in the 1950s and '60s.

But there is a danger here too. Most people, and perhaps clergy more than most, want to feel needed. The ever-available pastor is a busy and needed professional. The teacher is not quite so sought after. When the family is falling apart, not many folks call for the teacher—though perhaps they should!

Nevertheless, these two aspects of ministry, pastor and teacher, are mutually dependent, and when one goes or eclipses the other, a ministry and minister get out of balance in funny ways. All teacher easily becomes distant, didactic, and interesting but not all that useful. All pastor turns into something that may not be very different from my golden retriever: ever present but not having a lot to say. But the pastor who is a teacher does teaching in the context of a relationship, which is the way most good teaching happens. The teacher who is a pastor not only provides the comfort of presence but the gift and challenge of perspective, alternative ways of interpreting experience, and most of all a call to faithful response in the midst of life's relentless unfolding.

The conjunction of pastor and teacher also means that while the approach and methods of some teaching ministers look like other kinds of teaching, with a classroom and books, much of it looks different and takes place in other, less formal settings. Ministers teach, as my field-based scholar idea suggests, in the midst of life and in relation to ongoing experience. While this is certainly true, ministers and those who prepare them ought to give more attention to both the teaching office and teaching methods. Our preparation and ongoing education as pastors is given great priority through Clinical Pastoral Education, training in family systems dynamics, grief counseling, and the like. Training in teaching methods has no equivalent emphasis of which I am aware. While teaching may be a gift and some pastors more disposed to it than others, it is, like all gifts, a developed one. Teaching skills can be learned and practiced. More clergy ought to serve as apprentices to master teachers by availing themselves of skilled observers who provide feedback on their teaching. In addition, they can pay attention to the ample literature on the skills of the gifted teacher. We clergy may not all become great teachers, but we can all become better teachers. If congregations are to be grounded in the core convictions—the saving truths—of Christian faith, ordained clergy must once again become teachers of the faith.

The balance of this concluding chapter offers practical suggestions for ordained ministers who would be teachers and theologians of the faith and for congregations that hope to grow as teaching and learning communities. You shall discover other modes and means that have not occurred to me. (Drop me a note or send me an email at www.anthonybrobinson.com and tell me about what you have discovered and what you are doing.) The ideas that follow are not surefire schemes or steps to dramatic numerical growth. They are things that have been tried and used and have enjoyed reasonable, though not spectacular, success. They are some ways in which pastors can be teachers and theologians and congregations can become teaching and learning communities. For fun, I have organized this as my "Top Ten" bright ideas for learning congregations and teaching pastors.

1. A Foundations Course

"Foundations" may be a good name where you are, or it may not. The name is not important. The point is a course that does the basics. What are the foundational convictions as well as central practices of Christian faith and living? As an example of each, grace is a foundational conviction, while a foundational practice is weekly worship together. Make the course an introduction that assumes nothing. You won't promise to cover everything (you can't), but you will cover some of the most important things.

You can make preparing such a course or learning experience a teaching moment in itself by asking either an existing group, such as an education committee, or an ad hoc one, such as the Foundations Course (or Christianity 101) Planning Team, to help you plan and lead it. Figure out who your audience is for this class: existing church members, new members, nonmembers, seekers, visitors. (My preference is new members or seekers, with a sprinkling of more mature believers as part of the teaching team. Some congregations might have one Foundations course for new folks and another one for those who have been around a while but feel they never really got the basics.) Get some of your intended audience involved in planning it too. Be clear about course objectives, which ought to include both the material to be covered and the experience of being together with others and building relationships through the course. Plan the learning to happen in different ways—lecture, interviews, site visits, group discussions, case studies. Assign homework that relates to the week's theme, so that the ideas aren't just dropped between sessions, but people have a chance to reflect and build on what is presented each week.

Some congregations are doing Foundations or Christianity 101 with video series. There are three series of which I am aware, The Alpha Course (alphacourse.org), Living the Questions (livingthequestions.com), and Beginnings (beginnings.cokesbury.com). Some congregations use texts for such a class. I like and recommend Martin Copenhaver's *To Begin at the Beginning* (United Church Press, Cleveland, OH, 1994) or Stanley J. Grenz's *What Christians Really Believe and Why* (Westminster John Knox, Louisville, KY, 1998). I also like Pastor Rick Floyd's self-published *A Course in Basic Christianity*.[2]

Maybe you serve a smaller congregation and aren't sure you will ever have enough people at one time in your target group to make it fly. Then consider joining forces with other similar congregations and do your Foundations course together. The point is to regularly offer something that does Christian basics while building relationships. This opens a door into your congregation and says, "Seekers are welcome here."

2. The Ten Essentials

Credit for this wonderful idea goes to my friend and colleague in Seattle, Diane Darling, pastor of Alki United Church of Christ. Out in our neck of the woods, we all have some familiarity with "The Ten Essentials" for going hiking or backpacking in the wilderness. These include things like a map, a compass, and water. Diane piggybacked on this and developed "The Ten Essential Bible Stories." "The world is simply too dangerous for you to go out there without these stories," she told her congregation.

She did the Ten Essentials as a sermon series. It could easily be dovetailed with small groups or with Web site supplements. It provides a way to build biblical literacy and comfort in your congregation, laced with a note of urgency. Preachers and teachers using this series would not only have to lay out the story, they would also have to make a case for why it is essential, and why every Christian who venturing out into the world needs this story. After a pastor has taught the Ten Essentials, ask the congregation to come up with its own list, and together the church can turn it into a brochure for newcomers and visitors. It would also be relatively easy for a season or two to build the whole church program for children, youth, and adults around the Ten Essentials idea.

3. The Forest (and a Few Trees)

Week by week in worship, people hear different passages, snippets of this and bites of that, from the Bible. They see, to change the metaphor, lots of trees, but often have no clue about the forest. Do a "Through the Bible in One Year" aimed at seeing the forest, the big story, the overall drama. In his book, *The Story We Find Ourselves In: Adventures of a New Kind of Christian,* Brian McLaren does the big story in a series of *c* words: creation, crisis, call, covenant, conversation, Christ, church, and consummation. Others have other memorable summaries or devices for getting the big picture, but you gotta have it, the overall story line. Pastors need to remember that many (most?) feel intimidated by the Bible, and rightly so. The Bible is not an easy book! Imagine someone with no historical knowledge or relevant literary background trying to pick up the collected works of Shakespeare and make sense of it.

As the year-long class winds down, challenge students to tell the big story in one sitting, or, if they prefer, either to write out the drama in their own words or draw it. Then turn last year's students into next year's teaching team, because the very best way to learn something is to teach it yourself. You may develop your own curriculum for this or draw on some of the best existing curricula from the *Kerygma* series (The Kerygma Program) or from the *Disciple Bible Study* program (Cokesbury). Both can be located on the Internet. Or just offer those series, which have been very helpful for people who want to see both the forest and the trees.

4. A Class on Worship

Worship is the one thing every church does, the one thing that churches do that other groups and organizations don't do. Worship is the one thing the most people participate in, and what we do week after week. But what in the world is worship? Where did our pattern of worship come from? What are the sacraments and why are they important? What is the role of music in worship? How about this thing called "the lectionary"? What is a sermon and what is it supposed to do? How can people in congregations interact with, help, or respond to the preacher? What is the role of art (dance, drama, architecture, sculpture) in worship?

The questions go on and on. Worship is not the same as a lecture, live performance, television show, or concert. How is it similar and how is it different? Without worship education, congregations cannot be blamed for measuring worship against a television program or some sort of performance. What ought people expect to bring to worship and take from it? How can the experience of worship be deepened, strengthened, or improved?

On what basis and according to what standards is worship properly evaluated? Take a field trip or two to services of other families of faith. What do you notice and learn, not only about them but also about yourselves? Bring in a rabbi to talk about Jewish worship, because Christian worship grew out of the synagogue. Have participants in the class complete weekly worship feedback forms. Have the class plan and lead a service of worship as its final project. Offering classes on worship is not only a way to strengthen worship but also to teach and explore the core convictions of Christian faith.

5. This I Believe

Invite members of the congregation to put their personal credo into words with this caveat: they have to talk about God. In the church, you want people to speak about more than generalized values, such as "the power of love," as important as they may be. You want God made explicit. Where is God in this? Lay people's testimonies to their faith and convictions are sometimes (always?) more compelling to ordinary folks than those of clergy, who get the "clergy discount": "He's a minister, he has to say that!"

A variation on the "This I Believe" idea that perhaps puts speakers on the spot a little less is a series of faith journey stories. Members of the congregation are invited to talk for 30 to 40 minutes about their life and their faith. The congregation I most recently served did a faith journey series between services on summer Sundays and found it a continuing hit. We asked people to talk about the following kinds of questions: What have been your experiences of God's presence or God's absence? Who is Jesus Christ for you? How has your faith changed? What people and events have formed your faith? How does your faith affect your job or your family? Leave 10 minutes at the end for the listeners to respond, asking them "What has touched or spoken to you in what you have heard today?" The point of such a series is to give speakers the chance to reflect on their faith, the challenge to put words to it, and the opportunity for others to hear someone like them work with questions people in congregations want to ask but seem never to find the opportunity to.

6. Gifts Discernment

Start with baptism and ministry and the notion that baptism is, at least in part, the call of each of us to ministry, that is, to lead a life as loving response to God's grace and mercy and in service to our neighbors. Open up some of the great call stories of the Scriptures: Moses, Samuel, Mary, Paul, and Priscilla. Look at what Paul has to say in 1 Corinthians and Romans about many gifts and one Spirit and about gifts given to all for the common good. Build community among the participants. Then move into exercises and inventories that help people identify their gifts for ministry. (A number of such gift inventories and related exercises and worksheets are available in print and on the Web.) What gifts have they long known that they have had but not recognized as gifts from God for ministry? What gifts have they left untouched or undeveloped? How do these gifts and their possible use thrill or terrify them? Where in the church or wider community can people's gifts be more fully put to use? What kind of congregation do we need to become to support a culture where gifts are cultivated?

Be sure to acknowledge that for many people their primary ministries are through their work; for some fortunate folks, their job is their primary vocation. Of course, it is true for the reformers Martin Luther and John Calvin, a job is usually a Christian's calling. It might not be one we enjoy, but it's still an opportunity to serve neighbor and God. They also acknowledged not all jobs are callings, but those are rare, such as activities that are downright dishonest or that do not benefit others. In fact, for Luther and Calvin vocation must be considered alongside salvation, not because we are saved by our vocation but because vocations that are difficult for us remind us of our dependence on God for all things, including salvation. Despite the reformers' teaching on this matter, some may consider their primary vocation has to do with relationships, whether at work, in the home and family, or in the congregation or community. How can people be supported and strengthened in these ministries? What further, periodic opportunities for training or reflection might they need? Discerning gifts for ministry is part of developing a congregational culture of shared ministry. (Recall the chapter on church and ministry, chapter 10.)

Then close the loop. When people have spent time identifying their gifts, take the next step of getting them involved in a practice of discipleship appropriate to their gifts. That may be fixing meals in a homeless shelter, building a Habitat for Humanity home, visiting the aged and infirm, teaching a class, leading a prayer group, tutoring kids in a neighborhood school, doing a ministry through music, or being a volunteer chaplain at the youth detention facility. It may mean convening a gathering for those who work in health care or law or business and who are trying to understand it as a calling. Whatever the ministry, figure out ways to get people together and reflect on their experiences. Ask them three questions: What did you give? What did you receive? Where and how did you experience God in this? If people are organized in teams or groups for particular ministries, this reflection on experience can be a part of the team's ongoing life. In this way, by intentional and ongoing reflection on experience, the church becomes a learning organization.

7. Pilgrimage

A pilgrimage is an old practice making a comeback under a new name, "mission trip." A pilgrimage is a long journey or search with a sacred or moral purpose. More and more people today are going on mission trips. Some trips are for youth. Some are for adults. And some (this has great potential) are intergenerational. Most go to developing countries. More trips to different parts of our own country also need to be planned. Mission trips are rich in teaching and learning potential of many forms, but before focusing on those, be aware of this: a pilgrimage puts the travelers into a liminal space. Liminal spaces are "spaces between." They are what the Celts called "thin places." Pilgrimages take us from our known worlds and thrust us into strange places where God can get at us. By and large, being a tourist doesn't do this. Tourists mostly travel in a special world, one that is designed for tourists. Through the church, we often have a deeper entrée into another culture and country than a tourist can ever have.

At least two kinds of learning take place on such border-crossing pilgrimages. The first is learning about another culture and its people, learning what being Christian in another world means. What is worship like in that place? How do they do church? What challenges are Christians up against in another culture, and where do they find strength and hope? Who is Jesus for them? Often mission trips are all about doing. We build houses or clinics or schools. That's fine. But build in some time for being, for listening, for just hanging out with the people.

The second huge learning opportunity of such trips is for community building— being church—with one's fellow pilgrims. Few things draw people closer together and help them to know each other as readily as travel in a land and culture not their own. In the course of such a journey, things happen that reveal us to ourselves and to one another. Facades fall and we are exposed. Build in times of shared reflection on what people are experiencing. I have often found mission trips a great place to do Bible study. Pick a book or theme that may have some particular tie to where you are going. For example, for a mission trip to Nicaragua, we focused on the Gospel of Mark, because Mark's whole picture of Jesus is of the crucified one, which speaks in a powerful way amid the widespread suffering of people in Nicaragua. Amid the suffering and joy of that country and culture, Mark came alive in new ways.

8. Retreat

Another ancient practice with new meaning and appeal is that of the retreat, or, we might say, the monastery. I mean a spiritual retreat during which participants enter into an ordered life of prayer and work in community, not a weekend of camp. It might be three days. It might be a week. It might be one day. It's a great time to teach something like centering prayer or the Ignatian art of praying the Scriptures. Silence in a group is different from silence alone, but both can be a part of such a retreat. Go someplace where people can take walks in a garden or along a lake or seashore. Have healthy, wonderful meals (preparing them may be someone else's gift and ministry!). If people fall asleep while praying or meditating, bless them and assure them they won't fail Retreat 101. Sleep is probably what they most need.

If you are planning a retreat and haven't done it before, visit a Catholic retreat center (they are all over the country). Do a retreat with Franciscans or Benedictines, or do a three-day retreat on the Jesuit model. (Warning: the Jesuit retreats involve a lot of silence and are not for everyone.) Experience the guidance of a spiritual director. Experience praying the Scriptures. Make retreat days a regular offering to begin seasons of the church year, such as Advent or Lent. Figure out ways and resources for people to do mini daily retreats. Doesn't that sound more enticing than daily prayer? But what a wonderful way to start people in a practice of daily prayer: their own daily retreat. Put the resources for daily mini-retreats on your church's Web site.

9. Newsletters and Web Sites

Don't underestimate the humble newsletter! The congregational newsletter is a great teaching instrument, especially if your congregation publishes one weekly. Pastors can write a series of columns on a topic that ties in with other aspects of a congregation's life, such as a series on vocation for Epiphany or another on sin and bondage for Lent. Pastors who reflect on events in the congregation's or wider community's life can (and should) put those in a larger faith and theological framework. You can use the newsletter for a series on worship. You can carry a "This I Believe" feature written by a different layperson each week. Far too many church newsletters are chockfull of stuff no one reads. Try this test. If people had to pay for a subscription to your church newsletter, how long would you be in business? The newsletter needs to include more than a calendar and bold-print reminders of upcoming board meetings. It can be an engaging teaching tool, a spiritual journal, a community celebration, and storytelling device.

Increasing numbers of churches have Web sites. Having someone with expertise design and maintain the site for you is worth it. Think twice about accepting someone's offer to do this as a favor or as a volunteer: their skills may not be up to the task, or their time and interest may wane. Pay $1,000 to have a great Web site built and $25 to $50 per month to have it maintained. And once you have it up, keep it current, fresh, and attractive. Think of it as a teaching tool, a spiritual journal, and a device for telling the story and celebrating the life and ministries of your faith community. Include such features as weekly reflections on the lectionary texts, which you may prepare yourself or for which you provide links to other sites. Have a link to your denomination's Web site and a link to *The Christian Century* magazine or beliefnet.com. Carry a prayer for the day. Include sermons in both text and audio versions. Have your choir, soloists, or music ensembles record music that people can play or download at your Web site. Be sure, of course, to get the proper copyright permissions.

10. When the Sky (or a Chunk of It) Is Falling

When things fall apart, you are presented with a teachable moment. Things fall apart in different ways: death and birth, marriage and divorce, changes and challenges of many sorts. All of these are teachable moments. No one needs extended, abstract, or didactic presentations at such times. They do need to have the great truths and affirmations of faith brought to the moment in appropriate ways and words.

Things fall apart in other ways: earthquakes, storms, terrorist attacks, and assassinations. When the world caves in, people turn to churches, and every pastor should anticipate what cannot be fully anticipated. Every pastor should be prepared to give "an accounting of the hope that is in you" (1 Peter 3:15) that speaks pastorally to the moment and the need. And honesty is always good. Express and articulate your own shock, sorrow, and confusion, and claim faith's meaning in such times.

Another way things fall apart is when churches have fights. Never pleasant, they can be useful and a great time to bring to bear the core convictions of faith. It may be useful to spend some time learning how to fight, or put more positively, how to resolve conflict when no conflict is going on. For this purpose, study Acts 6, Acts 15, and all of 1 Corinthians, as well as the many contemporary resources.

When people are really angry, they don't hear well, so our messages must be clear, direct, and short. When people are hurting, they hear a little better; still, the messages must be to the point. When congregations have gotten themselves wound around the axle on some issue, the unwinding takes both patient listening and reiteration in many different ways of core truths, such as "Knowledge puffs up; love builds up," and "All have sinned and all have fallen short of grace." These need to be put in words people can hear. Life crises, societal turmoil and disaster, and congregational conflicts are not usually things any of us go looking for, but you can count on this: they will come looking for us. When they do, look for the silver lining of teaching potential in such cloudy skies.

Those are my top ten bright ideas for helping pastors be teachers and theologians and for congregations to become teaching and learning communities. Beyond these, congregations, or clusters of congregations, ought to be thinking about some ordered patterns of learning that become a part of their life together. At one church I served, we did this with what we called "Wednesday Night Live." A simple dinner was followed by class options in four tracks: Scripture, theology and church history, spiritual practices, and ethics. Each track was broadly defined. All the pastors taught. We asked retired clergy and nonparish clergy who were good teachers to teach. We brought in gifted teachers from the community. Members of the congregation taught classes. This kind of thing works well in some congregations but not in others. Teaching ministries too need to be contextualized.

Finally, and to repeat, much of the clergy's teaching will be in the midst of the life of the congregation and its people. This doesn't mean always having the answers; indeed, it may mean having the question. It does mean putting the little dramas of life in community and of our lives individually into the context of the great story of God's redeeming and relentless love and purpose. It means making the connections between God's story and our stories, because in reality they are not two different stories but one story. Tell the story with love. Tell it with confidence. Tell it with joy. Amen!

Questions for Reflection and Discussion

1. Think of a great teacher you have experienced. What made him or her a great teacher? What are the qualities of great teaching?
2. Pick one idea from the author's top ten that most intrigues you. Why does it excite you? How might it be tried in your congregation?
3. Do you have a number 11 teaching and learning strategy you have experienced or would add to the top-ten list?

Questions for Reflection and Discussion

Notes

Introduction

1. Kenda Creasy Dean, *Practicing Passion: Youth and the Quest for a Passionate Church* (Grand Rapid, Mich.: Wm. B. Eerdmans Pub. Co., 2004), 9–10.
2. Ibid., 25.
3. Douglas John Hall, *The End of Christendom and the Future of Christianity* (Harrisburg, Pennsylvania, Trinity Press International, 1995), 47.
4. Fleming Rutledge, "A New Liberalism of the Word," *Loving God with Our Minds: The Pastor as Theologian*, ed. Michael Welker and Cynthia A. Jarvis (Grand Rapids, Mich.: Wm. B. Eerdmans Pub. Co., 2004), 252.
5. Anthony B. Robinson, *Transforming Congregational Culture* (Grand Rapids, Mich.: Wm. B. Eerdmans Pub. Co., 2003), 26–28.
6. Daniel Migliore, *Faith Seeking Understanding: An Introduction to Christian Theology* (Grand Rapids, Mich.: Wm. B. Eerdmans Pub. Co., 1991), 2.
7. *The Columbia World of Quotations* (1996), s.v. "Gertrude Stein," *Everybody's Autobiography*, chapter 4, 1937, http://www.bartleby.com/66/37/55537.html (accessed Oct. 20, 2005).

Chapter 1

1. Edward Farley, *The Fragility of Knowledge: Theological Education in the Church and University* (Philadelphia: Fortress Press, 1988), 88.
2. Richard Osmer, *A Teachable Spirit Recovering the Teaching Office of the Church* (Louisville, Ky.: Westminster John Knox, 1990), 140.

Chapter 2

1. Martin Copenhaver, *To Begin at the Beginning: An Introduction to the Christian Faith* (Cleveland, Ohio: United Church Press, 1994), 109–110.
2. Daniel Migliore, *Faith Seeking Understanding: An Introduction to Christian Theology* (Grand Rapids, Mich.: Wm. B. Eerdmans Pub. Co., 1991), 20.
3. Ibid., 24.
4. L. Gregory Jones, "Tale of Two T-Shirts," *The Christian Century* 121, no. 18 (September 7, 2004): 47.
5. Belden C. Lane, *Landscapes of the Sacred: Geography and Narrative in American Spirituality* (New York: Paulist Press, 1988), 11.

Chapter 3

1. Norman Perrin, *Jesus and the Language of the Kingdom: Symbol and Metaphor in New Testament Interpretation* (Philadelphia: Fortress Press, 1976), 52.

Chapter 4

1. Migliore, *Faith Seeking Understanding,* 10–13.
2. John McManners, ed., *The Oxford Illustrated History of Christianity* (Oxford: Oxford University Press, 1990), 49–50.
3. Copenhaver, *To Begin at the Beginning,* 77.
4. Paul Tillich, *The New Being* (New York: Charles Scribner and Sons), 152.

5. Copenhaver, *To Begin at the Beginning,* 36–37.

6. Eugene Wehrli and Douglas Meeks, "Toward a Theology of Evangelization," study paper of the Iowa Conference of the United Church of Christ, 1983.

7. John Leith, *The Reformed Imperative: What the Church Has to Say That No One Else Can Say* (Philadelphia: Westminster Press), 1988, 98.

Chapter 5

1. Anthony B. Robinson, *Transforming Congregational Culture* (Grand Rapids, Mich.: Wm. B. Eerdmans Pub. Co., 2003), 35–37.

2. Robert Benson, *Living Prayer* (New York: Putnam Books, 1994), 1.

3. Jürgen Moltmann, *The Theology of Hope* (New York Harper and Row, 1968), 22.

4. Shakespeare, *Macbeth,* Act 5, Scene 5, *William Shakespeare: The Complete Works,* ed. Alfred Harbage (Baltimore: Pelican Books, 1969), 1133.

5. Copenhaver, *To Begin at the Beginning,* 17.

6. Wendell Berry, *Jayber Crow* (Washington D.C.: Counterpoint, 2000), 49.

7. Abraham Joshua Heschel, *The Sabbath: Its Meaning for Modern Man* (New York: Farrar, Straus and Giroux, 1951), 32.

Chapter 6

1. Nathaniel Hawthorne, *The House of Seven Gables* (New York: Signet Classic), 42.

2. Migliore, *Faith Seeking Understanding,* 131.

3. Kathleen Norris, *Dakota: A Spiritual Geography* (New York: Ticknor and Fields, 1993), 97–98.

Chapter 7

1. Barbara Brown Taylor, *Home by Another Way* (Boston: Cowley Publications, 1999), 34–35.

2. Roberta Bondi, Turner Lectures, Yakima, Washington, 1996, author's notes.
3. Copenhaver, *To Begin at the Beginning,* 36.
4. John Garvey, *The Prematurely Saved and Other Varieties of Religious Experience* (Springfield, Ill.: Templegate Publishers, 1986), 15.
5. Fred Craddock, "Have You Ever Heard John Preach?" *A Chorus of Witnesses: Model Sermons for Today's Preacher,* ed. Thomas G. Long and Cornelius Plantinga Jr. (Grand Rapids, Mich.: Wm. B. Eerdmans Pub. Co., 1994), 39.
6. Copenhaver, *To Begin at the Beginning,* 38.
7. Gabriel Fackre, *The Christian Story* (Grand Rapids, Mich.: Wm. B. Eerdmans Pub. Co., 1978), 116.

Chapter 8

1. Migliore, *Faith Seeking Understanding,* 165.
2. Copenhaver, *To Begin at the Beginning,* 77.
3. Migliore, *Faith Seeking Understanding,* 166.
4. John Gardner, *Leadership* (New York: The Free Press, 1990), 124.
5. Ibid., 121.
6. "Archbishop Desmond Tutu: Peacemaker in a Diverse Nation," *Christian Science Monitor,* October 26, 1994.
7. Barbara Brown Taylor, *Speaking of Sin* (Boston and Cambridge: Cowley Publications, 2000), 86.
8. Long and Plantinga, *Chorus of Witnesses,* 92.
9. Taylor, *Speaking of Sin,* 90.
10. Dietrich Bonhoeffer, *The Cost of Discipleship* (New York: MacMillan Publishing Co., 1963), 45.
11. See Dorothy C. Bass, ed., *Practicing Our Faith: A Way of Life for a Searching People* (San Francisco: Jossey-Bass, 1998).
12. See Diana Butler Bass, *The Practicing Congregation: Imagining a New Old Church* (Herndon, Va.: The Alban Institute, 2005).

Chapter 9

1. Ellen T. Charry, "Sacramental Ecclesiology," *The Community of the Word: Toward an Evangelical Ecclesiology,* ed. Mark

Husbands and Daniel J. Treier (Downers Grove, Ill.: Intervarsity Press, 2005), 201.

2. Ibid., 204.
3. Ibid., quoted from book cover.
4. Michael Foss, *Power Surge* (Minneapolis: Fortress Press, 2000), 15.
5. Ibid., 19.
6. C. Kirk Hadaway, *Behold I Do a New Thing* (Cleveland, Ohio: The Pilgrim Press, 2002).
7. Ibid., 11.
8. Ibid., 117.

Chapter 10

1. Frederick Buechner, *Wishful Thinking: A Theological ABC* (New York: Harper and Row, 1973), 82–83.
2. *Book of Worship* (Cleveland, Ohio: The United Church of Christ, 1986), 143.

Chapter 11

1. *The Pilgrim Hymnal* (New York: The Pilgrim Press, 1987), 461.
2. *The New Century Hymnal* (Cleveland, Ohio: The Pilgrim Press, 1995), 616.
3. *The New Century Hymnal*, 369.
4. *The New Century Hymnal*, 610.
5. Migliore, *Faith Seeking Understanding*, 242.
6. Douglas John Hall, *Why Christian? For Those on the Edge of Faith* (Minneapolis: Fortress Press, 1998), 74.
7. Robert Jewett, *Jesus against the Rapture: Seven Unexpected Prophecies* (Philadelphia: The Westminster Press, 1979), 25.
8. Molly Ivins, address delivered at Carleton College, Northfield, Minn., 1995, author's notes.
9. Migliore, *Faith Seeking Understanding*, 233.
10. Philipp Nicolai (1566-1608), *The Pilgrim Hymnal*, 108.
11. Jewett, *Jesus against the Rapture*, 25.

Chapter 12

1. Martin Copenhaver, Anthony Robinson, and William Willimon, *Good News in Exile: Three Pastors Offer a Hopeful Vision for the Church* (Grand Rapids, Mich.: Wm. B. Eerdmans Pub. Co., 1999). See the chapter on the church's teaching ministry, "Christian Formation and the Teaching Ministry: Becoming Christian."
2. Richard L. Floyd, *A Course in Basic Christianity*, 27 East St., Pittsfield, MA 01201, 1997.